THE CAMEL

ITS USES AND MANAGEMENT

THE CAMEL

ITS USES AND MANAGEMENT

MAJOR ARTHUR GLYN LEONARD

GYAN

Published by

Gyan Publishing House
5, Ansari Road
Daryaganj, New Delhi-110002
Phone: 011-47034999, 9811692060
E-mail: books@gyanbooks.com

Distribution Network
gyanbooks.com
India, USA, Canada, UK, Australia, France

ISBN : 978-81-212-9238-2 (PB)
First Published, 1894

2nd Impression 2023

Printed at: Gyan Press, Delhi.

THE CAMEL ITS USES AND MANAGEMENT
Author: MAJOR ARTHUR GLYN LEONARD

THE CAMEL

ITS USES AND MANAGEMENT

BY

MAJOR ARTHUR GLYN LEONARD

LATE 2ND EAST LANCASHIRE REGIMENT

LONDON

LONGMANS, GREEN, AND CO.

AND NEW YORK: 15 EAST 16th STREET

1894

I have the honour to dedicate this work to My Old Comrades of the 59th (2nd Nottinghamshire) Regiment, and to their successors of the 2nd Battalion East Lancashire, as a slight mark of esteem and affection for those who taught me my duty, and among whom I passed sixteen very happy years.

PREFACE

THE following pages are principally the result of sixteen years' practical observation and experience of Camels in India, Afghanistan, Egypt, and the Soudan, and the elaboration and expansion of diaries kept by me on different campaigns under every variety and extreme of condition and circumstance.

My object in offering them for publication is manifold and obvious, as a perusal of the work will show. In a few words—

(1) To awaken and to stimulate an interest in, as well as to encourage the proper treatment of, Camels, under all phases and conditions.

(2) To explain the various uses to which both the riding and the baggage Camel can be put.

(3) To act as a guide to every soldier in the above, and also in the most useful and most practical doctrines of transport.

(4) To promote and improve the breeding of the animal, so as to ensure the production of a superior class of riding and baggage Camel.

(5) To urge a more universal use of both riding and baggage Camels, especially in Australia, and in the southern and central portions of Africa.

(6) To advocate the establishment of a system by which Nos. 1, 3, 4, and 5 can be effected, and by which

No. 2 can be utilised with the soundest and most practical results.

These are questions which, not only from a military, but from a national and even international, point of view require immediate looking into, and a serious attention to which cannot fail directly to benefit the animal, and indirectly humanity.

To accomplish this the more readily, also as an inducement to the young soldier, who dislikes the dry detail of a purely technical work, I have done my best to make it readable, by clothing it in plain and simple language, and by rendering it interesting through the relation of incidents and anecdotes.

At the same time, I venture to hope that it will find favour with all those who take an unselfish interest in animals, and with zoologists as well. For though I am not one myself in the strict sense, and have not written from a scientific point of view, I can claim without hesitation the undoubted advantages of having studied deeply the customs and characteristics of this little known and strangely unsympathetic animal, during a long, close, and continuous contact with him, and of having done so on purely and eminently practical principles.

In laying down rules and in suggesting principles I have done so altogether conditionally, basing them entirely on the broad principle that all rules and regulations depend naturally on circumstance and on the nature of the case, and are therefore subject to alteration. I have endeavoured, however, to look at each question from all sides and from various standpoints.

Much of the anatomical information I gleaned from interesting conversations that I held during the Nile campaign (1884–85) with Major PHILLIPS and Captains BENNET and GRIFFITHS, of the Army Veterinary Department, with whom I frequently came into close contact. Also from an essay on Camels by Veterinary-Surgeon STEEL, which appeared many years ago in the 'Veterinarian,' so clear and concise in its views that I have taken the liberty of quoting several extracts from it. Finally, to Mr. M. L. WESSELS, of Cape Town, I am extremely indebted for his kind assistance in placing his library and classical knowledge at my disposal. To him, and to others who have incidentally helped me, I tender my sincere and hearty thanks.

Twenty years ago I read 'Dombey and Son,' and the 'Cuttleian' philosophy inculcated by that wooden-legged and worthy old salt, the guiding principle of which—'when found make a note of'—made such a firm impression on me that I have always since acted upon it.

Experience is knowledge—knowledge derived from practice, use, trials, and a continuity of observation. And if this species of knowledge is not always power, it is, at least, practical, and as such will, I trust, prove universally useful.

ARTHUR GLYN LEONARD, MAJOR,
late 2nd East Lancashire Regiment.

ARTHUR'S SEAT, SEA POINT:
December 1, 1893.

CONTENTS

THE CAMEL

INTRODUCTION

HISTORICAL

THE Camel is one of the oldest mammals now living, is essentially a domesticated animal, and one of the earliest ever domesticated. It has never—at least to my knowledge, but I am open to correction—been found in a wild state, nor have any traces ever been discovered of its having been so at any period of the world's history.

Prejevalsky says that wild camels frequent the wastes of Lake Lob-Nor in Central Asia, and I have read elsewhere that herds of wild ones of the Bactrian species have been reported to exist in Turkestan, as also in the desert tracts of Shamo on the Chinese frontier; but I have never seen these statements verified or confirmed. In Nubia and the Soudan large herds are allowed to run wild by their owners, and this is what also occurs in Central Asia, I should imagine, there being a vast difference between wild camels and camels that are allowed to run wild. Up to the present, naturalists have failed in their endeavours to unearth any reliable evidence of the existence in the prehistoric ages of its wild ancestor; though, on the other Wild camels hand, they have been able to indicate with tolerable accuracy and certainty the progenitors of all other domestic quadrupeds.

Fossil camels

Fossil remains have been discovered in the Sewalik Hills, in India, deposited in the Tertiary strata, and of a species slightly larger, but otherwise hardly distinguishable from recent specimens. Andrew Murray, writing on this subject, says, 'The difference is so slight it pleases us to think that we have here in this most ancient animal a species which saw the Miocene epoch, and which has survived all the chances and changes which have taken place since then,' and there is much soundness and a great deal of common-sense in his remark. Excavations have also been made in Algeria, and large fossil remains have been found in the Quaternary deposits. Professor Cope has traced a long line of descent from the Miocene Poebrotherium to the modern forms, and Marsh and others have described primitive forms from the Eocene strata. It is a curious fact that the former description of the family seems to be much wider than the natural habitat of the forms now extant—a fact which may, perhaps, be attributed to the Deluge, and the sundering of what in those days were vast globes into smaller and insulated continents. That the camel was in use in Assyria long ages ago is evidenced by the fact that traces of it appear in the Assyrian sculptures, while the fossil remains of the Helladotherium, which were discovered at Pikermi, near Athens, in 1853, and commonly supposed to be those of the giraffe, are nothing else, my friend Mr. Wessels thinks, after a careful comparison of the engravings of the skeletons of each, than those of the camel. The camel was, as we know, a native of Arabia or of the regions adjacent, and could have easily crossed over into Greece in those prehistoric days when Europe and Africa were joined together, and the Mediterranean was a huge lake.

So far as we can gather from the oldest manuscripts Mosaic records extant, the camel has been employed as a beast of burden since the beginning, at all events, of Mosaic traditions, and prior to the formation of the Jews into a nation. Mention is made of it several times in the earlier books of the Old Testament. Arabia, according to these ancient records and traditions, has been longer associated with him than any other country, and there seems to be no doubt, as previously remarked, that he was indigenous to that country, or some adjoining portion of South-west Asia, from whence he must have spread into the countries contiguous, extending gradually into the arid regions of Eastern Asia and Northern Africa. The natural inference is that he was reclaimed from a state of nature, and domesticated by the patriarchal Arabs, long before the days when Abraham was driven into Egypt by famine, and was presented by Pharaoh, in a style truly Oriental in its magnificence, 'with sheep, oxen, he-asses, and men-servants and maid-servants, she-asses, and camels.' Curiously enough, Rawlinson, in his 'History of Egypt,' can find no traces of the camel in the hieroglyphics; and yet, connected by dry land as Egypt was to the very birthplace of the camel, as well as by commercial transactions, it stands to reason that the camel must have been in general use there about that time. The story of the courtship of Isaac and Rebekah is familiar to some of us. How that Abraham, in his anxiety to secure for Isaac a wife from out of his own kindred, sent his servants with ten camels to Nahor, in Mesopotamia; and how she was wooed and won by proxy at a well without the city of Nahor; and how, like a true Mesopotamian maiden, she watered and fed the camels, accepted the golden offerings of earrings and bracelets, and with the consent of her parents returned to become Isaac's wife—neither the first nor the last romance, I expect, with which a camel has been connected. We are also acquainted with the anecdote of Joseph and his jealous brethren. How through hatred he was thrown into a pit by them, was rescued by some Midianitish merchants, and sold for twenty pieces of silver to a company of Ishmaelites who came from Gilead with their camels bearing spicery, balm, and myrrh, going to carry it down to Egypt. And we know that the Queen of Sheba, when the report of Solomon's fame reached her, and in order to satisfy her own curiosity, came to Jerusalem with a great train, with camels that bare spices and very much gold and precious stones. Isaiah, too, when he threatened the Jews for their confidence in Egypt, speaks of them carrying their riches upon the shoulders of young asses, and their treasures upon the bunches of camels; while among the Mosaic laws none were more stringent than that which prohibited the Jews from eating the flesh of certain beasts, the camel coming within this category. 'Nevertheless, these shall ye not eat of them that chew the cud, or of them that divide the hoof as the camel; because he cheweth the cud, but divideth not the hoof, he is unclean to you'—facts which go far to prove that even in those days the camel was, and had been, a most useful slave to man, providing him with the means of livelihood, and forming a great source of wealth to him, at the same time that he was looked upon among the predatory nomads, who were perpetually raiding one another, as one of the spoils of war; Job, for example, with his flocks of 7,000 sheep, herds of oxen and she-asses, and 3,000 camels, being counted a man of great substance 'and of a very great household, and the greatest of all the children of the East.' 'The Midianites also, who oppressed the Israelites, came up with their cattle and their tents, and they came as grasshoppers for multitude, for both they and their camels were without number, and they entered into the land to destroy it.' David, when he smote 'the Geshurites, Gezrites, and Amalekites, inhabitants of the land as thou goest to Shur, even unto the land of Egypt,' took away their sheep, oxen, asses, and camels.' The tribes of Reuben and Manasseh when they destroyed the Hagarites took away their cattle—of their camels 50,000, and of their sheep 250,000, and of asses 2,000. And again we read that when Job's misfortunes were falling thick upon him, 'not single spies, but in battalions,' the Chaldeans formed three bands and made a raid upon his camels, and took them away, and slew his servants with the edge of the sword, the narrator being the only man who escaped to tell the tale; while to show that the value of the camel was considered and appreciated, amongst David's several officers who were in separate charge of his treasure—his fields, his vineyards, his flocks, &c.—an officer had the special control of these animals: 'Over the camels also was Obil, the Ishmaelite,' the Ishmaelites being a nomadic tribe who lived in the desert, and whose principal wealth consisted of camels; hence Obil's selection for the post as a man of practical knowledge and experience. And in Solomon's reign, 'barley also, and straw for the horses and dromedaries [New Version, 'swift steeds'] brought they into the places where the officers were, every man according to his charge,' showing that riding camels kept for fast work were in those days looked on as valuable, and were especially well cared for; while in later days, about A.D. 1616 (see Gibbon's 'Decline and Fall,' chap. xlvi.), when giving a description of Chosroes' wealth, he writes: 'His tents and baggage were carried into the field by 12,000 great camels, and 8,000 of a smaller size.'

General utility

In those olden days, more so even than now, men were in more ways than one entirely dependent upon the camel for their living as well as for their means of support, and this general utility was, if anything, more extensive than it is now, and in every way greater than that of the reindeer to the Laplander. The camel can be ridden, driven, and used as a pack animal. The milk of the female is used in many forms of nourishment. When sour it is mixed with flour, and made into a paste called 'aish' (a kind of bread); when sweet it is boiled with rice and flour, and called 'behatta'—common and favourite dishes with the Bedawins; while the Arabs who breed camels in the deserts of Nubia and the Soudan exist principally on camel's milk and corn. Its constituent parts are nearly identical with those of mare's milk; but it is considered more nourishing and productive of greater stamina.

than the milk of any other animal by the Panjabis, Afghans, Persians, and Arabs, who feed their colts on it. Aristotle mentions camel's milk as being very strong, but good when mixed with two or three parts of water. It is said that butter cannot be made from the milk, and that the Arabs use its grease as a substitute; but I have seen this contradicted, and a statement to the effect that both butter and cheese can be made from it. The flesh of the camel is eaten, being forbidden to the Jews only; and that of the young is considered delicate, and said to be like veal, the hump being also called a delicacy; and in Sennār the different tribes, who are chiefly Mahometans, often eat the entrails. The skin is tanned, and turned into harness and shoes. Clothing and tents, which are waterproof, are made from the hair; while in Europe brushes for painters and toothbrushes are manufactured out of it; also camlet, formerly woven of silk and camel's hair, but now with a mixture of wool as well. It is also mixed with cotton, forming the warp, and the cotton the woof, of the famous Persian camel haircloth; and a coarse kind of hair is imported for various uses. Aristotle tells us that the genitals are of such a nature as to be useful for bowstrings. The dung is used as fuel in Arabia, Persia, Egypt, and India, and, in fact, in all countries where the camel is employed as a beast of burden; and sal-ammoniac is extracted from the soot of burnt dung, as well as from the urine, and used for purposes of commerce—at least I believe so; at all events, it is strongly impregnated with it.

Classical records

Aristotle, in his 'Natural History of Animals' and of 'Parts of Animals,' alludes frequently all throughout these works to the camel, and shows by what he has written that, in addition to having a love for animals, he must have been a keen observer, profiting by his experiences when he probably accompanied Alexander the Great in many of his expeditions, as well as from many specimens which were procured for him by that monarch; but his remarks apply chiefly to the breeding and procreation of the animal. Pliny, in his 'Natural History,' also devotes some matter to the camel, but appears to have copied from Aristotle, and where he tries to improve on him is generally wrong.

Herodotus—who travelled a great deal in Egypt and in the Levant—in i. 80, 4 says that the horse cannot endure the sight or smell of the camel, and he attributes the defeat of Crœsus at the taking of Sardis (B.C. 557) by the Persians under Cyrus to this fact. The Persians brought a corps of men mounted on camels into the field, which created such a panic among the horses of the Lydian cavalry that they became uncontrollable, and fled precipitately in all directions. As this historian flourished about sixty or seventy years after the event, his authority may readily be accepted; the more so as recent researches have established beyond doubt the accuracy of much that he has written. This undoubtedly is the first precise mention of the camel being employed for warlike purposes—in other words, the first camel corps that was ever formed—the great difference between its ancient and modern application being that the Persians fought on the camels, whereas in these days of the deadly breechloader they are only used as a means of mobility to move men rapidly from one point to another, and so save time and fatigue, the camels being left in the rear and the men employed as infantry.

In the account of the battle of Magnesia, fought between the Romans and the Syrians, under Antiochus the Great, in 190 B.C., a similar camel corps is also mentioned. Gibbon too, in his 'Decline and Fall of the Roman Empire,' in chap. xli., speaking of the eunuch Solomon's battles after leaving Carthage (about the year A.D. 535) says: 'The Moors depended on their multitudes, their swiftness, and their inaccessible mountains, and the aspect and smell of their camels are said to have produced some confusion in the Roman cavalry.' And in a note he adds: 'This natural antipathy of the horse for the camel is affirmed by the ancients;[1] but it is disproved by daily experience and derided by the best judges, the Orientals.'[2]

Supposed antipathy of the horse to the camel

This, I maintain, is wrong, horses that have never seen or never been brought into contact with camels show a distinct dislike, almost dread, of them at first, and will shy tremendously; while well-bred horses and those of a highly nervous disposition will not go near them. Of course they can very soon be broken of this habit, especially the latter class, and with proper management will quickly grow accustomed to them. But a horse will not as a rule make friends with or show any affection for a camel, though they will do so with animals of an altogether different species from themselves, such as sheep, goats, cats, with

[1] Xenophon, *Cyropaedia*, vi. 488, vii. 483 (ed. Hutchinson). Polyaen. *Stratagem.* vii. 6. Pliny, *Natural History*, viii. 26. Aelian, *De Naturâ Animal.* iii. c. 7.

[2] *Voyage d'Olearius*, p. 553.

which one would imagine they would not have anything in common.

As to this natural antipathy, my experience is that it is more the result of external causes, and the effect that the uncouth and awkward appearance of the camel produces on a fresh horse, or one of a fidgety disposition, or of a nervous organisation, which any thing new or strange to him for the first time, such as a train, tram, or bicycle would produce, and that it does not spring from any internal reasoning or instinctive fear or animosity, and is in no way due to their offensive smell.

Gibbon again alludes to the matter in chap. liii., when describing the armies of the Arabs: 'Instead of waggons, they were attended by a long train of camels . . . and the horses of the enemy were often disordered by the uncouth figure and odious smell of the camels of the East.

Biblical records

Yet we can surmise with tolerable accuracy that ages prior to this the Arabians and all the nomadic races in the south-west portion of Asia rode as well as drove the camel, and it is not at all unlikely that they fought on them as well. Rebekah, when she left her people to marry Isaac, 'lifted up her eyes, and when she saw Isaac she lighted off the camel.' In the time of David they were not only ridden, but evidently employed for warlike purposes, and we read that, in retaliation for the destruction of Ziklag by the Amalekites, the shepherd king 'smote them from the twilight even unto the evening of the next day, and there escaped not a man of them save 400 young men which rode upon camels and fled.' Riding camels or dromedaries were employed for postal purposes in carrying despatches in the days of Ahasuerus (or Xerxes), who reigned from India even unto Ethiopia over 120 provinces, when Ahasuerus commanded Mordecai to write to all the Jews in the provinces to avenge themselves on their enemies in return for Haman's persecution of them. 'And he [Mordecai] wrote in the name of King Ahasuerus and sealed it with the king's ring, and sent letters by post on horseback, and riders on mules, camels, and young dromedaries [New Version, 'riding on swift steeds, mules, and young dromedaries'] . . . . So the posts that rode upon the mules and camels went out, being hastened and pressed on by the king's commandment. And the decree was given at Sushan the palace.' Isaiah speaks of the dromedaries of Midia and Ephah, and we have already alluded to those kept by Solomon. It was Isaiah also, when he bewailed the captivity of the Jews, who saw in a vision the destruction of Babylon by the Medes and Persians: 'Go set a watchman, let him declare what he seeth. And he saw a chariot with a couple of horsemen, a chariot of asses, and a chariot of camels' (the New Version speaking of a troop or chariot).

Xenophon when he commanded the 'Ten Thousand,' during their retreat after the death of the younger Cyrus, had frequent opportunities of observing the camel, and in his 'Cyropaedia,' VII. i. 27, also alludes to the panic among the Lydian cavalry, but he merely says, 'Such things the horses suffer in the presence of camels;' and he does not, however, mention the effect that either seeing or smelling camels is said to produce on horses. Sufficient examples have been adduced from the classics to prove incontestably the extremely ancient origin of the camel, and its adoption and adaptation by the nomadic and warlike races from the East, not only as a peaceable beast of burden and post-riding animal, but also as a fiery steed of war; and yet here we in this enlightened nineteenth century know less about him than about any other animal under the sun.

Introduction into Europe

The camel has been introduced into Europe at different periods, but without success, not because the climate and country have been unsuitable, but through neglect and mismanagement, I should think, and because he has never become a favourite like other domestic quadrupeds. His first introduction, as far as I can trace, was when he accompanied the soldiers of the Fiery Crescent into Spain in 1019. Even after the conquest of Granada in 1492, when Ferdinand V. put an end to the Moorish kingdom, the camel still remained in the southern provinces, but, despite the suitability of the country, was finally allowed to die out.

Gibbon, in the 'Decline and Fall,' chap. lvi., when speaking of the conquest of Sicily by Roger, quotes Malaterra, who states that the Arabs had about A.D. 1058 introduced the use of camels into Sicily. And in the battle of Ceranico (between 1060 and 1090), where 50,000 Saracens were overthrown by 136 Christian soldiers, 'without reckoning St. George, who fought on horseback in the foremost ranks, the captive banners with four camels were reserved for the successor of St. Peter.'

At the solemnisation of the nuptials of the Emperor Frederick II. of Germany with Isabella, the sister of

Henry III. of England (A.D. 1235), at Worms, 'the Imperial Court was completely Oriental in character, and the historians of the time speak with astonishment of the camels which attended its movements.'[1] These animals, it is evident, came from Sicily or Rome, and not from Africa direct, as Frederick was also King of Naples and Apulia, and it is very probable that they had not up to then been allowed to die out since their introduction by the Arabs.

When the Turks under Mahomet II. conquered Constantinople in 1453, they brought the camel from Asia Minor, using him to carry their baggage and families. He is still employed in European Turkey, but not to any great extent.

In 1650 Ferdinand de Medici II., Grand Duke of Tuscany, imported some camels, presumably from Northern Africa, and established a stud at San Rossora, where there is a large sandy plain, employing them to carry goods between it and Pisa and neighbourhood. This stud, averaging about 180, was kept up until 1840, and since then it has gradually but very slowly increased to 200 in 1887, but has never grown numerous. Camels of the Arabian species from the Moorish States in Northern Africa have penetrated the Sahara to the Niger and Senegal, and have been employed on some parts of the West Coast, but not to any great extent. It must have been from Morocco that they were imported to the Canary Islands in the early part of this century—to Fuerteventura, which lies about fifty to sixty miles from the mainland, and they are still bred there,

[1] See English translation of Wenzel's *History of Germany*, i. 530.

being sent to Santa Cruz de Santiago and Lanzarote, where they are used for carrying merchandise and also in agricultural operations.

Introduction to the New World

About fifty years ago, for the first time, some camels were imported to South America from the Canary Islands, and a few also to the West Indies. Evidently the scheme was a failure, due possibly to the unsuitability of the lower lands of tropical America, and the moisture and humidity of these latitudes, but more probably the result, I expect, of the ignorance of those who were in charge of them. As is well known, the llama, which is indigenous to South America, and known as the 'camel of the New World,' is a much smaller animal, and belongs to the *Camelidæ*—a small family which includes the camels of the Eastern and the llamas of the Western Hemisphere; but of these latter it is not my intention to speak.

A little over thirty years ago—in 1857, I believe—ten camels were landed in New York, but they very soon died, except one male and one female. This pair were sent to Nevada on account of the soil, which is sandy and covered with prickly shrubs, and they produced in all twenty-four young, all of which survived. These having interbred, the number increased, until in 1875 it had reached to ninety-six, all of which were born and bred in Nevada, which speaks volumes in its favour. What has since become of these animals I cannot find out; but, without wishing to discredit the statement, I would only remark casually that 50 per cent. of newly-born camels are generally supposed to die. Whether, therefore, this is an American story or not, I would not like to say; but such a very remarkable physiological fact, so directly opposed to all preconceived opinions, should certainly receive a world-wide circulation, being far too valuable to be confined exclusively to the limited tract known as Nevada.

Importation to Australia

About the same time (1860) twenty-four camels were taken over from India to Australia for Burke's and Wills' exploration, and a little later on Warburton crossed the great Central Desert with a caravan. Since 1884, when the Australian Contingent was at Suakim, a wider experience has been gained, which has given a fresh impetus to their employment—an impetus which came just in time to restore the interest in them which had begun to flag and droop; and the movement seems to be meeting with general success, the number on the continent having now increased to over 2,000.

Napoleon's camel corps

Napoleon the Great was the first general of modern times who made use of a camel corps. Where he got the idea—whether he borrowed it from the Persians at Sardis; or during his Italian campaign (1796–97) he came across the camel at Pisa and made a mental note of it; or whether, again, it was a flash of genius which revealed it to him, and he saw with one of those lightning glances—so marked a feature of his—when he found himself in the Egyptian desert in 1798, the undoubted utility of the animal for military purposes, is not, so far as I am aware, generally known. At all events, to him is due the credit of reviving an ancient custom, and applying, but modifying it to suit modern usages, in accordance with the marked changes in the science of ancient and modern warfare through the increased development and advancement of intelligence resulting in modern firearms. At first detachments of 100 men only were mounted on camels, increased subsequently to battalions of 700, formed into flying infantry columns, the camels being also employed, when the necessity arose, for transport purposes—a twofold use which Sir Charles Napier also adopted on occasions when campaigning in the Murree and Bugti Hills.

The French in Algeria

The French, who undertook the conquest of Algeria in 1830, after thirty years' experience of trials and failures, chiefly conducted on the hire system, abandoned this temporary transport, and established a permanent camel train at the maintenance of the State as the only way out of their difficulties, and as the only sound principle to work on. It will be seen that they did not come to this conclusion in a hurry, but after various attempts on active service against the Arabs, and it would be well for us to learn a lesson from them. However, more of this hereafter. In connection with this train they have established a stud farm, and the breeding has been attended with great success.

The Russians also utilise the camel in their steppe campaigns in Central Asia, but I do not think we have anything to learn from them. Not many years ago a general officer on the Russian staff visited Algeria, inspected the French system of transport, and wrote a eulogistic report on it; but whether the Russian authorities have since adopted the French system or not, I cannot with any certainty say.

India

The camel has been known to us certainly since the days when Clive decided the fate of India on the plains of Plassey (1757), and even prior to that event, and it has been used both for riding and carrying purposes. But it is only within comparatively recent years (with one exception), and notably since the Afghan War (1878–80), that we have begun to understand something about him, and to find out his intrinsic worth. The exception I allude to is Sir Charles Napier, whom I look upon as one of our best all-round commanders, not only because he was a fighting soldier, skilled in the science and art of war, but he was his own commissariat and transport officer (an accomplishment which, as the Iron Duke said, every good general should possess). And as such he knew of what vital importance both branches were to an army, especially in the kind of country (Sind and Beloochistan, sandy, waterless wastes) in which he commanded—countries in which a force was absolutely dependent on its commissariat and transport. His observations on the camel, though few, are pithy and to the point, and well worth reading. What is more, they show that he was personally acquainted with its ways and habits, and fully recognised its extraordinary utility as a beast of burden and locomotion if properly treated and managed. Judging from these remarks, and from his action in forming a baggage and camel corps in Sind, he had a more practical knowledge of the animal, and a completer grasp of the subject, than any soldier we have ever had in India; and he, first of all British generals, fully appreciated and gauged the true capacity of the camel. And yet, in spite of the valuable lessons he inculcated, the result of a wide and varied experience, we, in 1878 in Afghanistan, knew far less about the animal than he had known some thirty years previous.

European ignorance of the camel

Up to then, it was astonishing the lamentable ignorance and unpardonable indifference that prevailed among Europeans generally—and for the matter of that, which still prevails—except among those who have lived and travelled in those countries where the camel is principally if not exclusively used. I may go still further, and assert that even amongst these a knowledge of the animal is confined to a small minority.

We ourselves, in spite of the common use that we make of the camel in nearly all our expeditions, especially in India, and despite the wholesale way in which we slaughter them, have in no way made an effort to study the camel. Nor have we attempted to lay down a system which would enable our soldiers to learn his customs and capacities, so that they could treat him in a rational and practical manner.

It will be my earnest endeavour in the following pages to give some idea, at all events, of the treatment and management of the camel, in all its phases, in connection with the military machine, and in order to be as clear and as explicit as possible I have divided the subject into the following chapters, viz.:—

I. Structural Peculiarities and Anatomical Notes.
II. Characteristics and Temperament.
III. Instinct and Intelligence.
IV. Species and Breeds.
V. Breeding.
VI. Watering.
VII. Feeding.
VIII. Loading.
IX. Marching and Carrying Power.
X. Ailments, Causes and Remedies.
XI. Equipment.
XII. General Management.
XIII. Comparison with Other Animals.
XIV. Purchasing.
XV. General Remarks.

CHAPTER I

STRUCTURAL PECULIARITIES AND ANATOMICAL NOTES

THE Camel belongs to the order of Ruminants, which is the most useful to man, the marked structural peculiarities of which are (1) cloven hoofs, (2) act of rumination, (3) absence of incisors; but it is in their dental and osteological formation (in the feet particularly) that they differ from other animals of the order, and are similar to pachyderms; in fact, it would appear that they form a connecting link between the two orders. V. S. Steel says: 'As readily recognisable instances of their differing from ordinary ruminants the fact of their having incisor teeth in the upper jaw, the possession of canine teeth both in the upper and lower jaw, and the presence of two pre-molars in the upper and two in lower may here be mentioned. The wedge-shape teeth of the lower jaw are evidently adapted for browsing on shrubby plants, and their dental arrangement altogether indicates that they are naturally herbivorous.'

General description The general appearance of this order is graceful and symmetrical—such as the deer and antelope—but the camel and the giraffe (which is even more distorted and disproportionate) are among the few with clumsy proportions. The limbs of the camel are not only ungainly, but out of proportion. His angularities and gauntness; his strange-looking head with small rounded ears perched on the thin, curved, elongated neck; his thick, mobile upper lip, slit in two and always twitching with a half-deprecating, half-cynical curl; the fringe of eyelash, long and thick, surmounted by a shaggy, beetling brow, a natural provision against the blinding glare of the fierce sun, shading eyes which the most critical must admit are large and soft and beautiful, if a trifle too prominent—a beauty which forms a redeeming figure to the animal's otherwise uncouth appearance. His large body well ribbed up in front and falling away behind, overtopped by a big hairy hump, which looks more like an exaggerated excrescence than anything else, and the short, almost stumpy tail which bears a terminal switch; his long, lanky legs—meagre extremities to such a great frame—at the end of which are great shapeless feet. His sprawling, shambling walk as he shuffles along is familiar to many, and has always made him appear to me in the light of a self-imposed caricature on nature, just as in the arboreal world the baobab-tree has similarly struck me. It is a curious coincidence, too, that he is more difficult to delineate than any other four-footed beast.

He is provided by Nature with a flat padded foot, which enables him to move over loose and heavy sand, but he is tolerant of shingle and rough ground. During progression, unlike the horse, he moves both legs on the same side simultaneously (first the near fore and hind leg together, then the off fore and hind, and so on), which gives his movements a jolting, swinging motion when you are riding him, something like that of a ship rolling and pitching at sea, and that accounts for the intense stiffness which your joints and back especially suffer until you have ridden one constantly. He is well adapted for carrying loads, but in proportion to his size is not up to great weight. He is also an excellent riding animal, and in his native deserts cannot be surpassed for speed and endurance. His nostrils are so compressed that he alone of all animals can withstand the stifling blast of the 'khamseen' or 'simoom,' which blows across the desert at times to the inconvenience, and sometimes danger, of the unfortunate passer-by. His hind quarters are deficient in power, and there is a marked disparity between them and the fore quarters, which you can see at a glance have far greater muscular and sinewy development; consequently, as well as on account of (1) length of legs, (2) general clumsiness, he is a bad climber, though mountain camels, or, properly speaking, camels found in mountainous countries, have shorter legs than those belonging to flat districts. Camels when having sexual connection, for this reason, are obliged to assume a semi-recumbent position. Both these questions will be fully discussed later on.

And now I intend to examine in detail some of the more prominent features, which will at least give us an insight into the system and inner structure of the camel. Kindly recollect, however, that this is not from the pen of a scientific anatomist and naturalist, but of one who has always taken a deep interest in the creature, and who has never been above learning a lesson from anybody or any source, particularly from the camel himself.

The nostrils are constructed in the form of slits, Nostrils

which converge towards one another, with the extremities elevated, the upper one being capable of expansion or even contraction at will. This is another of Nature's wise provisions, and the reason is plain—to exclude the fine sand and other particles which are blown about in the desert by the frequent sand storms, which would cause intense irritation in the respiratory passages of the throat. When overtaken by a simoom the camel drops on his knees, stretches out his neck, and closes his nostrils tight until the storm blows over.

The upper lip is hairy, thickened, and divided, is extremely extensile, and slightly prehensile. It is used while browsing, on thorny shrubs in particular, as a feeler, to touch and examine the leaves before nibbling them; and it has invariably been a source of wonder to me how dexterously he always avoids being pricked or scratched by the thorn.

Teeth

In the upper jaw he has twelve molars on each side, but they are not all continuous. In front of these, and separated by a good space, is one pre-molar; while before these, again, and with a small interval, is a canine, large, strong, and pointed. He has four incisors, but the two central are only small milk teeth, which he sheds when rising five years old. The remaining two lateral ones being permanent, and resembling canines in shape, become full grown at six years; they are conical and laterally compressed.

In the lower jaw he has ten molars, but, as in the upper, not all continuous, with one similar detached pre-molar and one canine; while he has six incisors, compressed, oblique and pointed. Thus it will be seen that he has two pre-molars and two canines in each jaw.

The number of molar teeth varies, but usually there are one or two more on each side in the upper than in the lower jaw; in the true camel the foremost molar is placed considerably in advance of his fellows, and is of a conical form, closely resembling the true canine. By the time he is eight years old, or certainly when nine, he has his full complement of teeth.

He is provided with a hard substance upon certain parts of his frame, upon which he leans the whole weight of his body when kneeling down, either to rest or for the imposition of a load, or just prior to rising up. Kneeling, I may here remark, is his natural state of repose. The largest of these callosities is on the chest—a kind of boss, which rests always on the ground, and which should be round and full. He has also one on each elbow and knee, one on each hock, and a little one as well on the outer side of each hock. It seems doubtful whether they are natural or only artificially produced by long ages of servitude; but I am of opinion the former is the true state of the case, and that newly-born young have traces which wear and tear naturally harden and develop. Callosities

The feet are large spongy pads, that are placed like a cushion underneath the toes, which are elongated and tipped with small hoofs, terminating in short, slightly curved nails. The camel treads flat on his toes or on the cushioned pad that protects and connects them together by extending on both sides, the horny tips alone being free and separate; which though hard is springy and elastic, expanding by pressure each time the foot is placed on the ground. This is a decided advantage on soft sand or firm ground, Feet the elasticity not only being a safeguard from lameness, but giving ease to his movements. The feet are, in fact, specially formed to travel over sand, and the sole or lower part not being cloven but united is another clear indication that Nature adapted the camel for the desert, for this prevents his sinking in loose, shifty sand. This pad is also more adaptable for the burning sand than a foot like the horse or ox, made of hard, horny substance which is liable to become brittle and develop sand-cracks; on the other hand, excessive moisture causes swelling and inflammation both to the feet and legs, so that a dry climate and soil is more or less indispensable for the camel. Dallas says: 'The structure of the foot is very peculiar, the whole of the phalanges being turned forward in such a manner as to form an elongated foot, the lower surface of which is applied to the ground. These two toes are merely enclosed in skin, and the hoofs, which are of a very small size, appear more like nails than anything else. The hinder toes which usually occur in the ruminants are entirely wanting.'

Hump

This extraordinary feature tends to heighten the distorted appearance of the camel, but in reality there is no distortion of the spine or prolongation of the spinous processes. It consists principally of fat. Arabs and Asiatics say that it is a provision of Nature for endurance of long abstinence, and, speaking literally, they say that the camel feeds on its own hump. In other words, they mean that when he is obliged to go without food and water, and is thrown completely on his own resources, he draws gradually on this natural store of adipose matter, and is thus enabled to carry on for several days. One thing is certain—they are most careful in looking after it before starting on and during a long journey. This may or may not be, and sounds very plausible. The camel, it is acknowledged, when in first-rate condition has a full, round hump, and, *vice versâ*, when in poor condition the roundness and fulness disappear. In fact, as the animal fails the hump gradually but visibly wastes away and shrinks into nothingness. I have watched hundreds upon hundreds of camels closely when they have been underfed and overworked, with their humps failing perceptibly every day before my eyes; and the conclusion I have come to, which strikes me as far more reasonable, is that the hump is the true indicator or the barometer by which you can tell at a glance the health and condition of a camel. Some of the desert breeds I have seen in the Soudan have scarcely any hump at all, or at least it is so slight as to be almost imperceptible, and yet this is when they are in the best of condition. This to a certain extent would seem to support my argument, for the reserve upon which they have to rely is almost *nil*, and they are hardier than the large-humped animals, though of course it is naturally much harder to detect loss of condition by the hump in them than in the latter kind.

The hump as a reserve

I have always considered a failing hump a distinctly bad sign, because on service, or when a camel is doing extra hard work, even allowing that it is a supply which nourishes the animal when all else fails, it is, after all, only a temporary reserve which soon becomes exhausted, and which itself requires constant replenishing to keep it always full and well nourished—a condition that only extra good food and moderate work, and not short, scanty rations and extra work, will produce. And where is this supply to come from unless you carry extra rations; and when is this ever done? Even should he be fed fairly well and regularly, the increased exertion and work that the poor brute is called upon to do, invariably without any corresponding increase in his food, counterbalances the good effect of the food. The camel himself requires every bit of the food he eats to sustain, and so enable him to meet the increased tax on his strength. In a few words, the demand of work being greater than the supply of food, what earthly chance has the hump of keeping its reserve up to the mark? And it stands to reason that the camel is incapable of increased exertion on its hump alone, no matter how well nourished it might be.

The skin

But the hump is not the only feature by which you can judge of a camel's condition. The skin, consequently the hair, is, if anything, as good, if not a more infallible sign, as I will endeavour to explain.

Deficiency in perspiratory follicles

V. S. Steel says 'that the skin when placed under a powerful microscope has been found to be deficient in perspiratory follicles and ducts.' That this to a certain if not great extent accounts for his extreme liability to mange and other skin diseases, I think is more than likely. A stinted action of the skin must of necessity lead to internal complications, and a free, continuous action is a necessity to preserve condition. That dry food, insufficiency of water, overwork, &c., conduce to aggravate such complications and produce actual disorder among the digestive organs—the mere fact of the skin becoming diseased, dry, scaly, or eruptive (abnormal, in fact), the hair starring or falling off—seems to my unprofessional mind a clear indication, the skin in this case simply acting as an organic barometer, and each specific affection being a register of the actual state of the internal organs. **Affections of the skin and hair**

That these scorbutic affections are further aggravated by an excessive amount of grain I feel positive, grain being to camels the equivalent that meat is to us. That we as a nation eat too great a quantity of meat and too little of vegetables, in hot climates more especially, I have always considered. And in like ratio we treat our camels. As with human beings, so with animals. A green diet given judiciously acts on the digestive organs, relegating health and vigour to the system; while these in their turn react on the skin, which assumes a normal condition, a clear, smooth, soft, almost oily appearance, the hair becoming bright, clean, and glossy. **Dry food and grain an aggravation** **Green diet most necessary**

As the skin of the camel is deficient in perspiratory follicles and ducts, it is all the more necessary to give it all the artificial assistance possible to enable it to act properly in the elimination or expulsion of secreta. This is all the more evident because this deficiency in itself would seem to indicate a normal condition of congestion. Therefore the drier the food, the less water, and the greater the work you give them, it is only too manifest that you not only diminish the opportunities of, but actually prevent the skin from fulfilling its functions by clogging up the pores. The immediate result is that these openings, already too few in number, are closed. The digestive organs get out of order, the **Also artificial assistance, to promote action of the skin** animal becomes hide-bound, the skin acting like a waterproof sheet devoid of ventilation; and without any channels for the excretion of secreta the germ of organic disease is sown internally, and a break-out is the final and merciful result—merciful because it is a natural indication of internal complication, which if so confined would lead to far more serious consequences—and which enables the animal to throw it off, and man, who with all his knowledge had accelerated and aggravated it, to check it. This to my mind, irrespective of any other reason, clearly demonstrates the vital importance of water to the camel, as we will see in chapter vi.

Causes of unhealthy skin

There can be no doubt that an unhealthy skin arises from impurity of blood, also from a want or excess of it. This in turn must be due to a lack of vitality or of proper nutrition, or from a superfluity of one or both, in the system, the result principally of injudicious and improper diet. It is almost universally acknowledged that the majority or a large proportion of human ills spring directly from the above, while a careful and correct diet is the secret of an even digestion. In like manner, this remark as regards the camel when he falls into our hands is, I think, equally applicable. I look on superfluity of blood in a camel as great an evil as anæmia or, if anything, worse, as apt to be congestive (or to induce congestion) and to excite enteric mischief, because of his predisposition to congestion. We cannot, therefore, be too careful in respect to his management if we want to get a fair equivalent of work out of him, and until we do, we will never reduce the enormous death-rate that we have on service.

What we must devote special attention to is not only the quality and quantity of the food, but the description. The immense value of this cannot be overrated.[1] The two former may be all right, but the latter may be at fault, and may be (as it frequently is) quite unsuitable, and in no way adapted to the animal. In this case it is not assimilated by the digestive organs, therefore not only fails to give the requisite nourishment, but has the tendency to form into gas. The intestines soon become deranged, and the skin gets out of order, which (dependent, of course, on general conditions) may lead to diarrhœa, dysentery, and other serious diseases. Then he is either worked till he drops, or possibly he may receive medical treatment, and takes a very long time to recover. How much simpler would it not be in the first instance to give him the proper food, and so save useful life, infinite trouble, and much expense! Besides, such treatment ensures less wear and tear of the internal organs, more rest, and greater vigour. These remarks apply all the more forcibly to very young camels, who require the greatest care when they are weaned and able to feed on their own account.

Diet: quantity, quality, and description

Another point I must call attention to, for it is significant, and that is, that the abdominal layer of fat is not so well developed in a camel as it is in other ruminants. There can be no doubt that this organic defect in a great measure must account for his liability to enteric and pulmonary mischief, while it explains to a certain extent his constitutional delicacy. It should therefore in itself be a sufficiently strong

Liability to enteric mischief

[1] *Vide* chap. viii.

reason for taking greater care of the animal than we do.

Mouth

Professor Owen writes: 'The mouth seems formed to save for the animal every drop of the fluid excretion of the nose; a channel leads from each nostril to the mid-fissure dividing the upper lip, which is continued down into the mouth.'

Unlike the blood of a man, the blood of the camel has oval corpuscles, and the vertebræ in the neck remain, as they always have been, seven in number.

Palatal flap

During the rutting season the palatal flap of the males alone—an inflated organ which only appears when the animal is 'mast'—hangs from the mouth like a bladder, invariably on one side only—the near, if I remember right. It never appears until the animal reaches the age of puberty, which is usually in his fifth year. The female, although she possesses one, never produces it. V. S. Steel speaks of it as a peculiar membranous kind of bag which protrudes from the mouth accompanied by a gurgling sound; and he says that the popular and even suggestive idea that it refreshes itself by bringing water into the mouth and fauces is misleading, if not erroneous, as he failed after a most careful *post-mortem* examination to detect any duct by which water could enter from the œsophagus.

Professor Owen, however, thinks that 'the surface of' what he calls a broad pendulous flap hanging down from the fore part of the soft palate and usually resting upon the dorsum of the tongue 'shows the pores of innumerable mucous crypts, and in the ordinary state in both sexes the flap may supply its own secretion, and water regurgitated from the storage cells of the stomach to the extended surface of the pharynx and root of tongue so as to allay the feeling of thirst.'

I am altogether inclined to this latter opinion. The nature of this organ is unknown—at all events, appears to be extremely doubtful—as here we have two authorities expressing themselves adversely; and yet it must be acknowledged that Nature designed it for some rational purpose, and that all Nature's handiwork is purely and exquisitely practical no one will deny. It seems likely, therefore, that the use for which it is intended is, as Professor Owen's investigations demonstrate, to allay a special feeling of thirst. I know that I have seen camels in the desert, that if they were in a state of 'mast' were too exhausted to show it, some two or three days subsequent to the last watering produce this organ frequently during a few hours, and it always seemed to me that they were apparently rinsing out their mouths and moistening them.

And now we come to that portion of the camel's internal arrangements which for so long seemed to remain a mystery, simply through lack of scientific investigation, and the proper construction of which, even at the present day, is as little known among the masses as is that of the planets and great constellations in the firmament above us. We need not discuss the reason; we will do so later on in its proper place. Stomach

The camel, like all other ruminants, is said to have four stomachs; but in a strict sense there is only one organ, which occupies a considerable portion of the abdomen, and which is partitioned off internally into four cells or compartments, which act independently of each other. The four compartments are:—

1. The paunch or ventriculus (or rumen).
2. The hood or honeycomb (reticulum).
3. The monyplies (omasus).
4. The rud (abomasus).

The herbage, having been nibbled and drawn into the mouth, is first of all coarsely ground between the molars, rolled round the tongue, mixed with a certain amount of saliva and mucus (a fluid secreted from the lining membrane of the mouth), and then forced down

First compartment

the gullet into the rumen or first compartment. This is by far the largest cavity, and the food remains in it in a comparatively dry state, and undergoes a process of softening—in other words, the paunch being full of partially digested food, the camel kneels down and rests, and experiences a sense of repletion, while the food is gradually propelled through a valvular aperture into the hood or second compartment.

Second compartment

This is of much smaller size, and the sides internally have numerous folds forming polygonal cells: hence the name. Here the food is compacted into pellets, which are returned one by one, in regular order, through the gullet into the mouth, to be remasticated by a voluntary effort more thoroughly—the operation commonly called 'chewing the cud'; and V. S. Steel says, 'in the camel the food is ground alternately in opposite directions from side to side; in other ruminants this is not done so regularly.' When the food is sufficiently remasticated, and once more mixed with saliva, it is again swallowed in a pulpy state and passes along into the third compartment, being conducted along the upper margin of the second through a canal formed by a muscular ridge, which contracts with so much force as not only to open the orifice of the second compartment, but so as to bring forward the mouth of the third into the second, by which action the muscular ridges which separate the rows of cells are brought close together, so as to exclude these cavities from the canal through which the water passes.

This third compartment contains various leaves or folds of lining membrane, similar in appearance to the leaves of a book, which are so covered with a number of prominences and so placed that any aliment which comes from the reticulum must fall between them, and describe three-fourths of a circle, before it can reach the orifice of the abomasus. Between these folds it receives still further trituration, or grinding into fine powder, and mucous admixture, and it is compressed into flattened portions, which are gradually conveyed through a valvular orifice into the fourth compartment. Third compartment

This is the true digestive cavity, where the food mixes with the juices, which by their action entirely alter its properties. The most active of these is the gastric fluid, with which it first comes into contact, and which is secreted in the inner membrane of the abomasus. It is then conveyed to the first small intestines, 'the commencement of which,' V.-S. Steel says, 'forms a distinct pouch in the camel,' where it is subjected to the action of yet two more juices, bile from the liver, and the pancreatic secretions; here the aliment becomes fit for the separation of the blood material, which is taken The fourth, or digestive compartment up to certain glands and conveyed into circulation by means of a set of conduits, named lacteals from the milk-like appearance of the fluid contained. The remaining mass is passed on through the small and large intestines, during which passage still further nutritious matter is selected from it, until ultimately superfluities are expelled in the form of excrement, this being particularly rich in ammonia, as proved by sal-ammoniac being prepared from it. The gastric juice is well known for its power of coagulating milk, and when taken from the calf, salted, and dried, is called 'rennet,' and used in making cheese.

The young camel's stomach

Before we proceed any further, a few words as to the internal machinery of the young camel. In these animals, as in all ruminants, I believe, the operation which takes place is extremely simple, yet beautiful; for the milk, then their only form of nourishment, neither requires nor undergoes the process of rumination. When the young one is fed the milk is conveyed direct from the mouth, through the gullet, into the fourth compartment, passing by the second and third compartments, which in this stage are only partially developed, and avoiding the folds of the third compartment, which are closed up altogether. Dallas, writing in 1860, says: 'In young ruminants this structure of the stomach is not distinctly visible, the first three cavities being very small, and the milk passing directly into the fourth or true stomach; and in the Camelidæ it has been recently found that the psalterium, or third stomach, is entirely deficient.'

Water cells

This brings us down to a subject of even greater interest, if not importance, in connection with the wonderfully complicated and peculiar mechanism of a camel's interior—a subject upon which the greatest ignorance prevails, and about which a great amount of doubt still exists, and that is, the water-carrying capacity of the animal itself.

Water capacity

The camel, it must be distinctly understood, has not what in a strictly technical sense can be called a special or extra stomach for the storage of water, but it has an arrangement of deep cells attached to the rumen, for the reception and preservation of water, and the enlargement of the cells of the reticulum for the same purpose. The rumen is divided into two portions, a right and a left, by a longitudinal ridge of muscular fibres which begin at the mouth. In the right is a series of cells capable of holding about a quart of water, while on the left is a larger series, which when full contain from one to one and a half gallon. When these cells are full, the liquid is prevented from being mixed with the food by the contraction of the orifice of each cell, and it can be forced out at pleasure by the action of a muscular expansion covering the bottom of this cellular apparatus.

The deep cells of the reticulum are arranged in twelve rows, and are formed by muscular bands intersecting each other transversely. This second compartment in the camel appears to be destined exclusively as a reservoir for water, never receiving solid food as in the ox or sheep; and, as we have already seen, the remasticated food passes by the entrances of the first and second compartments, along a passage direct into the third.

Sir E. Home has observed that 'while the camel

is drinking the action of the muscular band opens the orifice of the second cavity; at the same time it directs the water into it, and when the cells of this cavity are full, the rest runs off into the cellular structure of the first cavity. It would appear that camels, when accustomed to journeys in which they are kept for an unusual number of days without water, acquire the power of dilating the cells so as to make them contain a more than ordinary supply for their journey—at least, such is the account given by those who have been in Egypt.' This power of dilatation I question very much, for the fibre of which the cells are composed is not capable of much expansion. The camel may be able on a special occasion, such as above referred to, to blow himself out (to use a vulgar but forcible expression) with an extra gallon of water or so—nothing more, and I doubt very much whether the surplus will enable him to abstain and endure any longer. After a long abstinence the camel, if given the opportunity, will overdrink himself; but we will postpone the discussion of this important question to chapter vi., on 'Watering.' It is utterly erroneous to suppose that these cells do not require frequent replenishing. On the contrary, if you wish to husband the animal's strength, never lose an opportunity of watering him, and the oftener you water him the better. This supply of water is a special reserve, and, as in the case of the hump, do not draw upon it until you are obliged to.

I cannot leave this subject without quoting what V.-S. Steel has written, and so clearly expressed himself on; but I am surprised that he does not even allude to the cells of the reticulum, or second compartment, as being set apart solely for water—a fact which to me seems indisputable. Having described the rumen, he continues: 'The remarkable peculiarity of this stomach in the camel, which I wish to describe, is that appended to it are pouches arranged in two groups, disposed in parallel rows, separated by strong muscular bundles, given off from a large band of fibre, which commence at the extremity of the rumen and proceed in a longitudinal direction, dividing the entire cavity into two compartments. Muscular bundles of fibres are arranged transversely, and are otherwise distributed so as when contracting to close these square-shaped mouths of the pouches. This arrangement, all comparative physiologists agree, is a provision for the especial stowage of water, enabling the camel above all animals to tolerate upon an emergency an abstinence from that fluid; but let the word "emergency" be remarked, for it has been mentioned that, although the animal is thus enabled to travel on a short supply, it does not follow that he is not better with his tanks frequently replenished. This interesting provision has been made much stock of by lecturers, and I am afraid in their enthusiasm erroneous impressions have been conveyed; for instance, I recollect one who said that when he found the camel to possess two extra stomachs for the conveyance of water, the object of which was to supply him with refreshment during his passage through the desert, he could not help ejaculating, "How wonderful!" and went on to enlarge greatly upon the jealousy with which the supply was drawn upon, conveying the idea that it was only when the animal arrived at an extremity that these stomachs were opened, and even then but just sufficient quantity of water exuded to moisten the parched palate for fear the store should too soon be exhausted. True, these water pouches may be called extra stomachs, but they are not large reservoirs. It is equally true that their muscular mouths prevent lavish expenditure, but we must not in our enthusiastic admiration of Nature's provision run away with the idea that camels are absolutely independent of frequent watering; it is a dangerous doctrine to adopt on a campaign when we want by every means to economise the animal's strength, and draw as little as possible upon this reserve.'

It seems very probable that the term 'two stomachs' above alluded to is only a misnomer arising from a confusion of ideas, and that two compartments were meant to be implied; though the idea has always been prevalent that the camel has four stomachs—a misapplication of words purely and simply. Even Aristotle speaks of the camel, on account of his size and the nature of his food, as having several stomachs, and that he ruminates but has no bile, showing how very old are the fallacies regarding this strangely unsympathetic animal, and altogether accounting for the superstitions which have prevailed as to his extraordinary powers.

A popular fable

It seems to be generally believed that the Arab and other nomadic tribes, when placed in jeopardy through want of water, kill some of their camels in order to get at the precious fluid; but this, again, is a popular fable, although many travellers and naturalists have credited it, and Buffon cites a case of a dead camel that had not been watered for ten days being found with a pint of *pure water* in its stomach. Water when mixed with food becomes stinking, so that it is more than probable that the supply found in a dead camel would be impure and undrinkable; besides the overpowering stench that comes from a camel when opened, to say nothing of the extreme probability of the supply either having been entirely exhausted by the camel himself, or of its being so small as to be of no real use. Only a pint of dirty water in some cases —in others not so much; and in others, again, that have been without water for some days, none at all—has been found in dead camels that I have seen cut up. Other naturalists, and among them M. de Quatrefages, think that the water found in these reservoirs is in reality a secretion of the animal; but I should think there can be no doubt that the supply comes from the water which the animal drinks, and is intended as a reserve to quench his thirst on an emergency only, saliva and mucus being the secretions which assist in moistening and lubricating the food.

I once more take the liberty of quoting V.-S. Steel: **Lungs** 'The lungs are spongy bodies composed of air-tubes and cells, bloodvessels, and a tissue which connects the parts together. They are divided into two, right and left, which are subdivided into lobes, the peculiarity of those of the camel being that the latter division is less marked than in most mammalia. The lungs are covered with a fine membrane of a serous nature called pleura, which is also reflected upon the inside of the chest, the secretion from which performs the office of lubrication, and by its means any attrition during the motion of inspiration and expiration is avoided.

There are peculiarities in the anatomy of the liver **Liver** and some few specialities in the form of the pancreas, but it will be sufficient for our purpose to notice the absence of the 'gall bladder' as an appendix to the former; this proves that as in the horse a continuous flow of bile is intended, and we consequently infer that digestion in both animals is a continuous and not an intermittent process, as is more or less the case with those that possess 'gall bladders.'

Kidneys

The kidneys are glandular bodies situated in the abdomen under the loins; they perform an excreting office, and it is to be particularly remarked that the urine of the camel corresponds with the dung in being rich in ammonia.

Staling

Another peculiarity about the camel is the way in which he stales. He does not discharge his water like a horse or ass in one continual stream, and have done with it; nor does he stop to do it, but he dribbles a few drops at a time, and keeps stalking steadily on—then a few more drops, and so on; and he does this even when he is standing about. Parthey says that the camel urinates very scantily, and does this at regular intervals, so that Bedawins and Arabs are enabled by this means to trace the direction or route taken by the caravan. In 1886–87, when I was in command of the 2nd Camel Corps in the Egyptian Army, we were stationed at Mograkeh on the Nile—then our southernmost outpost, about a hundred miles south of Wady Halfa. The main body of the Dervishes was at Dongola, with an outpost at Abou Fatmeh, while their scouting parties used to come to Ras Dalgo, which was fifty-one, and sometimes to Absarat, which was only forty miles from Mograkeh. I was out constantly patrolling to Absarat and south of it, and frequently some of my men who were very clever trackers were able to tell by the traces left by the camels how many days previously the enemy's patrols had been there, and in time I became quite expert at this myself.

CHAPTER II

CHARACTERISTICS AND TEMPERAMENT

THE Camel has always been looked upon as a patient, docile animal, more capable of endurance and abstinence from food and water in sandy and arid regions than any other animal: hence the poetical name, 'Ship of the Desert,' which the unpoetical Arab has bestowed on him. That he is essentially a denizen of a flat country, and that Nature never really intended him for a cold and mountainous region, his peculiar structural formation pretty clearly demonstrates. Those of the Arabian species which are found in Afghanistan (and other parts of Central Asia of a similar nature) have, I should imagine, become acclimatised, and inured to the different conditions to which they originally were unaccustomed; after many centuries of living in cold, hilly countries, Nature has come to the rescue and clothed them with thick, long coats of hair. But for all this they have never become mountain climbers in the strict sense of the word, and never will, for reasons already given, although, of course, through sheer force of habit they are far more at home than the camel from a plain country would be. In a few words, the camel was never meant for climbing, and it is useless to compare him with the mule, donkey, or hill pony, all three of which are as handy and as active in a hilly district as the wild goat of the mountain.

In the sandy wastes of his own desert, for which Nature clearly intended and created him, the camel undoubtedly is the most invaluable of all animals for riding and carrying loads, and here he will defy competition. The fact, therefore, of his not having spread so universally as the horse, the ox, and the ass is thus accounted for. Outside his own domain, although his value is diminished, he is, nevertheless, for military purposes a very valuable acquisition. He is said to have an antipathy to crossing streams of water, which stamps him wherever he goes with the hall-mark of his desert origin. I cannot vouch for the truth of this statement from my own experience, for I have seen thousands wade through streams of icy cold water without showing any disinclination to do so, or even refusing, or giving any trouble whatever over it. Of course, they may have got over their objection by then, and whether they would have done so if left to their own free will and choice I cannot say; but what I have seen them object most decidedly to has been the descent of a steep and slippery slope. General view

The camel's temperament is decidedly passive and anomalous, for he cannot in my estimation be said to have either a good or a bad temper. He is looked upon as being vicious, but I must admit that my experience has been to the contrary. Every rule has an exception, and there are times, however, when roused, or especially when he is 'mast' (rampant), that he becomes highly dangerous and savage to man and beast, biting and kicking most severely. As a rule, though, he is a most Temperament long-suffering creature, and his forbearance is positively marvellous, and in no sense can he be called an aggressive animal. Whether, as in the case of the Egyptian fellah, centuries upon centuries (like the huge boulders piled one upon another which constitute his ancestral pyramids) of slavery and oppression have crushed all the spirit out of the camel I do not know, but imagine that it must have gone a long way towards it; or whether a spark of it, inherited from his prehistoric progenitors, still lies dormant, and requires an extra excessive, if I might be allowed to use the phrase, amount of cruelty to bring it out, I cannot say for certain, but he can bite and kick very severely, and now and then retaliates by attacking his driver, mauling and savaging him in a terrible manner. Aristotle mentions that in a fit of rage or madness he will bite a man's head off, but the old sage does not say that he himself ever witnessed a case. I have seen one mangle a driver's arm so badly that it had to be amputated, while I have been present when a man's leg has been broken by a kick from the hind leg of a camel. They rarely, if ever, strike out with their fore feet, and this, again, must be due, I imagine, to the weakness of the hind quarters, as well as perhaps to their laziness and general clumsiness of shape. This is not to be wondered at, for hired drivers are unnecessarily and brutally cruel to them. The only marvel to me is that it is not of more frequent occurrence, and goes far to prove that the animal's forbearance is almost inexplicable.

Revengeful He has been accused of being revengeful, and to this, and not to the reasons above given, may be due these sudden fits of passion. The history of the human race has taught us that, even as the worm will turn, so man, enslaved and downtrodden by continuous tyranny and coercion, will seek revenge by fair means or foul, invariably the latter. Why not the camel, then? Too dense to think of a way in which he can outwit his driver by putting him off the scent, and so taking him unawares, and roused to that pitch when even the crawling worm will rise to the occasion, he works himself into a perfect fury, and, rushing at the tyrant open-mouthed, his formidable teeth and powerful jaws do serious damage. I have read somewhere that the Turks in Asia Minor used to train their camels to fight, previously muzzling them; that then the camels would get up on their hind legs and regularly wrestle with each other, using their fore legs, and striking each other on the head with them. Whether this barbarous practice is still indulged in I cannot say, but it is a fact worth noticing as throwing a fresh light on the disposition of this very peculiar animal, for it would seem to demonstrate that a certain amount of the spirit of aggression is still left in him, and only requires some encouragement to bring it out; though I imagine, if the truth were known, these fights most likely took place in the rutting season, when the camel's temper is uncertain, and he is prone to be irritable and fierce. For my own part I would not call the camel vindictive, but he is undoubtedly liable to periodical outbursts of passion or fits of temporary insanity, especially when in the state just described. That shrewd old observer, Aristotle, among other things, mentions three facts that are worthy of note—viz. (1) 'Liability of the camel to madness'; (2) 'excessive anger with man or other

Liability to periodical fits of rage

camel at time of connection'; (3) 'objection to have connection with his dam,' to obviate which owners cover up the latter and deceive him; and he goes on to say that should the camel detect the fraud he will kill the perpetrator. The two former are well known, and have been already alluded to, but the latter is a most curious thing, which if true will support the theory of his vindictiveness. I see no reason to doubt its veracity, though I am bound to say that I have never heard of the custom existing in the present day. I have seen it stated elsewhere that the camel is decidedly revengeful, and in satisfying this passion is said to display a far thought-out malice scarcely consistent with the extreme stupidity attributed to it by Palgrave. Of this vindictiveness the driver is aware, and of the certainty that sooner or later the camel will seek revenge. Accordingly, it is customary for the person who fears his malice to throw his clothes before the camel, meanwhile hiding himself until his fury has been expended in tossing and trampling on them, when the injury, real or supposed, is at once forgotten. This agrees with and quite bears out Aristotle's statement, but whether due to retaliation, revenge, or whatever cause, argues a distinct power of reasoning in the camel which I, for one, have never seen exemplified, and is endowing him with a superabundance of intelligence which I feel sure he does not possess. I must confess, however, that on service there is little time left to the poor beast to exercise anything but a long-suffering forbearance. Nor can I agree with the writer who speaks of Palgrave's inconsistency in attributing extreme stupidity to the camel in face of persistent vindictiveness, for I consider that it is this very stupidity which accounts for the revenge, and which is nothing more than the law of self-preservation inherent in every animal, which an excess of cruelty provokes to retaliation. Besides, surely it is a well-established fact that the more ignorant and stupid man is the harder he is to rouse, but when once roused the more revengeful is his disposition, and the more dogged persistence he shows in carrying through a scheme of revenge. And in a similar manner I think the same rule applies to animal nature in general, and to a camel in particular.

The camel has been called obstinate, but this depends entirely on circumstances. He is not naturally obstinate, and a young camel if treated kindly and brought up properly has no sign of it in his disposition. It is only when he falls into the hands of men who do not know how to manage him and who vent their ill-humour on him that he develops this characteristic, and once he does, his extremely passive dulness assists materially to intensify it. It is my firm belief that the so-called obstinacy and vice of many animals is nothing but the result of an early vicious training by cruel, ignorant men. Surly, sullen, morose, churlish, are all epithets, coupled with strong adjectives, that I have heard hurled at the poor brute, but I hardly think any one of them is applicable. Painfully gloomy and lugubrious, and always so, I have never in the whole course of my life seen a camel, even a young one, playful or sportive. His view of things is far too serious. He is so absorbed and preoccupied that he has no time to waste on the

Obstinacy

gambols indulged in by other young animals. It is a case of the old saw, 'All work and no play'—in other words, domestication—which has kept his nose so unremittingly to the grindstone, that has evidently altogether done for him.

Patience

As to his patience, no one who has worked with him as I have done—struggling against almost impossible difficulties in long, tedious campaigns—will hesitate to award the palm to the camel above any other animal. See him as he stalks along, with a mingled air of discontented resignation, or resigned discontent (if I may use a seeming paradox), and as if life had no zest or flavour for him, but was a stern necessity which had to be borne! Or again, look at him standing quietly under a heavy load for hours at a stretch, immovable as a statue, the very personification of patience, the truest type of it on earth, and a splendid example to impulsive, impetuous man, who drives him to suit his own aims and ends until he falls down from sheer exhaustion to die.

Submission

And not only is he patient, but submissive—as a rule, exceptionally so—nor is he easily provoked. It is only when he is cruelly treated and habitually thwarted that he becomes exasperated and assumes the offensive, and then only after a long and constant course of such treatment. Once he does become unruly and disobedient it is extremely difficult to manage him, and as a rule he gets beyond all control; but these cases luckily are few and far between, in spite of the atrocious treatment he generally receives—not usually at the hands of owners and breeders, be it remembered, but from soldiers, British and native, and always from hired drivers, who, as I shall point out hereafter, in all our expeditions are composed of the scum and scourings of the population—lazy, ignorant scoundrels who have only been attracted by the high rate of pay.

Imperturbability

The camel, it is almost needless for me to remark, is not an excitable animal—on the contrary, his calmness and imperturbability are beyond precedent. You may annoy and disturb him, and even make him grunt, but you cannot excite him, and I should think it is almost an impossibility to upset his equilibrium when under control. Under fire he is coolness itself, and the firing and noise seem to have no effect on him. I have seen three camels hit within a few seconds by rifle bullets—one through the head, which he only shook once or twice; the second through the hump, at which he made a snap; and the third in the hind quarters, who made no kind of movement; all three resuming their ordinary attitude, and going on with their day's work as if nothing had happened. I am inclined to think that the sense of feeling in the camel must be strangely wanting, and that his nervous organisation is scarcely developed. That he is deficient in this power there can be no doubt.

Normal condition

The normal condition of the camel is one of moral torpor and insensibility, out of which it is almost impossible to rouse him, and it is to this that his calmness and coolness are due, though I have seen young, untrained camels that have been running wild in the desert very restive and skittish at times. This is when they are first employed for riding or carrying, but it soon passes off under the wear and tear of hard work.

Docility

As to his docility, if to be docile means tractability and easy management, then there is no doubt of it.

If it means that the camel is ready to learn and easily instructed, then I cannot answer with the same readiness or certainty. For though on the one hand he is very tractable and easily managed, on the other he is not ready to learn, and not so easily instructed, because he is undoubtedly a slow, dense animal. What this docility arises from it would be difficult to say, and I doubt the deepest physiological research ever revealing or accounting for it. It may be that over-domestication has been too much for the camel, or that, backed up by his own retiring, unsympathetic nature, he has developed this extreme density, the outcome of which is blind docility; but it is certainly not due to instinctive intelligence. Docility to him, like everything else, is a matter of course.

A gregarious animal

He is soon taught to kneel down, rise up, and to carry a load, but any task out of the common he is slow to, if he will ever, learn it at all. He is essentially a gregarious animal, and should be ridden or driven in couples. He shows a decided disinclination to part company from other camels, and at times will absolutely refuse to do so; and if beaten or bullied will throw himself on his knees and display great determination. If you do happen to leave a convoy to go into the bush, as long as the convoy remains in sight he will try his best to get back to it, for he hates isolation—a strange fact considering his coldness of character. But should you lose sight of the convoy he will meander along aimlessly, and never find his way back by himself. Should you lose your way in the desert, you would never think of trusting your camel to find it, as you would your horse.

That he is stupid is undeniable, and though I will not go so far as to say that he has no instinct, I maintain that this quality is certainly not well developed in him, and that centuries of assiduous drudgery have dulled, if not extinguished it. It may burst forth at times—at all events, he is credited with showing it on occasions—yet from amid the memories of the past I can personally recall but few instances that came either under my own observation or within my knowledge. It is extremely difficult to get him out of the groove—the force of habit is so strong within him. Try and coax him to do something out of the beaten track, and you might as well attempt to stem the mighty torrent of the Nile. To gain your object you must drive him, teach him you never will. He is a willing enough machine, that you can do anything with or take anywhere, but he is only a machine, and must be guided. **Stupidity**

His stupidity is shown in various ways, but in none so strongly as in his want of judgment or discrimination in selecting proper herbs to graze upon. By means of his strong olfactory nerves he is reputed to detect poisonous herbs and shrubs and discriminate between them, but such has not been my experience. He requires to be taken to suitable grazing grounds, and if left to himself will not find them out. He is not an adventurous or inquisitive beast. Thousands of years of slavish domestication have driven it all out of him, and if the herbage is scanty and poor he will not strike out for fresh pastures. Overwork in our expeditions may in a measure account for this, but in reality it arises, I think, from sheer stupidity and nothing else. **Want of discrimination**

V.-S. Steel, who was in Afghanistan 1878–80, says no case of a camel dying from eating poisonous herbs ever came under his notice, while I have seen several deaths in the same country occur through camels eating poisonous shrubs, such as the oleander bush, 'leghunai,' and 'gangao,' which are the commonest and the most deadly up there. Deaths from the same cause have also come under my notice in the Soudan, and 'aroog,' a poisonous plant which grows in the desert, is often eaten by them; also a parasitic plant named 'nikabit,' with very brilliant green leaves, is devoured eagerly, and I have been informed of this fact by the natives over and over again.

Sir Samuel Baker, in his 'Albert Nyanza,' substantiates my assertion, and bears witness to the extreme dulness of the camel; for while other animals in feeding select wholesome herbs, he is stupid enough to eat indiscriminately every green vegetable, and is thus often poisoned through eating a plant known to Arabs as 'camel poison,' and on this account it is customary to set watchers over them while grazing in districts where this plant is found. With all deference to V.-S. Steel's opinion, I am still quite convinced that the camel does eat poisonous herbs. Whether this arises from his inability to distinguish one from the other, in spite of the acute sense of smell which is attributed to him, or is due to the fact of his being greedy and voracious, or yet again is the outcome of stupidity, is a moot point, though I am more inclined to attribute it to the two latter reasons than to the first.

Tenacity

Tenacity of life the camel possesses in a marked degree in comparison to its physical strength. This is called 'obstinacy' by some, but the poor brute, in addition to ill-usage, is a much maligned animal, and I prefer to use the word 'tenacity,' and without any stretch of imagination I should call it 'pluck.' It is simply wonderful to see him plod along although utterly worn out. He does not give in easily, but clings to life, and goes on and on until he drops; and when he does drop, you may take it as a foregone conclusion that he will never get up again. Of course there are cases when they recover, but they are rare, and the chances are a hundred to one against it. His calm, stoical endurance under intense pain and suffering has excited many a time my compassion as well as my admiration. It has often been a puzzle to me how he could have possibly undergone what without exaggeration must have been positive torture, and some of the things I have seen, were I to relate them, would hardly be credited except as 'Munchausen' fiction. I know I could hardly believe at first that I was an eye-witness and an unwilling participator in them, but custom soon makes one callous, and familiarises one to the most heartrending and sanguinary scenes, though my pity for these poor sufferers was great, and I always did what I could for them.

Here, at all events, Nature, if sparing as regards meting out a due amount of intelligence to the camel, has been lavish with her gifts, and given him acute sight, smell, and hearing, though I must again confess that I myself have never seen any unusual evidence of the powers of any one of them. So keen is the first, travellers and others have asserted that, aided by the elevation at which he can carry his head, he can detect Senses the verdure of an oasis as it stands out like an island in the surrounding sea of sand; so acute is his sense of smell that he can scent far-distant water and fresh or pleasing pasture over a mile off, and more, and to this sense has been attributed the salvation of many a caravan. I cannot contradict these statements from personal observation, as no instance of them has ever come under my notice; however, as I have just pointed out, the power certainly fails him in the detection of poison and of danger, as I will show in the next chapter.

Ornaments

He delights in the jangle of bells, and Orientals invariably decorate their camels thus, also with cowries (shells) and silver neck and head ornaments, but it is most probably on the principle that, guided by the sound, a herd or string will keep better together. It is interesting to note that this custom is as old, probably, as the date of the domestication of the camel, or very ancient at all events, for when Gideon revenged the death of his brethren on Zebah and Zalmunna, he 'arose, and slew Zebah and Zalmunna, and took away the ornaments that were on their camels' necks,' the word 'crescent' being used instead of 'ornaments' in the New Version of the Bible. And when, according to Gideon's request, the Israelites gave up their booty, 'the weight of the golden earrings that he requested was a thousand and seven hundred shekels of gold; beside ornaments, and collars, and purple raiment that was on the kings of Midian, and beside the chains that were about their camels' necks.'

A silent animal

The camel on the whole is a silent beast, but there are occasions, when, being loaded or mounted, he gets noisy. His cry is slightly shrill, and inclined to be plaintive. As a rule, I have found the younger the camel the noisier he is, and, what is worse, he will give tongue without almost any reason for it, and howl if you simply go near him. If you do so with the object of mounting he will howl at you in the most dismal fashion, turning his long, unwieldy neck and head, open-mouthed, as if he were going to bite you, and looking at you out of his beautiful eyes in a semi-reproachful can't-you-let-me-alone kind of way. He will continue grunting until you have mounted and got some little distance on your way, when he will cease, but not altogether, breaking out occasionally, especially when you want him to go a bit faster. Of course, some are noisier than others, but for any exceptional service where silence and secrecy are necessary, and steadiness a *sine quâ non*, never employ a young or an untrained camel. Two or three times when stalking gazelle in the Nubian desert I have lost a splendid chance and easy shot through having a young camel, whom I had dismounted and left two or three hundred yards behind, howling without any seeming cause, except because he had been left to himself. Another thing is that if left alone like this a camel will get up and bolt, and leave you perhaps in an awkward predicament, unless you have previously taken the precaution of securing him firmly—a most necessary measure always.

Special service

The older the camel, the quieter and more amenable he is, either giving a gentle grunt of dissent or, if well trained, more frequently remaining quite silent, not even deigning to look at you appealingly, but treating you as if he had made up his mind to tolerate you and make the best of things. The older he grows the

The older staider

steadier and more sedate he becomes; but naturally there are exceptions, and when bad-tempered, or in a 'mast' condition, he is usually very noisy and snappish.

The average specimen

To sum up the average specimen of a camel. He can abstain from food and water—the latter more especially—longer than any other animal. He is stupid and patient to excess, submissive and tenacious to a degree, docile and obstinate to a certain extent, vindictive and passionate when roused, not easily excited nor usually alarmed, though at times liable to a panic or stampede—an animal, in fact, whose characteristics are every bit as peculiar as his structural peculiarities.

Prevailing ignorance

We have previously remarked on the widespread ignorance of the camel that prevails, even among European residents and travellers in the East, but in a measure this is not to be wondered at, and the reason of it is more or less self-evident. It may be that the apathy and nonchalance of the camel better suits the sluggish and conservative temperament of the Eastern than it does the rapid, radical disposition of the Western races. Or is it that in the good old days, and even nowadays for the matter of that, in this go-ahead, practical age, few people have troubled to learn his peculiarities and characteristics, and fewer still have studied his capacities and ailments under the variable conditions and circumstances that he has been subjected to?

The reason of his unpopularity

Because, with all his docility and patience, in spite of his domestication, and notwithstanding his large, soft, sympathetic-looking eyes, the camel is uninteresting and unattractive, and has been looked upon more in the light of a strange natural curiosity, valuable only to certain tribes in certain countries. And yet, to those who know him, not uninteresting in the strict sense of the word, for the camel has a curious conglomeration of characteristics not to be found in other animals, and not only is he well worth the study of an ardent naturalist, but would well repay his researches. To the ordinary observer, however, his intense, Medusa-like composure, far from attracting, is repellent. Nor does he ever break that composure, no matter how old and how long your association with him. He steadily declines your advances. He refuses to become your friend. He will not identify himself with his rider or driver in the smallest way whatever. His eye never lights up with love or even interest at the approach or approval of his master—in fact, it never lights up at all with any feeling inspired by affection. This is a quality which Nature seems to have entirely forgotten to insert in the composition of the camel, and his best friend and most devoted admirer cannot accuse him of being a sentimentalist in any sense. No endearments and no blandishments (to me it seems the height of ridicule even to imagine a sane person making a pet of one), not all the coaxing in the world is of any avail. You cannot appeal to him as you can to almost any other domestic animal—through his stomach, to put it literally; in other words, by feeding and pampering him. In fact, you cannot appeal to him at all, for he has no feeling to appeal to. I do not know how it would succeed if you took a newly-born camel in hand, as I have never attempted it, but I imagine the difficulties, though perhaps not insuperable, would still be very great.

Though he is very tame, and gets to know you, it is only to a strictly limited extent, and though he will go so far as to eat bread out of your hand, and perhaps give you a low grunt of recognition when you come near him—a mark of great condescension on his part—somehow or other you cannot get any further with him. Should you attempt to pat or caress him, he shows not the slightest appreciation—on the contrary, he usually objects to it in a very decided manner, drawing his head away and giving vent to a low growl of disapproval, with a don't-take-any-liberties-with-me kind of expression.

No liberties

The fact is, you must not take any liberties with a camel. He is not like a horse or a dog in this way; though he may be good and faithful to you according to his lights, you cannot make a friend or a companion of him, like you can of these. Life and its hard conditions are taken for granted. Good treatment or bad makes no difference to him, or at least his countenance, stolid and stony in its expression, does not reveal it. No one but a keen observer would detect in the young camel a slight look of reproach in its beautiful eye, or a fine touch of pathos and appeal in its wailing grunt; while the old battered veteran accepts his fate with supreme and calm indifference, not unmingled with a dash of supercilious scorn, as if he were the only creature in existence, and you had nothing whatever to do with him. It is this indifference and want of interest that he shows to man, this entire want of confidence in him, that in a great measure widens the breach between them. A horse endears himself to you and shows his affection for you in many ways, neighing and whinnying at your approach, rubbing his nose up against you, licking your hand, and learning his name like a dog. Who so keen in a clinking run after the wily fox or the mighty boar as a good horse? When you are on him, he has a fellow-feeling with you—reciprocates your sentiments, shares your ardour and excitement in the chase, enters into the spirit of it with a fire and a will, a kind of animal magnetism, which passes between you, which makes your very heart go out to him, and you almost feel as if you and he were one and the same being! You not only look on him as an old friend, but feel for and cherish him as one; and what better friend or companion has any man in the South African veldt, or in the Australian bush, than his horse? He will do for you what he will not do for a stranger; to a camel there is no distinction. What makes a horse fly a five-barred gate or a stone wall; what makes him face the tusks of an infuriated boar; or, if he scents danger round about, what adds to his courage but confidence in his friend and master whom he trusts? The horse is a gentleman, and the camel is a boor. In a few words, it is a question of united self-interests and hearty co-operation between man and horse. The mule and the donkey, too, if you treat them kindly, will appreciate your attention and reciprocate it. Not so the camel. He neither gives nor takes. He is wrapped up entirely in himself and his grievances, and they are on occasions very grievous, poor wretch! Like the tortoise, he prefers to keep himself to himself, for out of the shell of his impenetrable reserve he will not come, and, what is more, no inducement will make him.

And so it is, I imagine, that few people have taken an interest in the camel, and he has been looked on merely as a useful brute, that as long as you gained your object with him it mattered little or nothing whether it was at the cost of his life or not. Another reason, perhaps, is that he has been looked upon with a certain amount of awe and mystery, as the only animal of its kind, strange and exclusive, with a complicated internal machinery that enabled him to march impossible distances under impossible conditions. By degrees, without proper study or inquiry—in fact, people seemed purposely to avoid it—it was believed that the camel could carry almost any weight, and travel any distance without food and without water; and that these, especially the latter, were merely secondary considerations—luxuries, and not necessaries—which could be dispensed with altogether. Never was there such a fallacy; but we will discuss these questions later on, under the separate headings of 'Watering' and 'Feeding.'

CHAPTER III

INSTINCT AND INTELLIGENCE

On a subject so exhaustive as the above I have been obliged to alter my original plans and devote a special chapter, although I have casually alluded to it in the preceding one, which, however, was already quite long enough. General remarks

In approaching so deep a question as this I must confess to a feeling of diffidence in giving expression to my views, which are crude even to simplicity. But in a period extending over twenty years it is scarcely possible, and somewhat improbable, to go through life without learning something about the ordinary domestic animals that are more or less mixed up with the daily routine of our existence—all the more so when one has been placed in almost every possible conceivable position with certain of them; it is more than likely that you get to know a good deal as to their habits and characteristics without even going out of your way or putting yourself out to make a special study of them. It is this which has emboldened me to put on record my thoughts and feelings on so weighty a matter, in the best language at my command, yet in spite of this weakness I feel that some of my experiences deserve a certain amount of attention and consideration. In fact, anyone taking an ordinary interest in animals, and possessing an average amount of the power of observation, is bound to learn to a certain extent, while, if you are at all careful in your obsèrvations, and use a little intelligence, you do not require to be a zoologist (in the strict sense of the term) to become acquainted with the temperament and characteristics peculiar to the different kinds. I regret extremely that I am no zoologist, and I deplore my want of technical knowledge, which has been a great drawback to me in writing this work. But though I cannot in any way say that I have been a student of natural history, I certainly can affirm that I have always taken the very greatest interest in animals of every kind. And it has invariably afforded me not only much amusement and pleasure, and a deep and intense satisfaction, but, above all, information and instruction in watching closely their little ways and manners, so that the time thus spent has in no way been thrown away.

One does not need to be a Darwin or a Quatrefages —I say this in all meekness—to see a distinct and decided connection between the lower animals and ourselves, and, for the matter of that, with the vegetable kingdom, though the links which bind them are in many instances extremely subtle or vaguely shadowy; while on the other hand, again, so close is the connection that it might almost be said to amount to relationship. Of course, it is to Darwin and such able men, who have devoted their lives to science—by whose genius and patient research and investigation certain facts have been established beyond doubt, and certain theories, amounting almost to fact, have been so clearly and logically worked out and expressed—that we owe our present knowledge, and to whom the world at large is greatly indebted; and it is they who have materially assisted in confirming the doubt and wavering belief of all lovers of Nature and of animals on certain points in connection with the close alliance that exists between the different kingdoms of Nature; and it is they who have taught us lessons that have hitherto been vague, shadowy, and undreamt of in our philosophy. And if we are in any way desirous of learning more, or of seeking further truths, we must be more than keen observers. We must do as they did, and make it the study of a lifetime; and not only a study, but a devotion. Not only must we dip below the mere surface, but plunge headlong into it, diving into its deepest depths. Like Byron, we must love not man the less but Nature more. And to this we must add genius.

And what is genius, after all, but a patient, persistent perseverance, a dogged, determined application that will neither give way nor give in, that will not acknowledge defeat; a perseverance and application, combined with a certain clearness of intellect and a length, breadth, depth of mental vision that is telescopic and yet microscopic in its range and compass—a vision that not only grasps an object at first sight, but retains the impression for good and aye on the retina of the mind: in two words, a vision that is keen and retentive?

Affinity between man and man

That there is an electrical affinity between man and man, which springs from some secret source of hidden spiritualism as yet unknown to us, which eternity alone will discover and unravel, I have a strong conviction. But that this will not be until we have been educated up to, and have reached such a stage of intellectual development, as will find us morally and spiritually mature enough to deal with the subject with the same ease and simplicity as we now do with the ordinary A B C of commonplace life, I feel equally convinced. What this affinity is, and whence it is, is almost idle speculation and waste of time to conjecture and surmise about.

Whence its motive power?

Let us be satisfied that it is; and there can be little or no denial on this point. What else can draw and attract two organisms, who have never known or seen each other in this phase of their existence, from the opposite ends of the earth? Mere accident, chance, or coincidence, say the sceptical. 'Kismet,' says the Mahometan. 'Fate,' replies the fatalist. But call it what you will, it is something more than this. Whoever or whatever it is, unseen and unknown, it is a force which makes itself felt, controlling, directing, and guiding us, through our wills and consciences, like wave-tossed weeds or wind-wafted straws, imperatively and irresistibly—a power from which there is no escape.

Is it fate?

In this stage chance or destiny appears to have something to do with it. Two people are apparently thrown together accidentally. Granted. But what is it that draws them towards each other? Whence this mutual attraction? Why to them in particular? Why not to any of the other individuals among whom they are thrown? A common sympathy may have a good deal to say to it. Feelings, sentiments, ideas, and opinions may also be in common. Sympathy at first attracts. Communication leads to an interchange of thoughts, which results in a mutual understanding. Then comes companionship, followed immediately by affection—that quality commonly called love, which poets dress in all the imagery of choice metaphor, culled from amid the weeds and flowers of fanciful and riotous imagination, and for which they have their own individual definitions. But even granted for sake of argument that simple coincidence is accountable for all this, how are we to account for antipathy,—the diametrically opposite feeling—the feeling of deadly repulsion, of intense inimicality, between two individuals who presumably have never previously met? Does Fate also provide for this eventuality in like ratio?

Coincidence?

Is it not probable, is it not at all events possible, and quite within the bounds of human intelligence to admit, that our life on this earth, varying as it does from an hour old infant to the allotted span of seventy years and upwards, is simply an existence in a certain sphere, a probation, a phase of an eternal life of which this planet is but one stage? A life which has existed in various grades, each one gradually working up to a higher level? A life that will continue to exist in other phases, until it reaches the highest level attainable? And is it not also possible that these two souls have met in one of the previous stages, and so have either been attracted or repelled according to the existence of affection or revulsion which has formerly existed between them? I fail to see why not, and I believe it to be not only highly possible, but extremely probable. Here again, however, we are confronted with the same difficulties, and with the same want of education. The

Or the phase of an eternal life?

day will come in its own sphere, and in its own time, when we shall know; but it will come to us in a future stage. Therefore it is simply an elaborate loss of valuable time to argue on possibilities or probabilities, for time alone will unfold the mystery.

Affinity between man and beast

In the same way, there is a distinct affinity, I firmly believe, between the human and animal kingdom, but of a material and inferior grade, more in the form of a species of animal magnetism, which is first of all set in motion by a mutual feeling of sympathy, that creates a bond of fellowship which age and association ripen into affection. In like measure, I believe that it is this force which accounts for the extreme fancy or intense dislike that a horse or a dog, the latter especially, will contract on first coming into contact with an individual. This is usually attributed to instinct, and inasmuch that it springs into existence all of a sudden, and on the impulse of a moment, it is instinctive.

Is its motive power instinct or reason?

But the question is, whence the instinct? How and why impelled into being, without previous provocation or knowledge of any kind? Instinct is but simply impulse. Here surely behind this impulse is something more—a motive intelligent reasoning power, that causes the animal to think and act. At all events it is a thought worthy of consideration; and that this affinity exists between man and certain animals only—notably between the horse and dog, animals to whom man bears a distinct analogy in some respects—I feel quite certain, and I will endeavour to explain myself as clearly as I can as I go along. That it does not simply spring from use and association only is, I think, admissible. But that it is more than this, and originated ages and countless ages ago in some such affinity as I have tried to describe, I have an inward conviction which I cannot clearly express.

Want of sympathy between us and camels

At all events we have been quite as long associated with other animals, such as the cow, sheep, goat and camel, which are quite as, if not more, useful to us, but for which we have little or no affection, because of this very affinity and analogy which they lack. Camels especially, though gregarious, seem to have little if any sympathy for each other, and mutual affection, except of the mother for its young—and that is not very marked—is an unknown quantity. That this want has always prevented it from being on the same friendly footing as the horse with the Bedawins of the desert, there can be no doubt; and that this is due, either to a tacitly antagonistic feeling, or, which is more likely, to the non-existence of an affinity between itself and man, seems quite possible.

Noble qualities of horses and dogs

Horses and dogs, more so than any other animals, have in their natures certain noble qualities and characteristics which not only endear them in our eyes, but which call for our respect and our admiration, and which are worthy of our imitation, among them unswerving fidelity, obedience, constancy, patience and submission, which human nature may equal but not excel, and the examples of which many of us would do well to follow. Even the much maligned camel is a living and everlasting monument to us of submission and long suffering, which is in marked contradistinction to the impatience, impulse, and impetuosity, as well as to the wilful lawlessness of human nature,

Patience of camel

which requires the constraint and control of law and society to keep it properly in subjection.

Affection between man and horses, dogs, &c.

That it is this magnetism between the human and animal creations which, though in degrees, developing from affinity in certain animals, and therefore of a stronger and higher order, brings us nearer together, and that it is man's superior intelligence and intellect which enables him to trace the connection which unites the different kingdoms, seems quite a reasonable deduction.

Affinity due to similarity of nervous development

There is, however, another way to look at it. It has been asserted that man seeks his affinities; and we have all heard of the old saying that 'a man is known by the company he keeps,' another way simply of saying that his nervous system and that of his associates is similarly developed. But if this were true, why should he seek his affinity any more than that it should seek him? The chances are, if chance has anything to say to it, that in nine cases out of ten the stronger development draws the weaker towards it; or, if they are equal in strength, the attraction is mutual. And so it is equally possible that the nervous system of man and certain animals (dogs and horses) is on a similar but comparative scale; and the latter, looking up to the former as a being of a higher order, are so attracted and impelled towards him.

Physical analogy between human and animal creation

Schweinfurth, in his 'Heart of Africa,' calls attention to 'the remarkable law of nature which provides that similar conditions of existence should produce corresponding types amongst all ranks of animal creation.' In other words, to the striking analogy that exists between man and certain animals. But he alludes exclusively to physical conditions. Now it is equally possible, and quite as probable, that this resemblance does not simply extend to external characteristics, but to mental and internal qualities as well. There certainly can be no reason that I can see why an animal brought into constant touch with man should not develop certain like mental tendencies. There can be no doubt, for instance, that, in any field of game or sport, man, the horse and dog meet on common ground. No one who has ridden an Arab or a country-bred horse on the plains of India out pig-sticking, or who has careered across country in the shires on a thoroughbred hunter after the wily fox, will for an instant deny that his horse enters into the spirit and excitement of the hunt as much as his rider, all the more so if they know one another. And who will deny that the pack of hounds—who allow nothing to discourage or stop them, even when Master Reynard is clever enough to throw them off the scent—do not keenly enjoy the sport? Who can dispute the sporting proclivities of the pointer, the setter, and the retriever? Take a fox-terrier who is not specially trained, and watch him when he is worrying a rat or chasing a cat. Keep your eyes on his face, and watch the intense expression of intelligence that comes into it when his master simply repeats the magic words 'cats' or 'rats,' which act as an 'open sesame' to his heart. What a train of associations—happy hunts, thrilling chivies, fierce fights, glorious victories—do they not evoke in his little brain! What pleasant memories to be awakened, refreshed, and satisfied once more by an indulgent provident master, who is always kind and ever ready to

Also mental

Reasons in support of this

assist him in his favourite sport. Look at him as he still sits on his haunches, uncertain whether to move or not, and rather incredulous as to the genuineness of the thing, for his master has more than once taken him in on previous occasions and raised a false alarm. All the same, he is quite ready for any emergency, and he shows it, too, by the eager knowing way in which he looks at his master, with his ears cocked and his eyes brimful of wistful expectancy and eagerness. Then, when the magic words are repeated, and he concludes that his master is in real earnest this time, see him jump to the conclusion and to his feet in a bound, all action, life, and energy, prepared to battle with any number of the feline or rodent species. And when his master does not move, as a reminder or an incentive to him, see him rush away a short distance barking, return, look up into his master's face, wag his tail, bark, as if reporting the result of his scouting, then off a second time, repeating the same performance over again. Who will not admit that his keenness and readiness for sport are inherent and instinctive in him, and that he wants no encouragement, but is only too ready to accompany his master at any time or anywhere? And who can doubt but that the force of reason is impelling him all this time to give an outward expression of his thoughts through his actions, and that had he the power of language he would say 'Come along, do, my good master, I see a cat up that tree; come quick, and help me to tackle him'; or, 'A rat has gone down that hole; come and help me to dig him out'? Even in the borderland of dreams his true sporting nature reveals itself, and when his dormant fancy runs riot, many is the clinking run and row he takes part in, as vivid and exciting as the reality. What an eventful history could a poacher's dog unfold were he gifted with speech! How stirring, adventurous, and hazardous a life, requiring the keenest perception of the senses of sound, smell, and sight, all ears and eyes in fact. A history, too, that would let in a flood of light on the vagaries of human nature.

Fidelity and obedience of horses and dogs

Regarding the fidelity and affection of horses and dogs, and the obedience of the latter, no one who has made pets of them will for a moment deny. Some will say, more especially as regards horses, that it is purely and only an affection of the stomach. It may in the first instance so originate; but if you are in close and constant touch with your horse or dog in hunting, shooting, and other sports, and if you show sympathy and affection for them, they in their turn will reciprocate your feelings with ardour and devotion. And, after all, how is an infant's or even a child's affection derived, but through the same material medium of food, prompted and aided by an instinctive feeling which germinates from affinity? And that a dog has a conscience—in other words, that he possesses a consciousness which enables him to distinguish between right and wrong, or has a sense so akin to it as to arrive at the same result by some mental process of reasoning—I fully believe. One has only to watch a dog closely, as I have done scores of times, when he has misbehaved himself, or done something wrong—stolen a piece of meat, for instance, or gone into a room that he had no business in—and when he is spoken to you can see by the look which comes into his eyes, and by his manner all over, as he crouches down or shrinks

The conscience of dogs

away abashed with his tail between his legs, that he knows and feels himself guilty. This may be put down to fear; but as a rule, when you understand a dog's character, you can easily analyse the two, and discriminate between them; and I feel sure that his conduct on these occasions is as often due to conscience as to fear, dependent in a very great measure on the character, breeding, and bringing up of the dog. The better these, the more conscientious and sensitive the animal. Of course it is a variable and elastic tendency, but in comparison, or relatively, no more so with them, I do believe, than it is with humanity.

Darwin's opinion

Darwin only touches on this point, but he says enough to show that he was a believer in canine conscience, i.e. 'Besides love and sympathy, animals exhibit other qualities connected with the social instincts which in us would be called moral; and I agree with Agassiz that dogs possess something very like a conscience.' That all these social instincts so closely resemble what in us are moral qualities, and that they are the outcome of mental affinity and contact with man, and that the dog is the only animal who seems to approach us in this respect, seems to me evident enough. But that some of these self-same animals evince in certain qualities a depth and intensity almost human, and that it is only through want of inferior reasoning power that they cannot distinguish as we do the finer moral distinctions, is also clearly evident. As Darwin says, 'I fully subscribe to the judgment of those writers who maintain that of all the differences between man and the lower animals the moral sense or conscience is by far the most important.

But there are other lessons for us to learn which only time can unveil, and science, tunnelling and burrowing steadily and earnestly, will unearth. And of this there can be no doubt. Apart from this, however, even with our imperfect knowledge, and inclined as we are to look down on and treat animals as brute beasts, there is much that we can learn from them by studying and making ourselves intimately acquainted with their habits and characteristics. And the more we know of them, the less inclined we will be to class certain specimens as mere brutes or beasts. It is by virtue of our intellectual attainments, by our powers of reason and moral discrimination more particularly, that we altogether rise above them. And yet there are many of these animals that have more intelligence in them than we, in our deepest philosophy, have ever dreamt of, confined as the majority of us are by the narrowest of narrow-minded prejudices to a cramped and contracted sphere, and blinded by our own vain egoism as we have been—an intelligence which only requires the cultivation and education of closer associations and stronger magnetism to improve and develop it. And that all animals who have a sharp and well-defined instinct are capable of this expansion is, I think, tolerably clear to those who know them. Necessity of studying domestic animals

'My object in this chapter' (iii. Part I. 'Descent of Man'), says Darwin, 'is to show that there is no fundamental difference between man and the higher mammals in their mental faculties.' And in the same chapter, speaking of reason, he writes: 'Of all the faculties of the human mind it will, I presume, be admitted that Reason stands at the summit. Only a Darwin's views on the mental faculties of animals few persons now dispute that animals possess some power of reasoning. Animals may constantly be seen to pause, deliberate, and resolve. It is a significant fact that the more the habits of any particular animal are studied by a naturalist, the more he attributes to reason and the less to unlearnt instincts.' That Darwin must have been alluding to scientists and lovers of animals, and not to the masses, as to general knowledge of this fact, I cannot help thinking. For the amount of ignorance that still prevails on the subject is positively marvellous; and I have heard educated and presumably intelligent people scout the very idea of such, even among dogs and horses, as utterly ridiculous. As to the significance of the latter fact there can be no question whatever. I have been in close contact with many animals—viz. horses, dogs, cats, elephants, mules, donkeys, oxen, camels—and in all but the two latter I have seen unmistakable signs of intelligence and reasoning.

The camel a drudge from time immemorial

That the dog and horse, owing to their constant association with man from the earliest days, and owing to the mutual bond of sympathy between them, which has strengthened these ties considerably, have undoubtedly developed the natural instincts inherent in them into an intelligence which clearly amounts to a distinct form of reason, I venture to think there can be little doubt. And that the distinction between their reason and man's is not radical, but due to a difference of condition and to a want of inner and upward development and expansion, is easy enough to understand. But as far back as we can trace, and even further, if I may use the anomaly, surmise and conjecture can weil imagine

—no matter what part of the world, whether on the confines of China or in the northern parts of Africa—the uses and treatment of the camel have been identical, also the conditions and circumstances that have surrounded him. And he has toiled, drudged, and slaved for man from the very beginning until now with the same stolid patience of stupidity, and the same wrapped-up conservatism of character. In fact, I quite believe, if the truth were known, that the camel was a purely conservative evolution, evolved solely for the purpose of domestic drudgery.

Remarks on the want of instinct and intelligence of camels

It is my invariable rule to take a man as I find him, and I have always acted on this principle with regard to the animal species. I am speaking now of the camel as I have found him, under every degree and variety of condition and circumstance, and I must confess that I have never seen a single specimen that was gifted with intelligence, while I have never come across one that showed any special form of instinct, except the ordinary ones of existence, propagation, and preservation. On the contrary, taking camels as a class, I have found their instincts to be of a decidedly low dull type. I will even go further and say, that I do not think if we took a camel in hand from its very infancy, subjected it to quite a different mode of treatment, one of kindness and fellowship, as in the case of a favourite horse or dog—an impossibility, I should imagine, this latter—and if we continued this treatment for several generations, or say longer, that even by then would reason have been developed in the offspring; though I think it quite probable that this humaner and kinder form of treatment, necessitating closer contact and association

Improvement of instinct probable

with man, might generate magnetism, and would certainly improve their instinct, making it clearer, sharper, better defined, in fact, and more decided. This in turn would, I imagine, require something like a hundred generations of training and cultivation before it would be possible even to mature it sufficiently to attempt a further development of the reasoning faculty, and would then be a failure, because I quite believe the germ is wanting. I must admit, however, that the greater part of my experience with camels has been under the hardest and most unfavourable conditions, and it is quite possible that high pressure and starvation materially assisted in dulling a naturally slow dull instinct. Besides, they rarely, if ever, had a chance or were given an opportunity of showing or using it, because they were looked on and employed simply as machines, and nothing else.

Cultivation of reason doubtful

Whatever the true cause may be, I cannot help thinking that ages of domestication and servitude have had an overwhelming influence on the camel, and have very effectually helped to deteriorate and stultify the instinctive faculty, which in its original state must have been singularly defective.

Probable causes thereof

During all this time he has been a living machine, pure and simple, and never for a moment has he been allowed to think or act for himself. He has been ridden, burdened, and driven to suit man's aims and ends, and in order not to overstrain him man has consulted his convenience as to halting, watering, and feeding him. Man has lived on him and by him from the earliest times, and made every possible use of him; but there has been no sympathy, and no approach of any kind between them. In this way he has been under complete subjection for a time the limit of which we can simply approximate, and then only hypothetically, and his instinctive faculties have run down and become nearly played out. In other words, their development and expansion have been thwarted and checked generation after generation, until they have dwindled down into a condition of feebleness and attenuation.

He has never been allowed to run altogether wild; only occasionally, for temporary convenience—a condition that would have done much to resuscitate and renew these dormant faculties. Everything, in fact, has been done for him from such a very early period that thousands of years must have elapsed since his ancestors lost, if they ever possessed, any reason, except when in a wild state; and though we have as yet found no traces of this, it is quite possible to suppose that they were so once upon a time. He has not been permitted in any way whatever to exercise these faculties, but has accepted life and its conditions as inevitable with a long-suffering passivity truly phenomenal. Consequently, it is not to be wondered at that these faculties have gradually and steadily deteriorated until, if not actually extinct, they have become so wasted and blunted that it requires a very extraordinary effort to vitalise and bring them into requisition.

We know that animals will degenerate if there is not enough crossing of breeds; more so if there is a total exclusion of strange stock. We also know that if for generations the economic pressure has been so great as to deteriorate the physical constitution of their progenitors, the offspring will suffer and become more degenerate still. And if the physical condition degenerates, the mental will do likewise, for they are so closely connected as to be in a great measure dependent on each other. So that we cannot expect the transmission of superior qualities when they no longer exist, but on the contrary qualities which are in every way inferior. But if, instead of generations, we pile centuries on centuries, and ages upon ages, and when we know that each preceding generation has communicated inferior tendencies to its successor, it is not surprising that the present offspring are deficient in physical and mental vigour. And so it has been with the camel, and I fully believe that at one time his physical and mental powers, the former more especially but disproportionally, were far greater than they now are, at so remote a period, however, as to place it beyond the present reach of practical demonstration.

Massoutier's views traversed

Lieut. Massoutier, of the 1st Regiment of Zouaves, in a pamphlet on 'The Conduct of Convoys in Southern Algeria,' says that 'camels are easily frightened, and that when they are, or when they scent from afar off some more pleasing pasturage, it is astonishing to see the speed with which they "make tracks;" and thefts of camels will often take place, notwithstanding every precaution.'

As to their powers of smell, I have spoken of them in the last chapter as undoubtedly exaggerated; but, without wishing to doubt, or in any way to cast a reflection on the accuracy of this statement, I can only say that, after a long experience with various breeds, I never met one that showed such intelligence as Lieut. Massoutier attributes to the Algerian camel. For my part, I cannot help thinking that he is labouring under a wrong impression. The mere fact of his alluding, all in one breath, to their also bolting when *frightened*, as well as for *fresh pasture*, and coupling this with the thefts which consequently follow, lead me to infer that he has got a trifle mixed in his deductions.

Camels when grazing wander about loosely, especially younger ones, and they are then easily enough frightened. Here he is quite right, and a few men can cause a panic among them without much difficulty. It is more than likely that this has been the case when Lieut. Massoutier has seen them bolting, and that they were being scared by thieves towards good pasturage, there to be stolen, or by dissatisfied drivers, who were anxious to return to their own homes. I am not aware of the thieving propensities of the Algerian Arabs, but certainly the Pathans on our north-west frontier of India are fully capable of this, which is quite feasible in bush country.

Mental variability of breeds

I will admit, however, that it is quite possible that one particular breed of camel may possess a greater amount of instinct in it than another, just as in dogs and horses one breed has distinctly superior intelligence over others, and one horse or dog, as you invariably find, is far cleverer and sharper than the majority of his kind. For instance, it is pretty universally acknowledged that the poodle is the cleverest of the latter, while of the former my experience has been that those of the Arab breed are the sharpest. As Darwin says on this point, 'The variability of the faculties in and of individuals

the individuals of the same species is an important point for us, and some few illustrations will here be given. But it will be superfluous to enter into many details on this head, for I have found on frequent inquiry that it is the unanimous opinion of all those who have long attended to animals of many kinds, including birds, that the individuals differ greatly in every mental characteristic.' This I can certainly confirm. In the particular instance, however, that Lieut. Massoutier quotes, the fact—namely, that a camel can discriminate from a distance as to the quality of the pasture—is in itself not only a proof of his wonderful powers of smell, but argues a decided reasoning power which I for one have never found in the many breeds that I have worked with.

Instance of stupidity of camels

One instance, however, that came under my notice, which gave them an excellent opportunity of practically demonstrating their faculties of reason, or even of instinct, occurred in Afghanistan in 1878, which at the time created a very strong and unfavourable impression on my mind. We were crossing the river Lora, which lies between Quetta and Gulistan Karez, at the foot of the Kojak Amran range. It was not very broad, while the water at the drift was only about a foot deep, and not more than two feet in any part of the stream; but the bed was full of quicksands, in whose treacherous depths many an unfortunate camel perished. Here was an occasion, one would at least imagine, that instinct in one of its forms, the so-called law of preservation, would have undoubtedly displayed itself, and come to the animal's aid by intuitively warning it of an existing danger. At all events, it is only natural to suppose that an ordinarily intelligent animal would have learnt by sheer force of example to avoid the danger, by seeing those which preceded it in difficulties sinking deeper and deeper out of sight. Or that at least it would have got an inkling that something or other out of the common was up, and so have become careful and suspicious as to how and where it went. Or again, that there would have been a mutual exchange of sympathy in a common danger, which certain gregarious and associated animals do evince at such times; evidently too much to expect from a camel, however. For, in spite of numerous examples, before their very eyes, and under their very noses, our camels plodded on, and followed one after the other, neither sniffing nor seeing danger—utterly oblivious, in fact, to what was taking place around them, and supremely indifferent to their fate, walking anyhow or anywhere. A clearer case and a more convincing proof of sheer stupidity, arising evidently from a deficiency of either sense power or of instinct, or a combination of both, I have not experienced.

Compared with intelligence of elephants, horses, and mules

Not so with the elephants, horses, and mules. The contrast was most marked, and I was much struck at the time by the vast difference between these and the camels. None of them were lost, and no wonder, for they displayed throughout a marked and consistent caution which, I am quite convinced, was more clearly the result of reason than of instinct; a caution which may have at first been set in motion by the latter, but which was carried on and worked out by the former.

Instance of elephantine reason

One elephant in particular, which the officer commanding 6/11 Battery, Royal Artillery, lent me to assist in extricating some camels who were being engulfed in the quicksands, showed an amount of sagacity which was positively marvellous; a reasoning almost equal to human, and only inferior to it because of its inability to give expression to it in language, although his actions and movements were a clear indication of what was going on inwardly, and were evidently the consequence of a train of thought followed out connectedly. It was with the utmost difficulty that we could get him near enough to attach a drag rope to one camel that I wanted to rescue. In spite of our being about fifty yards from the bank of the river he evinced the greatest anxiety, while his movements were made with extreme caution. Despite coaxing, persuasion, remonstrance, gentle admonition, ending finally in a torrent of bad language and a shower of big blows dealt mercilessly over his head by the exasperated mahout, this elephant stubbornly refused to be guided by his driver, and would not go where he was wanted, but with his trunk shoved out in front of him he kept feeling his way with his ponderous feet, placing them before him very slowly, deliberately, and methodically, treading all the while with the velvety softness of a cat, and taking only one step at a time. Then suddenly he would break out in a suppressed kind of shriek, evidently a combined note of defiance and alarm, and retreat backwards in great haste. This went on for some time, and after several ineffectual attempts of the kind, when the arm and patience of the mahout were quite exhausted, and when the animal had nearly completed a circuit of the ground in the vicinity with the same determined caution and deliberation, he advanced to within about ten yards of the poor camel, but not another step nearer would he move. It was too late, however. Only the poor brute's head and neck were visible, and in spite of every effort we were obliged to abandon him to an untimely and yet a kindly fate, which spared him many an after ache and pain and much cruelty.

That this elephant knew the footing to be unsafe and dangerous he clearly showed by refusing to be forced, and by doggedly feeling his own way, as well as by expressing an anxiety amounting almost to timidity, which demonstrates, I consider, a high form of intelligence. For, knowing the existence of danger ahead by seeing the camel's predicament, although several men were walking between him and that animal without any signs of the ground giving way, an instinctive feeling, backed up by reason, that it would not bear his weight, but sink with him, must have actuated him to behave as he did. And that he was acting on no mere whim, or from stubbornness, obstinacy, or bad temper —on the contrary, that he was only too anxious to do what was required of him, provided it did not endanger or imperil his own life—his finally moving forward in one direction, without an application of force or persuasion, to a spot from which we could act, indicated plainly enough. Elephants, however, I look upon, with the exception of the dog, as the most intelligent animals in existence. Burton, in his 'Nile Basin,' says that not only might elephants be made useful to man, but that they appear to possess an instinct which is quite a match for the reason not only of the natives of Africa, but of some others of the bipeds who visit its inhospitable shores. If, however, he had substituted 'intelligence' for 'instinct,' which I imagine was what he intended to convey, he would have been nearer the mark.

Intelligence of horses considered

I have often ridden ponies and horses across rivers in South Africa and elsewhere in which quicksands existed, and I have always found that, if they did not intuitively discover the fact, at all events when they had received a practical demonstration of the presence of a quicksand by stepping into it, they one and all quickly drew back and extricated themselves before they had sunk any deeper, then refused either to go on or avoided the place, chose another line, and proceeded with the greatest possible caution. But in these cases, knowing my animals most thoroughly, and being on the most friendly terms with them, I invariably gave them their heads and let them go their own way, which was also my way, guiding them in reality by magnetism, and outwardly by an occasional gentle pressure of the leg, only so far as to keep the general direction. In fact, I made a point on such occasions of never bullying or forcing an animal to go a certain way; indeed, I was never once obliged to resort to such a course. There can be no question that this is the best method to pursue when rider and horse mutually know and sympathise with each other.

How to get in touch with a horse

In fact, the real secret of fathoming a horse's intelligence, fidelity, and working capacity, getting in practical reality the maximum return of all these qualities, is through the mutual existence of sympathy and love between yourself and him. And the stronger this bond the more you will get out of him in every way. In other words, the deeper the reciprocity, the greater the return. At the same time, you must have complete mastery over him, and let him know it without going out of your way unnecessarily to make him feel it. In this way you engender in him a feeling of confidence, and altogether strengthen the ties of sympathy and affection. Your mastery must not be only and purely physical—that is to say, a practical proof of your ability to ride him—but by working on and through his sympathy and affections, and by establishing confidence, you should exercise a moral ascendency—a species of moral magnetism—over him, that will give you the entire victory, and place him completely under your control and influence.

That the bond of sympathy between man and horse expands and ripens into affection on the part of the latter I fully believe. Although, of course, his intelligence being on a greatly inferior scale to that of humanity, his affection is naturally of a lower form and grade, originating as it does first of all from good treatment and kindness—literally through the stomach—but strengthened and developed from constant and continuous association, and it is therefore of a grosser, less retentive, and more variable nature than man's. I could more clearly illustrate my meaning and my contentions by producing examples and relating anecdotes of my experience with horses, but I am afraid I have already too far digressed.

It is usual to attribute the behaviour of horses on certain occasions purely to timidity or fear. But I think we are too apt to jump to conclusions when animal nature is concerned, and to put everything down entirely to fear or nervousness, especially with a horse, and in many instances I firmly believe we are quite wrong. That an animal's movements, more often than not, originally arise from these disturbing influences, I quite admit; but they are not due solely to them, but to the fear of consequences and results emanating from reason—an argument all the more in favour of their intelligence being of a high order.

Human rashness and its causes

It is, I believe, a recognised and admitted fact that very frequently young children, or ignorant uneducated people, who are ignorant of a danger show no signs of fear when in the presence of it, simply because of their utter unconsciousness of its existence. Though it may be staring them in the face all the time they can neither see nor feel it, owing to a want of intellectual development, and to the obscurity and limited range of their mental vision. In what other way can we account for naked savages rushing recklessly to certain death against a hail of bullets? At Ahmad Kheyl, when the battle was over, we found among the slain of the Ghazis who led the charge several hundred who were armed with stout cudgels only, while here and there many boys—mere children almost—and a few women who had also mingled in the rush, lay stretched alongside their kith and kin. At El Teb, where the Hadendowas came on so fiercely, similar corpses were discovered among those of the warriors who fearlessly led the attack. Of course fanaticism has a great deal to do with this rashness, but ignorance of the effect of modern rifle fire has more. For, as a rule, once savages feel it, they rarely, if ever, attack a second time, and they certainly do not come on with the same mad impetuosity. In fact, the Hadendowas are the only tribe I know that have ever advanced a second time with the old fierceness and pluck. But even granting fanaticism to be solely responsible, what is it, after all, but the offspring of downright blind ignorance, which springs from the overwhelming force of surrounding circumstances, which is intensified by the want of a higher and broader education, and by the want of the restraining, softening, and refining influences of civilisation?

That ignorance in such case is bliss, or, to be more explicit, is due to a deficiency of intelligence and education, and to nothing else, I believe. Unless, perhaps, it is due to a defective development of the nervous organisation, which would seem to deaden the sense of moral feeling, but which elevates and gives additional impetus to the physical; while a corresponding increase would tend to promote greater moral courage, although combined with a certain amount of physical hesitation, seems to me clear enough, though I have not, I am afraid, expressed myself as explicitly as I should like to.

The more highly educated and intelligent people are, and the deeper their knowledge and the wider their experience, the greater innate nervousness and trepidation do they feel in the presence of danger. At the same time they control and conceal it by a strong effort, and by sheer force of moral courage, while those of lesser intellect, or of coarser moral fibre, will betray emotion or fear. There are, of course, exceptions to this, when the nervous system is either blunted or deadened, or has never been actively developed, that the individual does not know what fear is; but these cases are very exceptional, unless we include the savages previously alluded to as coming within the category—a plausible and by no means unreasonable or illogical conclusion. But, as we are aware, those natures which have the most sensitive and delicate nervous organisations possess the highest and finest form of courage—viz. moral—and such individuals, when put to the test, evince at first marked internal nervousness, then determined courage, in the face of impending danger; while the more serious the peril, and the more delicately refined the organisation—a woman's, for instance—the greater the courage.

Comparison with that of other animals

So with animals. A horse, for example, although aware of a danger at which he will first of all exhibit distinct symptoms of alarm, will eventually face it, because his reasoning power comes to his assistance. But it cannot control its feelings like a man, on account of its comparative inferiority, in addition to its deficiency in that moral self-control which even in humanity is in gradations, increasing in intellectual refinement and advancement by classes, according to the standards we raise in, and the nice distinctions that we draw between, certain abstract qualities, and which is the distinguishing feature—the line of demarcation, in fact—which divides the human and animal kingdoms; whereas a man in the same predicament, although equally frightened, will conceal his emotions, or only betray them by a slight nervousness at the most.

Confidence due to reason

When, therefore, you persuade a horse to face this danger, which he will if well bred, or if you go the right way to work with him, he displays, I maintain, distinct intelligence and a clear connected train of reasoning—by placing confidence in you, and by going to work in his own systematic way, as the elephant above quoted did. If not the outcome of reason, what else is it? The feeling of fear is possibly due exclusively to the mere inherent instinct of self-preservation; but in such case what would be the consequence? No animal in the face of peril would budge an inch, and then force would have to be used to oblige him to do so. But when they do so without force, in the face of all this, something more than instinct must be at the bottom of it. For, after all, what is instinct but an impromptu, unreasoned prompting or instigation, a natural spontaneous impetus or impulse in an animal to act, or to carry out certain conditions, which are indispensable and essential for its existence, propagation, and preservation, an effort which is solely an outcome of natural laws, independent of instruction and experience; while reason is the special power of the faculty of thought.

Definition of instinct

and of reason

Darwin, speaking on the difference between the two, says: 'No doubt it is often difficult to distinguish between the power of reason and that of instinct. . . . We can only judge by the circumstances under which actions are performed whether they are due to *instinct* or to reason, or to the mere association of ideas; this latter principle, however, is intimately connected with reason.' Without in any way presuming to differ with the great naturalist, it always appeared to me that, under the circumstances, and with the class of animals that I am alluding to, the distinction between the two forces was clear enough; in fact, reason invariably followed after instinct. In other words, the initial instigation to avoid a certain danger was often due to

Difference between the two

instinct, but the after conduct of the animal, and its various actions in facing it subsequently to a knowledge of its existence, were distinctly the result of a clear systematic chain of thought. In other instances, however, when instinct was evidently at fault, or at all events did not come into play, the same consistent line of action was carried out, when the first intimation that the animal received of the existence of quicksands was by finding itself sinking in one.

The camel a fatalist

The incident which occurred at the Lora is all the more extraordinary as regards the camels when we take into consideration the hypothesis, that of the various forms of instinct inherent in man and animals that of preservation is the strongest, and though self-murder is indulged in by the former, it is practically unknown among the latter. As to the camel individually, he is altogether too apathetic, and has too much of the fatalistic principle in his organism, to be of a suicidal tendency, so much so as to be quite out of the question. But even though their instinctive powers are unusually dull and dormant, one would at least imagine that danger, which usually has an electrical effect on most animals, would in this instance have acted like a sharp spur, if not an electric shock, and have awakened these camels to a sense of their peril. Fatigue and exhaustion may in some cases have rendered them indifferent and callous, but, on the whole, it was due to the dulness and dormancy of their instinct.

On another occasion, when I was disembarking camels at Suakim, the boats which conveyed them from the steamer to the shore were so frail and narrow that in more than one instance they upset, throwing the animals into the water; when this happened they swam to the shore, which, however, was not very far off. This is the only instance that I can recall of this kind where they displayed a certain unusual amount of alacrity, though at first it took them some time to realise the situation. But a camel's natural aversion to external contact with water, and the sudden immersion in it, probably aroused their instinct, and their ability to swim naturally helped them out of the difficulty. On the other hand, instead of trying to get out of the Lora quicksands, they got into a kneeling posture—a sign of stupidity in itself—which, with their legs bent right under them, converted their position into one of utter and hopeless helplessness, and made it all the harder to extricate them.

Mutual confidence inspired among animals

The simple fact of the reposing by certain domestic animals, of confidence in man, seems to me sufficient evidence in itself to point to intelligence as being the motive power that actuates them on special and particular occasions. And it is this very confidence, I believe, which leads to still further steps—more links in the chain—all of which form a close connection, which clearly indicates the faculty of reason. So it is that dogs and horses willingly follow man into all kinds of danger, in the hunting field, when shooting wild game, or into battle; and the former will often fight in defence of their masters, even to attacking a poisonous snake.

The results of it

In a cavalry charge a horse will face anything; while in the hunting field one horse will negotiate a jump which is beyond his powers, because either his confidence in and attachment to his master, or momentary excitement, blinds his judgment, another, of a more phlegmatic temperament or of a subtler reason, will refuse. As a rule we are in the habit of putting this down to vice or obstinacy, and no doubt a refusal is frequently due to such causes; and we very occasionally attribute it to want of pluck, which, in reality, I consider to be more often the reason of it than the two former. Instinct probably warns a horse of the danger, and reason tells him that he will come to grief if he tries it. Loss of confidence in his own powers first fail him. Then confidence in those of his master to bring him over safely. Next he anticipates the result, and dreads it. Failure of courage follows, and finally he refuses.

Such conduct may also be attributed to a mere association of ideas; but Darwin himself acknowledges this principle to be intimately connected with reason, while it seems to me to be in itself a clear indication of the existence of that faculty. First of all, there is a mutual affinity and sympathy, ripening into affection or hate, and engendering confidence or incredulity. Then the subsequent actions as a natural consequence of the tendency of these conditions, one leading up to the other in fact, and each step in itself being almost conclusive proof of a thought-out intelligence.

Such occasions as a cavalry charge or an across country gallop, when a horse will rush at or over anything, may sometimes be the result of systematic training, or of excitement, by which horses are so easily carried away. But we ourselves must not overlook the fact that there are occasions when even the quietest and most reasonable men are blinded by excitement, overcome by impatience, and completely carried away by impulse; so that we can hardly hold this up as a hard-and-fast argument against animals, and we must accordingly make every allowance for them.

Further criticism of Massoutier's views

Lieutenant Massoutier, in the same pamphlet, also asserts that camels will not eat 'camel thorn' when saturated with moisture, and that it is then injurious to them, and he states that they should not on this account be sent out to graze while the dew is on the ground. As a rule, when I have been with camels, we have been marching at that hour; still I have seen them on certain occasions eating herbage that was moistened with dew, so that as regards the species generally I am in a position to contradict the former part of this statement. Of the latter portion we will speak in chapter vii.

Here, again, Lieutenant Massoutier infers a power of discrimination in the animal which, if not due to reason, is at all events a very highly developed instinct, amounting, if not almost akin, to intelligence. For he would seem to infer that a camel refuses to eat moistened herbage, instinctively knowing it to be bad for him. It may be so with the Algerian breed, who may possess a sharper instinct, and who may have been trained from infancy to avoid moist pasture, or yet, again, who may have learnt from their own or parental experience to do so. But if such is the case, it would appear quite unnecessary to me to take precautions to prevent them grazing at an early hour.

But I know that most camels who have been deprived of water will certainly eat moist herbage, in fact any moistened food, all the more readily, and when suffering from thirst it would be difficult to restrain them. All camels that I have worked with, irrespective of breed, will eat any food or drink any water after a long fast, though on an ordinary occasion they will be particularly fastidious as to the choice of either, and will altogether refuse food that is distasteful to them. The camel is, certainly when being worked, what I should call a greedy animal, especially where green food is concerned, and he has a particular predilection, a craving almost, for 'camel thorn' and similar prickly shrubs.

It may possibly be—as I have more often seen them under unfavourable than favourable conditions—that hunger and thirst have overcome discrimination, and driven them to commit indiscretions which in their natural state they would never have done. So much I will readily acknowledge and concede; but that their discrimination is more probably the result of early training on certain foods only and avoidance of others, and is not exclusively due to natural intelligence, I still maintain.

CHAPTER IV

SPECIES AND BREEDS

No matter what part of the world the camel inhabits there are only two species—the Arabian, or one-humped, found as a rule in a hot dry plain country; and the Bactrian, or two-humped, confined to cold and mountainous regions. To this there are exceptions: the Afghan, for instance, which comes from a cold mountainous country, although it belongs to the former species. And there are parts of Central Asia where both species are found, one of the results of this being the production of hybrids, which are not uncommon in some places, and which, I have seen it alleged, are occasionally fertile among themselves. When the breed is produced from male Bactrians and female Arabians it is said to be extremely hardy and tough, and able to stand intense cold and exposure. On the contrary, when the parentage is reversed (male Arabian and female Bactrian), the progeny is useless, being vicious and refractory. This is a curious physiological fact, and well worth the study of scientists. Very many years ago, General Harlan, I believe, employed 2,000 of the former kind for several months, and marched them nearly 400 miles across the Indian Caucasus over ice and snow, losing only one camel, and that by an accident. There are, however, various breeds, differing principally in size, shape, colour, and other characteristics, such as in texture of hair, length of neck, prominence of hump, powers of endurance, &c., due to the different geographical conditions of climate, and to the geological formation of the soil.

Arabian The Arabian species is to be found in India, Sind, Beloochistan, Afghanistan, Arabia, Persia, Syria, Asia Minor, Turkey, and in Northern Africa, Upper and Lower Egypt, Nubia, and the Soudan, including Sennar, Kordofan, Darfur, &c. In general this species is smaller and lighter than the other. The hair is soft, woolly, and very unequal, being longest on the throat, neck, and hump; while the riding camel shows far more breeding and class than the baggage camel, which is of stouter and coarser build.

Measurement and weight

Length.

(1) From nose to tail, 8 feet.
(2) From shoulder to tail, 5 feet 6 inches.
(3) Of forelegs, about 3 feet.
(4) Of neck and head, 3 feet 6 inches.

Height.

(1) From top of hump, 6 feet 6 inches.
(2) Without hump, 5 feet 6 inches.

The weight of a full-grown camel is from 1,000–1,150 lbs. These measurements are only approximate, as there is a great difference between breeds although of the same species, and the desert camels are as a rule shorter and less massive than those which, like the Lower Egyptian and Indian, are well fed and watered regularly.

Bactrian As I have only seen a few specimens when I was in Afghanistan, my experiences having been altogether confined to the other species, I can only speak from what I have read and heard. The natural country of the Bactrian camel is the great middle zone of Central Asia, stretching to the north of the Taurus and Himalayas—in other words, from the Black Sea to China, and northward to Lake Baikal. This species was originally confined to ancient Bactriana, now called in a general way Turkestan, but strictly speaking it is Bokhara, or the slice of country lying to the north of Afghanistan and to the south of Samarkand, with Balkh for its centre. Gradually this camel spread over Central Asia into Persia, and up to Tartary, Thibet, and China, and, as we have already seen, is reported to exist in a wild state in the desert tracts of Shamo, on the Chinese frontier. In measurement the average Bactrian is slightly shorter but much stouter all round than the Arabian; and his weight is greater also, his bones being larger, and his muscles more developed. As a rule the hair is dark brown, and it is long and thick at the top of the humps, the mane, the crown of the head, the neck, and the fore-arm. The first hump is on the shoulder, and the second is near the croup. The pads on his feet are harder than those of the other species, therefore are better adapted to stand the extreme changes wrought on the soil by the frequent variations of rain and drought; while to enable him to stand the severe winter he sustains northwards, his coat is like a fur, growing thicker and far more plentifully than that of the Arabian. In addition to his being different in having an extra hump, he is provided with a sort of a claw-toe projecting beyond the pad of the foot, which enables him to move over ice and snow, and which would render him better fitted to travel on wet marshy ground, and most certainly over slippery stony hills, the extra hardness of the sole of the foot being an additional reason.

Comparison Opinion seems divided as to which species is the better of the two, and one Russian writer says that the Arabian is far more enduring than the Bactrian, consequently is more expensive; but I am inclined to think that each is most suitable in its own climate and on its own soil, the geographical and geological conditions being so opposite, the former being better adapted to work in a cold climate and a mountainous country, and the latter in a hot and level one. And this remark applies equally to breeds. On the whole, however, from what I can gather, the Bactrian is perhaps the hardier of the two, and has the greater weight-carrying power; and the Arabian is the lighter and handier, consequently is more adaptable as a riding animal. As regards endurance and abstinence from water and food there is, however, a vast difference between breeds, depending entirely where and how the camel has been bred. Those of the Arabian, Syrian, and Nubian deserts are naturally far more enduring than those of Egypt, Anatolia, or India, which have always been accustomed to a greater supply of water, and to greener and more succulent food.

Dromedary It is generally supposed that by the term 'dromedary' is meant the Arabian in contradistinction to the Bactrian species; but from the derivation of the word I should say it applied to the running or riding camel, from the Greek *dromeus*, a runner, or *dromas*, running, the name having been given to certain special breeds of camels in the days of Cyrus or Xerxes, or most probably long prior to this, on account of their swiftness. I have also seen it stated that 'dromedary' was a name often applied to all the members of single-humped species, but properly speaking belonging only to a thin, comparatively elegant, and fine-haired breed, celebrated for its fleetness, and carrying its rider when necessary a hundred miles a day. Long ages ago, before the Arabian camel had spread east into Asia and south into Africa, it may have been the case that the name 'dromedary' was confined exclusively to one breed, but now there are as many various breeds of riding as of baggage camels. The later part of this statement is quite correct, however, and applies pretty generally to dromedaries, no matter what their breed, and they are distinguishable from the beast of burden by their slightness and wiriness, and by their muzzles being less swollen—greyhounds in comparison with mastiffs being an apt illustration. Their speed we will discuss in chapter ix.

This is an ancient heresy, and the proper meaning of the term does not appear to have been understood. Even Aristotle seems to have laboured under a wrong impression. Gibbon, in chapter xlvi. of his 'Decline and Fall,' refers to it: 'The difference between the two races consists in one or two humps; the dromedary has only one; the size of the proper camel is larger; the country he comes from Turkestan or Bactriana; the dromedary is confined to Arabia and Africa.'[1] Had he substituted 'Arabian' for dromedary

[1] Buffon, *Hist. Natur.* xii. 211; see also Aristotle, *Historia Animalium*, lib. ii. cap. 2.

he would have been right, for, as I have just pointed out, there is not only a distinction with a difference between the two terms, but a distinct difference, which has been misinterpreted during the Christian era at all events.

It must be borne in mind, however, that all one-humped camels are not necessarily dromedaries; on the contrary, the proportion of baggage to riding preponderates in favour of the former; whereas I am within bounds, I think, when I say that, as a rule, all two-humped camels are beasts of burden, they being of a heavier and clumsier build, conducive to strength and not to speed. There are, however, exceptions, few and far between, and it would appear that there is a swift breed of Bactrian which is in request in China; and I have read that the Chinese have a peculiar breed which is very swift, and which they call 'Fongkyo Fo,' or 'camel with feet of the wind,' presumably of the Bactrian species, as I am not aware of the existence of the Arabian in those parts; but this, I must admit, is the only case I have ever heard of.

Class distinction

While on this point I wish particularly to establish beyond all doubt the fact that there are, moreover, distinctly two classes—viz. the riding, called in Egypt and Arabia 'Hageen,' and in India 'Sawari'; and the baggage, known as 'Gamal' and 'Unt' respectively in Egypt and India, and commonly called 'baggager,' to use a transport phrase. And these two classes are, be it remembered, quite as distinct as the racer is in comparison to the carriage-horse, or as the hunter is to the cart-horse. They belong to the same species undoubtedly, but to a totally different class and breed, the one being a riding animal pure and simple, and the other a beast of burden or draught. Of course there are and have been exceptional cases when the riding camel has had to carry loads; for example, Napoleon in Egypt, and Sir Charles Napier in Sind, so employed them, but only on emergencies. So also can a baggager be ridden, answering the purpose much as a cart-horse would; but, given your choice, you would naturally select a 'Sawari.' Bear in mind too that, as with the horse you have hacks, hunters, and racers, so amongst riding camels you have degrees of comparison in and between breeds of good, better, and best.

I will now proceed to describe in as few words as possible some of the distinctive features and characteristics of many of the various breeds, but more especially those with which I have been in contact. I have also described some of the brands which are in common use in the desert on both banks of the Nile; and where, as in the case of the 'Bisharin,' more than one brand is given, each represents ('El Beit,') the house or family to which the camel belongs. Breeds

In Arabia itself there are several breeds of baggage animals, and one or two of the 'Hageen.' The former are thick built, heavy footed, and slow paced; the latter well bred, with slight sinewy frames, the hair being much shorter and finer, the prevailing colour light grey. Sir Samuel Baker speaks of a breed belonging to a tribe of Arabs who live on the western shores of the Red Sea which are especially adapted for carrying loads over mountainous districts, and he says that when he used them they accomplished feats in mountain climbing which would have been impossible to any other domestic animal so loaded. I do not for a moment doubt that Arabian this special breed is a peculiarly active one; but what I do say is, that the camel, as a mountain animal, is far inferior to the mule, or donkey, or the hill pony, and a comparison between them is sheer waste of time.

Aden — These camels show every appearance of high breeding. Slight, small, very wiry and muscular, hair very fine and short, colour a kind of whitish brown. Far more suitable for riding than baggage work. These animals were some that I worked with in the Suakim campaign of 1884, and were shipped from Aden, hence my reason for speaking of them as such. As a matter of fact, I believe they came from the near vicinity.

Shawam or Shami — These are bred in Syria, especially at El Arish. They are very large, powerful, and hairy; are great weight-carriers, but slow, and must be well fed and cared for. Used in the Egyptian army to carry mountain guns.

Delta or Lower Egypt — These are large and coarse. Colour a dirty brown, but varies. Up to good weight. Accustomed to green food, therefore soft and do not stand desert work well.

Upper Egypt — Those between Keneh and Assouan are average-sized and well-bred looking, very white in colour, and only moderate weight-carriers.

Bisharin — Light grey, wiry, active and medium-sized. Are essentially riding camels, and considered by the Bedawins to be about the best and fastest. The whole district of this tribe, which is the largest in Nubia, extends along the Nile to the sea, between Berber and Suakim, and is called 'Etbai.' It stops at Wadi Kokreb, a hundred and five miles from the latter place, and in a southerly direction the limit is at Gozerajup. It is chiefly in the northern parts of Etbai that the breeding is carried on, so as to avoid the roads, and keep out of the way of being raided or disturbed.

A. Circular mark on the right cheek.

B. 'Mekimmeh,' a slash across the cheek.

C. Line on either side of the upper lip.

D. Round blotch on the neck.

E. Short line across the fore-arm.

F. Line across the hind-quarters behind the saddle.

These are average-sized, muscular and hardy, and are essentially desert animals, of a lightish brown colour, better adapted as Hageens. This tribe is contiguous to the Bisharins, and they inhabit the deserts stretching between Suakim and Wadi Kokreb and down to Kassala, where camel breeding is extensively carried on, Fillik, forty miles off, being their permanent headquarters. Haden-dowa

Also riding camels, and very highly esteemed. Are said to divide honours with the Bisharin in pace and quality; both these breeds, however, are occasionally used as baggagers. Ababdeh

A. 'Na 'ala,' round mark under the ear.

From the same tribe and also used for carrying loads. Darhami

A. Two lines under each ear.

Bred in tens of thousands by the Kababish, who are the finest and most powerful tribe in Kordofan. The camels are large and hairy, chiefly baggagers, and particularly good for desert work. Kabashi

A. Line (El Bay) passing under the stomach or chest.

B. Three lines on hind legs.

These are bigger than the Bisharin or Ababdeh, but are not so good. They are used chiefly for riding, Arrafi and come from Mesalamieh, south of Khartum, on the Blue Nile.

A. Slanting line on either cheek.

Shukriya From the same neighbourhood as the above, but beasts of burden only.

A. Line from the nose to the eye.

Dongolese Bred at Dongola, but are naturally much softer than the camels bred by the Bedawins, and even than the Delta camels.

Abiroof Are raised in the vicinity of Shendy; purely baggagers; have long necks, and are hairy about the ears.

A. In shape of the letter T, the top of the letter running down the spine, the tail of the letter down the side behind the saddle.

Binni Genai In size and appearance rather similar to the Kabashi. Used as baggagers.

A. Line from eye to eye under the jaw.

B. Four lines on either hind leg.

Es Dariyat Same as above. Come from Siwa.

A. |—| 'Gaim saif,' on any part of the body.

B. > under either ear.

C. ϱ called 'Malf.'

D. ↑ called 'El Miara.'

In the north-west of Kordofan the Hamid, and in the west the Hamre, Arabs also breed largely, but it is a noticeable fact, which Prout, in his 'Province of Kordofan,' calls attention to, that south of latitudes 13° or 13° 30′ camels cannot be bred successfully, the animals being degenerate and without speed or endurance. In the north and east of Darfur the chief pursuit of the Arabs is camel breeding. At Om Badr, the headquarters of the Homr tribe, over 30,000 have been estimated; at Saya, 15,000; and at Millet the Zyadieh tribe have about the same number. Further to the west the Mahamid have countless herds; while the Beni Hamran and the Maganin, who live in the vicinity of Om Badr, also own large herds. In the Bayuda desert, which is inhabited by Bedawin tribes, chief of which are the Hassinyeh, Esu Arab, Fadniyeh, and Umiyeh, camels are also bred; so also at El Getaineh, near Khartum, and at Seril, near Darra. In fact, the tribes who inhabit the deserts on both banks of the Nile up to Khartum and who do not breed camels are quite the exception, the Baggara being the most noted.

Algerian These camels are medium-sized, short-haired, and light-coloured, and are able to carry on an average a load of 330 pounds, the better class carrying up to 450 pounds. The breeds from Morocco and Tunis are very similar to the above.

We will now transfer ourselves to India, where the variety of breeds is not very extensive, all of them belonging to the Arabian species.

N.-W. Provinces Good-sized tall animals, carrying hardly any hair, and of a dirty brown colour. Cannot stand great cold, at the same time should not be worked in the extreme Indian heat. If well fed, and on good roads, will carry heavy loads. Numbers of this breed are bred in Rajpootana.

Oudh The same as above.

Bikaneer These also are more or less similar to the two preceding kinds.

Panjab Are tall, large, and good weight-carriers, of a brownish colour; they also require good feeding and good roads. The best breeds are found in north of

Jhelum, and close to Hissar one called Bajri. In the districts round Rajanpore, Dera Ismail Khan, and Dera Ghazi Khan good breeds were formerly procurable, but are now, and have been for the last ten or twelve years, very scarce. There are also camels bred in the Panjab desert, known as the Bar-ke-unt, but they are an inferior class of animal altogether.

Sind — Are powerful, tall, fine-looking, short-haired, sometimes almost hairless, of a whity-brown colour. Only fitted for sandy deserts and a dry climate like their own, but not for hill work or exposure to cold and wet, to which they are extremely susceptible. They are very long-legged, and the disparity between their hind and fore quarters is most noticeable.

Brahui — Bred in the highlands of Beloochistan. Essentially for working in hilly countries. Average-sized, strong, and thickset, up to heavy loads, of a brown colour, and hairy.

Afghan — These are also short, thickset, hairy animals, born and bred in a cold mountainous country, therefore, like the Brahui, good climbers. Able to endure cold and stand exposure.

Persian — The Persian is similar in build to the Afghan, and carries a splendid coat. The curve of his neck seems to be deeper and more graceful. We had a few specimens, also some from Turkestan, when we were in Kandahar. Unless looked after, their long soft hair gets tangled and felted, and in hot weather drops off in wide patches, giving them a scurvy, mangy look. We also had some which came from Zenimdawar, on the border of the Seistan desert, which were of a very fine breed. They were always in good condition, and carried heavy loads, between 550 to 650 pounds, even in long and continuous marches; but they were specially well looked after by their drivers, got 4 lb. of wheat flour daily in addition to their rations, and condition balls of camphor and pepper every week.

V.-S. Steel speaks of the Pahari camel; but this is a Hindustani word meaning hill, and is a generic term for the hill in contradistinction to the plain camel, and does not refer to any special breed.

Bactrian breeds

As I have previously remarked, I have never had any dealings with the Bactrian species, so will leave them alone altogether, except to make casual mention of those bred in Turkestan, which are said to be up to great weight; while I have read contradictory reports of the Kirgeze camel, one stating that they can carry up to 880 pounds, the other that they were shaggy and undersized, and only up to average loads. I have likewise heard of a breed which is said to exist in Western Tartary, but is very rare, of a white colour, and supposed to be sacred to the gods of the country. Owing to its rarity and the sacredness of its character it is only occasionally met with. There is also a breed in Persia which is used to carry guns, there being a special corps of this artillery in the Persian army.

Which colours and breeds preferred

And now I think we have discussed this question sufficiently to give us some insight into the varying qualities of the various breeds. As to the colours which distinguish the different breeds among the Arabs, brown, it appears, is not esteemed, reddish or light grey being preferred. Black is rare, and in Arab lore the black camel is looked upon as a sign of death. Nubian camels, generally speaking, are white, or of a very light shade. In Nubia and the Soudan the tribes of the east and west of the Nile are the only breeders and carriers that cross the deserts that exist in that portion of Africa, and not only every tribe but every house has its own distinguishing brand. It does not follow that because one district is famed for a special breed that no other will be found there. Both Bisharin and Kababish camels can be purchased at Assiout, and at Assouan and other places various breeds can also be bought. It is therefore of some importance to detect the breeds. I have been informed that these distinguishing marks are never used fraudulently by the natives when dealing either with Europeans or among themselves; due no doubt to the fact that most of them are not only thoroughly well up in the brands, but can as a general rule tell one breed from the other without them. As to Europeans, so few of them comparatively ever go up country, and so great is their average ignorance of the camel, that it is simple enough to deceive them without troubling to perpetrate such frauds.

CHAPTER V

BREEDING

I REGRET to say that this is a subject with which I have had little to do, beyond having witnessed the birth of a few calves, and I regret it all the more because it is one of special importance, and upon which the ultimate utility of the full-grown animal depends. This is too self-evident to need any further explanation; but I am firmly of opinion that were the weight of European intelligence and science brought to bear on this very vital question, in co-operation with the experience and knowledge of the Arabs, the result would be extremely satisfactory; and just as we in England made such a vast improvement in the breed of horses by a judicious blending of breeds, and great care and attention, we can, I maintain, do equally well with the camel. Not that I mean to say that the Asiatic and African races are altogether careless and inattentive, but there is no doubt that they leave a great deal to Kismet, or chance. If more care and greater supervision were exercised among the young camels a far better result would be obtained; and a still greater improvement by the intermixture of good breeds, and by less interbreeding, which in the long run must tend to deteriorate the stamina and physique of the race.

At all events no harm can be done in trying the experiment, and much good may accrue. Already there is a good opportunity in Australia, where the adoption of the camel is only in its infancy, while the whole of South Africa, from the Zambesi to the Cape, with one or two exceptions, is the very country for the camel. It is a broad question, and one well worth the study of all deep-thinking men, who take an interest in the opening up of the vast wilds of Central Africa, and in the growth of civilisation and development northwards from the Colony. And not only broad but beneficial, for just as I feel sure that there is a great future before Australia and South Africa looming in the not far distant future, so I believe that the camel will assist materially in extending and establishing it, by piercing the unknown interior, and by accelerating communication with out-of-the-way places which cannot be reached by any other means.

Heredity and atavism

In order, however, to understand thoroughly and clearly this question of breeding, it is first of all necessary that we should be acquainted with the principles of 'heredity' and 'atavism.' The former is said to be the transmission of certain constitutional characteristics, or mental and instinctive qualities, of parents to their offspring; but in reality it is the transmission of tendencies, and not of conditions. The latter is a disposition, or tendency, in offspring to return to or resemble in some special feature—or it is the recurrence of a peculiarity or weakness of—the ancestral type. I cannot do better here than quote some very pithy remarks on the subject by Dr. H. Smith Williams :—

'The explanation,' he says, 'is found in the fact that

heredity implies not so much the transmission of conditions as of tendencies. Speaking loosely, we often say that consumption, insanity, and heart disease are hereditary. Strictly speaking, the statement is never true; an inherent weakness, or susceptibility of lungs, brain, or heart, a tendency of these organs, may be transmitted, but not the diseases themselves. And so of other conditions. The word "tendencies" is our "open sesame." Two parents having qualities unlike, and often mutually exclusive, cannot transmit these qualities to their common offspring; but they can transmit all their tendencies to that offspring, even though these tendencies be antagonistic. An organism cannot be two things at once, but it may tend to be many different things, antagonistic tendencies within it constantly struggling for the mastery. Aided by external conditions, the tendency at one time subordinate may at another time become dominant. Failing of such favourable conditions, tendencies may keep up an unequal and seemingly inefficient struggle throughout the lifetime of an individual, without once making themselves manifest, and yet be transmitted to the offspring with such potential force as there to become operative. . . .

'A tendency may remain dormant and perhaps unsuspected, not merely for one, but sometimes for many generations, becoming at last manifest again in a remote descendant. And this is as true of mental and moral tendencies as of physical. In short, the observed facts would seem to warrant the conclusion that the organism never relinquishes any tendency it has once acquired, but holds it in stock, if need be, generation after generation, awaiting a favourable opportunity to herald it forth. Only by such a supposition can we explain the commonly observed fact of inheritance from remote ancestors, or, as Darwin termed it, atavism.'

This will readily enable us to understand that every being, human or animal, which comes into a state of existence has blended and infused into its organism a number of issues of remote, or at all events previous, actions. In other words, this new evolution is not in the strict sense of the word *new*, for it has received from its progenitors, through generations or even ages, certain specialities or peculiarities—a legacy, in fact, either of health or infirmity, mental or physical, tendencies to which will develop themselves during growth from infancy to maturity, earlier or later, sometimes at a slow, sometimes at an accelerated rate, or which may be dormant for a generation or more, showing themselves in the offspring with marked development, according to circumstances and conditions.

Breeding a science

If we clearly understand this, we will readily acknowledge that the question of breeding is a science in itself, but that we cannot reduce it to such without taking into consideration the above vital principles. We have seen that an infusion of new blood is an absolute necessity to prevent degeneracy, and I have endeavoured to explain that countless centuries of interbreeding, and the transmission of inferior tendencies, have reduced the camel to a state of helpless organic inbecility which will require all the artificial aid of science to restore and improve. And when we have improved the physical condition, an advancement in the mental will follow. The simplest way of effecting this is to adopt every possible means of producing superior breeds, in conjunction with a humaner and better style of treatment. We may treat him as well as we do the horse, but we can never take him on the same footing, for he is not a sympathetic or a lovable beast, and, what is more, never will be. Nature is responsible for this, for Nature has been unkind to the camel in evolving a form so ungainly and so devoid of feeling; while man, not from inhumanity, but as an instrument, has materially assisted. But there is no reason that I can see why, after a certain period of close and constant touch with him under the new *régime*, he—the riding camel specially—should not evoke our sympathy at all events.

Degeneration of camel

The camel in proportion to his size should be a greater weight-carrier. But in proportion to his height he requires more depth and breadth, and greater muscular development, especially in his hind quarters, and that he has degenerated in these respects I think quite probable. Bearing in mind that he is specially adapted to barren wastes, where an acute instinct would seem indispensable to enable him to track water or pasture, we find that he is singularly deficient in mental qualities.

General causes of degeneration in animals

It is a recognised fact that the offspring of devitalised parents have defective mental vigour, while in those of overworked parents the physical development is insufficient, consequently the higher control centres of the brain attain imperfect growth. While on this topic there is one question that requires a careful and exhaustive examination, because it is one that we are inclined to ignore, although it has a strong bearing on the subject, and that is—exhaustion.

Exhaustion

Exhaustion is the draining or expenditure of the whole strength of an organism by exertion. If an animal is worked when in a state of exhaustion, or, in other words, if this is carried too far when the full contents of its strength have been emptied or drawn off, weariness or fatigue sets in, and in fatigue the muscles are slow to correspond to stimuli. 'The sense of fatigue arises from the blood becoming charged with waste products, and from the blood thus loaded bathing the higher nerve-centres.' If we keep on working animals who are in this state until their normal condition is one of fatigue, the physical results that ensue must, as a matter of course, be very terrible. And what makes it worse is, that the poor dumb creatures, unable to give utterance to their pangs, and as helpless as infants in our hands, toil and struggle on with a patient endurance and a meek submission too much for words, until the last stage, when they drop and die. But their helplessness is even greater than an infant's, for the latter, though unable to express, can by its cries convey some idea as to its wants and woes, and give us a clue, however faint; while the camel can only do so when it is too late and he can go no further, and from the fact of its being an unsympathetic creature it excites neither sympathy nor pity.

It is this want of sympathy between us and the animal that makes us utterly indifferent and callous as to its fate. Certain work has to be done, and it must be done, whether it is at his expense or not. This is all very well in an emergency. But apart from a humane point of view, and looking at it in a strictly economical sense, much money and animal life would be rescued if on ordinary occasions we watched them closely, and put them on the sick list before they reached the exhaustion stage.

When only suffering from exhaustion, it is not so easy to detect in the very early stage. Careful observation, however, will soon discover a stiffness in the muscles and joints, a want of elasticity in the movement of the limbs, a general languor and lassitude pervading the animal's whole system, a dulness in the eyes, and a general disinclination to exert itself. He will not walk with his usual stride and up to his ordinary pace. Then as he goes on he shows signs of lagging and falling to the rear. This disinclination for exertion may sometimes be due to natural laziness, or it may be the result of an inherited defective constitution, or, yet again, of recent overwork and want of nutritious food. Whatever the primary cause, the consequences, if not taken in time, must be injurious and, if allowed to go on, fatal.

Exhaustion, how manifested

Besides we must recollect that the individual power of endurance among animals is by no means equal—on the contrary, most unequal. One has inherited a better constitution and greater stamina, consequently will survive a journey that will kill another; and this is a fact that we never, on any account, take into consideration, but we make it a rule to distribute the weight equally amongst them, irrespective of age, strength, or condition. This is a point, however, that requires the closest inspection under any and every

Individual powers of endurance unequal

circumstance, a strict adherence to which cannot fail to bear most fruitful results.

Other signs

Another but later sign, and a very bad one too, is that an animal when overtired refuses its food. If allowed to get to this stage he ought at once to be placed in a sick depôt, put on diet, and all work stopped. If this is not done the immediate consequence is that he grows weaker and weaker; insufficient nourishment brings on anæmia and unfitness, listlessness increases to torpidity, vital activity diminishes, muscular elasticity decreases, his energy entirely deserts him, and he is quite incapable of an effort. In a few words, his condition is one of utter helplessness. Besides, we must not lose sight of the very important fact that one of the immediate after-effects of exhaustion in an organism is exhaustion of the digestive organs, which in this state are unable to digest food, especially if it is coarse and heavy, and which, if forced, soon become incapable of performing their functions. Here, again, rest and diet are the only resource. The digestive organs must be allowed to recruit, and every means taken to restore their vitality, and they must be coaxed and tempted by the lightest and most appetising food.

Evils of overwork

The sooner we recognise the common-sense fact, or, I should say, the quicker we put it into practice, that by overworking an animal we devitalise him (i.e. deprive him of vitality), the better. 'Overwork,' says Mrs. Woodhull Martin, 'produces unfitness by not allowing sufficient rest for recuperation and elimination of waste products. These products are poisonous to the organism, and it is to the advantage of the organism to get rid of them as quickly as possible. As long as an individual is working, these products are accumulating. . . .

'A certain portion of the twenty-four hours of the day can be devoted to work, and a certain portion must be devoted to rest, to rid the organism of waste products. The capacity for work, or the labour value of the individual, can only be decided by the amount of waste products produced and powers of elimination of the organism. . . . The organism becomes poisoned by the product of its biological activity. Labour beyond the power of elimination will devitalise the individual, and add another pauper to charitable institutions.'

These remarks apply with equal force to camels. Work in excess of the power of elimination will deprive a camel of his vitality, and if continued will add one more victim to an unending death roll, and leave another corpse for the delectation of the feathered and four-footed carrion.

Caution as to breeding

It stands to reason, therefore, that no stallions or females that are employed for breeding should ever be worked. Let them be kept exclusively for this purpose and no other. To keep them in condition give them plenty of exercise, but on no account work. The best way to obtain this is to let them run free in good pasture, only bringing them in morning and night to feed them on wholesome and nourishing food. If worked at all, it would be wiser to kill them outright than to work them to a state of devitalisation, because, as we have seen, the tendency to physical and mental weakness is inherent, and can be transmitted to offspring, and we cannot expect any but a still more inferior type from such a class of parents. For, as Darwin says, 'in the breeding of domestic animals the elimination of those individuals, though few in number, which are in any marked manner inferior is by no means an unimportant element towards success.' But it is more than this, it is of vital importance; and in order to produce a breed of the greatest vitality and vigour it is absolutely necessary to eliminate all animals of marked mental and physical inferiority.

If we take all these points into consideration it will be acknowledged that there is a good foundation to account for the mental and physical defects of the camel, the former especially. And though we can never hope to produce an animal equal to him in his initial state, we have every reason to expect a result that is worth the trial, and a considerable improvement on the present type.

It is on these grounds that I advocate special care and attention being devoted to the breeding of the camel. And there can be no doubt whatever that, if it is taken up seriously, and made purely a question of practical science, the results in a few years would more than repay the cost and trouble.

Rutting season

It is only at certain seasons during the year that both male and female camels begin to rut, and, as we have previously remarked, they become passionate and ungovernable, and the female is dangerous to ride and liable to run away; in fact, on the whole, the male is at all times the safer animal to ride or drive. Aristotle says that in Arabia the season commences towards the end of November, and ends early in December; but among the various breeds I have seen, I have not noticed that it was confined to any particular season of the year. The female is, if anything, smaller than the male, and more deficient in power behind, and when having connection she does so in the same crouching attitude as when at rest, the male being in a semi-recumbent position. When in the act they embrace each other in the ordinary way, like other quadrupeds, and not buttock to buttock as is commonly supposed; and unlike horses or oxen they spend the whole day in this occupation, and keep themselves aloof, allowing no one except the owner or driver to come near them. The camel does not usually arrive at the age of puberty until he is in his fifth year, and Aristotle, I think, must make a mistake when he says that they begin to have connection when they are three years old. It is during this rutting season when, as previously observed, the male camel produces a palatal flap, which is a tolerably certain sign of his condition; though there are other times out of season when, in a moment of irritation, and when moistening his mouth and throat to allay feelings of thirst, it also appears. After the female has conceived the average period of gestation is one year, though it sometimes happens that it only lasts eleven months, and occasionally is lengthened to thirteen. Only one calf is produced at a birth.

A newly-born camel of the Arabian species stands about two and a half feet high at birth, and after eight years is three feet or a trifle more, dependent, however, in a great measure on its breed. It is said not to reach full growth until its sixteenth year; and if there is any truth in this—and I see no reason to doubt it, as the camel's ordinary term of existence is believed to be Growth

Length of life

from forty to fifty years, Aristotle declaring it to be a little longer—this is all the stronger reason not to work him until at least he is rising six.

There can be no doubt that a camel is a long-lived animal, and Lieutenant Massoutier makes a great mistake when he says that he only lives from sixteen to eighteen years, though I can quite understand that a large percentage of them die at this comparatively early age, owing simply to incidental causes, such as (1) working them when too young, (2) excessive work, (3) excessive exposure under the most trying conditions. He can, as a rule, when taken moderate care of, work up to twenty-five years of age, and if really well looked after would continue to work until he was thirty or even more; but the causes just alluded to exercise the same baneful effect, and if they do not kill an animal because it happens to have superior stamina, they cripple its powers prematurely and past recovery.

The female suckles the calf from a year to a year and a half, and she does not rut again, nor will she permit connection, while this period lasts, although she continues to give milk until she conceives once more. Her milk is very rich, very thick, and very plentiful, and of a decidedly strong taste; the general use that is made of it has been previously mentioned. The French on their Stud Farm in Algeria feed the calves on oats up to two years old, but whether they commence before the animal is a year old I cannot say. When they are weaned, which is generally in a year, by all means give them wholesome, nourishing food, but certainly not betore; though it would be far better and wiser to let them continue to suckle as long as the mother will permit, being careful, however, to protect her from debility, and then give them a suitable and nourishing grain ration, so as to put stamina and muscle into them. Arabs and Bedawins allow the young of their riding camel to suckle, and exempt them from all restraint until they are two years old.

Bearing capacity

A female produces on an average one calf in every three years, and cannot, as already pointed out, produce more at a birth or in a shorter time. One male can serve from fifteen females up to fifty; hence it is usual among these Eastern tribes to geld a certain number of males that are intended exclusively for labour. This makes them quieter, and renders them more manageable, or at least it frees them from the periodical outbreaks to which they are liable; but I consider that it is a great mistake, as the camel is quite tractable enough, and this mutilation reduces his spirit and tenacity, hence diminution in his powers of endurance, but I do not think, as I have seen it stated, that it actually *reduces his strength*. Lieutenant Massoutier, speaking on this subject, says that in Algeria nearly all are geldings, a few of the finest stallions only being kept for stud purposes, in the proportion of one to about fifty females. These stallions are for the most part quiet, and can be used for transport, but occasionally, in the rutting season, they become wild and unmanageable, and are then dangerous to men. This bears out what I have just said against castration, for during the 'mast' period means could be adopted to isolate a camel and prevent him from being dangerous or doing any damage.

Castration

Proportion of stallions to females

One stallion to fifty females is rather an unequal

proportion, though he might do it easily enough; still I have read elsewhere that the State Train in Algeria employ them at the rate of one to sixteen, which is more likely to be correct, and for many reasons is better—for instance, at this rate he would have more vigour, while a greater choice of sires increases the chances of transmitting good mental and physical qualities, and diminishes the possibility of transmitting defective tendencies.

Females also have their ovaries removed and are used to carry loads, but only to a limited extent, because as milk-giving and breeding animals they are far more valuable to their owners than as beasts of burden, and as such they are fed exceptionally well and exempted from all work. Aristotle refers to this, and says that even females are so treated that they should not become pregnant in time of war, and he further adds that they run very fast when in this condition, a fact which I rather doubt—for a spurt perhaps, but not for any length of time, as running is not the camel's natural pace. Unfortunately, it is not always the case that breeding camels are kept from work, and I have seen them in India, not only carrying heavy loads when near confinement, but with the calf actually protruding and being born on the march, and this state of things, I regret to say, also occurred in Afghanistan. Fortunately this is not, I imagine, of frequent occurrence in breeding countries, because, in addition to their value as suppliers of milk and of young, the fact of their only bearing once in three years enhances their value, and it is only in such emergencies as the Afghan War that owners, the smaller and poorer especially, who cannot afford to part with their working animals, are tempted by the price, which on these occasions is twice or three times the market value, to sell. I have seen it stated that the proportion of females to males should not exceed one-third. From an ordinary point of view I see no reason for this, because they carry quite as well as males, though they are rather more uncertain, and at times more inclined to be unmanageable. From a breeding point of view, however, the smaller the proportion is the better, I should imagine, and no female which is fruitful ought on any account to be worked at all.

Great mortality among young camels

Great mortality among newly-born camels up to four years old, generally put down at 50 per cent., has already been casually mentioned in connection with the importation of a small batch of camels which were first taken to New York and finally to Nevada, where a pair are said in about eighteen years to have produced as many as ninety-six camels, all of which survived. As one who is deeply interested in this subject I should like very much to learn the exact history of these particular camels, as it would bear me out in a theory which I formed many years ago, in entire ignorance as to the very existence even of camels in America, that with great care and attention this excessive mortality could be reduced to a minimum. As far as I can see, there are only three causes that can account directly for this excess—viz. (1) Because the mothers are worked during gestation, and too soon after; (2) the calves are weaned too soon; (3) and worked too young.

First cause

It is said that a female should not be worked within three months before bringing forth, and the same time afterwards should be given them to regain their strength, and to enable the little one to get strong too and run about after its mother. But, as a matter of fact, this is utterly inadequate, and she ought not to do any work during the period of gestation and until the calf is weaned, or at all events for a year after. To obtain a good class of animal, with good powers of endurance, speed, and stamina, it is absolutely essential, as previously remarked, to keep both stallions and females from work of any kind, and exclusively for breeding purposes. Needless to say that, with care, good feeding, and special selection for their physical fitness and superiority of breed, the results would be a hundred per cent. better, and the mortality among the young considerably diminished.

A young one should not be weaned before it is one and a half to two years old; and a female that is worked a few months after her confinement cannot do this—so that both the mother and calf suffer from such treatment, and deteriorate in consequence. This is only to be expected, and in itself would account for the excessive mortality among the young.

Second cause

One fact seems pretty certain, and that is, that the newly-born camels do not get nearly so much milk as they should, and that they are weaned much sooner than they ought; and this in a very great measure would account for want of stamina in an animal so brought up, but is an evil that can easily be remedied, as shown above. It has been already pointed out that some tribes exist almost entirely on camels' milk, while others use it largely for their own consumption; others, again, give it to their foals, the consequence being that the young camels are stinted, and put out to graze before their time; in other words, they are forced like hot-house fruit. However good the result may be with the latter, it stands to reason that with the former it must prove prejudicial if not decidedly injurious. Deprivation of natural food and the supply of unnatural is bad at any time, but more especially so in the young ruminant before his internal organs are in a fit state to undergo such an unnatural condition of things. We have already seen that the structure of the first three divisions of the stomach is not fully developed, and that milk passes directly into the fourth compartment; therefore, to wean the calf and graze it before this internal structure is ready for the process of rumination is utter folly, and must eventually lead to serious mischief. Nature must have her way, and you cannot force her without seriously injuring the animal.

Third cause

As to the third cause, there is little or no doubt that as a general rule young camels are made to carry loads before they are fit to work. It is as a rule quite exceptional for Arabs and Asiatics to work them before they are four—in fact, for their own purposes they rarely if ever do; though I am surprised to see, according to Lieutenant Massoutier, that in Algeria they are used as beasts of burden from their third year; and if this is at all widespread it is all the more in favour of my argument. It is only in emergencies like the Afghan War, 1878–80, when the Indian Government required them in such great numbers, that the breeders parted with so many two- or three-year olds, possibly because they got a good price, but probably to get rid of as many camels (which at the time were useless to them) as possible. On the other hand, it is also quite the exception to wait until the camel is five years old, and the great tribes of Asia and North Africa, who are the Pickfords of their own portion of the world, have not always got a sufficient supply of older camels with which to meet the demand, so, will-he-nill-he, are obliged to fall back on the four- and five-year olds. And even during his fourth and fifth year a lot of mischief can be done, and I maintain that it is too young to begin. If the camel not has done growing until he is sixteen, or even, for the sake of argument, say ten years of age, to work him at four or five years is to work him too soon, and it would be wiser to wait until he was seven, or at all events six years old; but though this is a point that I feel positive about, I should like to establish beyond doubt the exact age at which the growth of the camel does terminate before committing myself definitely to any opinion. Besides, one cannot depend on Orientals in a case of this nature, for they are not only indifferent but careless as to age, keeping no written records, and trusting entirely to memory, a faculty which with them especially is apt to be faulty, untrustworthy, and treacherous as well.

Direct evils

In this way and no other can the great mortality among young camels be satisfactorily accounted for, and the evils that spring from them are obvious. In the first place the young animal is forced before its time, its legitimate supply of nourishment stopped, and a supply of food given it that its internal machinery cannot cope with, the organs that do the grinding and masticating being still closed, and not fully formed for the ultimate purpose for which they were designed. By thus interfering with the regular order in which

Nature works out all her creations, even to the minutest details, these organs, which only Nature in her own time, and acting on her own laws, would have completed and perfected, are developed prematurely, and Nature thwarted; resulting internally in impaired digestive powers, and loss of stamina; externally in a deficiency of muscular development and a stunted, enfeebled frame. In the second place, before the animal's osteological structure is complete, while the bones are soft and unformed, and still pliant and plastic, and his frame is actually growing, the effect is equally disastrous, checking the growth and causing the animal to be undersized and deficient in muscular power, and, should he be worked hard and continuously, ending in complete exhaustion and total collapse, the one following rapidly on the other.

Feeding of breeding camels

There is one question that I intend to allude to, although to a great extent it belongs to chapter vii., and that is, on the way in which camels that are set apart exclusively for breeding should be fed. As I deal most exhaustively with this subject in chapter vii., all I will say here is that three points especially require consideration, and they are, (1) the quality, (2) quantity, and (3) special adaptation of the food, which, in addition to the finest pasture, ought to be supplemented by nourishing cereals and a certain amount of farinaceous food. In a few words, abundance of water and of the most nutritious food, combined with freedom, is what is necessary. But there is one point on which I speak more fully, because of its direct connection with the subject, and that is salt.

The undoubted and inestimable value of salt to all

Value of salt

animals cannot be overestimated, and a regular and systematic use of it would have a marked effect on their health and condition. Not only is it a vermifuge, and the very best remedy to expel worms, which are unable to survive the action, but it purifies its blood and invigorates the system. It also has a good effect on its quality of milk, because both the quality and quantity are regulated by the quantity of the food which is digested; and as the milk depends upon the health and condition of the milch camel, and is naturally greatly affected by it, great care should be exercised in the giving of salt to all female camels, especially those set apart for breeding purposes; and for the matter of that to all stallions as well, because their condition requires an equal amount of attention.

Salt should be given daily, but judiciously, with food, and in this way it is undoubtedly a great aid to the digestion; and it is in fact indispensable to the health and condition of all animals that feed on vegetable matter. If given separately, as a dose for worms or other cause, it must not be given in too large quantities and too continuously, as it causes intense thirst, and becomes injurious, even dangerous, while an excess of it is liable to poison the system.

Worms, their causes and prevention

It is, I believe, a recognised fact that game, which abound in countries where there is an absence of saline vegetation, suffer extensively from worms. This also is the case in the Upper Nile region with the cattle, amongst which it appears that great losses from internal disorders frequently occur. These takes place after the rains, when the pools in the desert, which are left, stagnate, and turn into active and prolific breeding centres for worms and other intestinal parasites, which teem in myriads, and which are swallowed by the animals when drinking.

Schweinfurth, in his 'Heart of Africa,' speaks very strongly on this point, and in a great measure attributes the degeneracy of the Dinka cattle to this, in addition to interbreeding and exclusion of strange stock. 'Again, the cattle of the Dinka,' he writes, 'are not provided with salt in any form whatever, which may in a measure account for the degeneration, and it may explain the prevalence, all but universal, of the worms known as "kyatt," which cover the first stomach or paunch of nearly all their cattle. . . . My milch cow was an almost invaluable possession. In spite of its yield of milk being somewhat meagre, it supplied me for eight months with a morning draught, and in the subsequent season of necessity its contribution to my diet was still more precious. Half the cattle sickened and died with all sorts of internal disorders, and the greater proportion of the animals that were slaughtered would not much longer have endured the climate. I am sure, however, that, notwithstanding the fact that these breeds have been entirely unaccustomed to salt, its admixture with their food would infuse new life and vigour into them. Nothing but this, I feel convinced, kept up my own supply of milk, and prevented my cow from being emaciated.'

The fact already referred to in the previous chapter, as to the degeneracy of camels south of latitude 13° or 13° 30′ in Kordofan, points to the same cause—prevalence of worms due to want of salt, in addition, perhaps, to the enervating nature of the climate; though this, I imagine, is merely secondary, and would have but a trifling effect were the former to be removed.

Camels or any animals which have been brought up on saline herbage are always healthier and more vigorous than others, and if such is not procurable salt must be given to them as a ration. Looking at the question simply from an economical standpoint, this daily ration is to be strongly recommended, as it would often save the ultimate use of more expensive drugs, and camel-flesh as well, and the sooner we adopt it the better, for, in addition, it cannot fail in breeding to have a marked effect on the offspring.

Summary of hints to camel breeders

Before concluding this chapter, I will summarise what I consider the chief points that are necessary in order to improve the various breeds of camels, as well as to check the excessive mortality among the young. They are—

(1) The elimination of all markedly inferior types.

(2) Selection of the best breeds, and of the finest specimens of each, mentally and physically.

(3) Cancellation of interbreeding.

(4) Encouragement of cross-breeding.

(5) Selection according to age.

(6) Strictest care and attention in general management, especially to hygienic conditions.

Here we have the whole question in a nutshell, and enough has already been said on the first four to convince even a sceptic of their essential importance.

Of the fifth, I can only say that, as with us, parents in the prime of life produce the most vigorous children, so with camels the ages of sires and dams should be carefully considered, the extremes of old age and youth being naturally prejudicial, and being another cause of the degeneracy of offspring. This I imagine has been a prominent feature in assisting to degenerate the camel, as Orientals keep no records and are altogether careless on these points.

In the last point a great deal is embraced. It is, as it were, the text to a sermon. But as the whole object of this work is to lay down a certain treatment and management of the animal which should be productive of the best results, it will be waste of time to enter into any specially elaborate explanation of it. In a few words, by hygienic conditions are included feeding, cleaning, sanitary and all other arrangements that ensure health. That these are all-important factors in this most vital question—which if neglected have a highly and directly injurious effect on the animals, and indirectly on the offspring by the transmission of tendencies—no one will deny.

It stands to reason, therefore, that the closer and stricter the observation on these points, the greater the certainty of success. And it is only vain repetition to say that the better nourished and better cared for are sires and dams, the healthier and better fitted are they to produce a vigorous progeny; and in the same way it follows that a cultivation of the mental faculties will also tell. As I have previously remarked, however, although the Eastern and African races do not specially ill-treat their camels, they do not, on the other hand, devote any special attention or care to sires and dams, and with the exception of their riding camels, of which they are careful, they pay no heed to class, quality, or any of the points above enumerated. There is no doubt that such details, small as they may appear to be in themselves, eventually exercise a marked effect, as I have endeavoured to show; and on the attention or neglect paid to them depends entirely the improvement or deterioration of breeds. On the other hand, I do not accuse the natives of neglect in the general management of their animals and caravans, and, as I point out later on, we can learn a great deal from them. But in this one question of improvement of breed we might teach them many valuable lessons if we only chose to do so. Indeed, science has a splendid field before it—to assist Nature, as it has done so successfully in other directions.

Stud farms

This is a question the careful examination of which I cannot too strongly impress on our Government, and the most practical way to do so is by the establishment of breeding depôts in Egypt, India, Australia, South Africa, and last, but not least, England. If it is to be adopted at all, let the adoption be purely practical, and not simply theoretical. In the long run practice is economy, theory is extravagance. The history of our transport has always been summed up in one word, 'failure,' while the less said about its financial aspect the better. Why? Because (in a sentence) experience has been despised, and experiment—in other words, theory—has reigned supreme. No transport in the world can be worked except on a broad and solid basis, a foundation built on the rock of hard practical experience, and not on the loose and shifting sand of theory. Then when the fierce flood of war breaks on it with unusual violence, and contrary to all recognised rules of science, it will stand the strain, though it may have to bend and swing to it, while the other has been swept away and become a total wreck. The enormous advantages which would accrue from the suggestion I have made (when the scheme has had sufficient time in which to develop) I think are almost too evident to require explanation or admit of argument. In fact, it is a question broader even than one would at first sight imagine it to be, for it comes within the grasp of that question of a Greater Britain and Imperial Federation which is one of the possible, if not probable, achievements of the future—a conception so grand and glorious that it almost turns one's head to look at it, while the bare thought dazzles you with its blinding glory. But to resume. Not only would we be able to produce special breeds of riding and baggage camels, superior in every respect, the former in speed, the latter in weight-carrying capacity, and both of them in stamina and powers of abstinence, but we should be independent of the natives, and our men would learn the treatment and management of an animal which at present they look upon as the incarnation of all vice and contrariness; quite oblivious of the fact that to their ignorance, and not to the animal's iniquities, is due most of the troubles that are attendant on the line of march.

CHAPTER VI

WATERING

It is on this point, and that of feeding, two of the greatest importance in connection with the camel, that his powers or capabilities have been grossly exaggerated, and the most culpable ignorance and negligence have been displayed. The theory of his being able to go days and days without water—as long as fourteen days and more, as I have frequently seen stated—is utterly ridiculous. He can go days, and that to his detriment, but not days and days. He can also do without food for a few days, but a very few, and at the end of the time he is decidedly the worse for want both of water and food. He can go longer without water than without food.

Various opinions

A great deal has been written by various travellers and naturalists on this subject, but in the former the camel's powers have been judged by special and individual cases; in the latter, the information of naturalists is chiefly hearsay, and has been gleaned from travellers, whose experience has been confined to special breeds and a particular journey. Calmet says that 'camels will continue ten or twelve days without eating or drinking, and keep water a long time in their

Masius

stomachs for their refreshment.' Masius, a German naturalist, in his 'Zoologie,' says that 'the camel can go from eight to ten days without water.' Ensor, in his 'Incidents of a Journey through Nubia to Darfur,' says that he rode a camel for sixteen days in February, and that it never drank during that time. This was with a temperature seldom exceeding 70° Fahr. by day, with cold nights. In June, with a temperature of 100° Fahr., his camels were often without water for ten days, and worked fairly during the time, but they were picked animals. This cannot be taken as any criterion, for these were exceptions, remember, and, what is more, they were exceptional camels. Even Ensor, after allowing that there are many different versions as to the number of days a camel can travel without water, admits that generally they will work better if permitted to drink every five or seven days. Had he, however, watered his camels on every available opportunity, he would have arrived at the same conclusion that I long ago came to, that they would have then worked still better. Ensor

Sir Samuel Baker says that 'an Arabian camel carrying a load of 400 pounds requires water every third day, or every ninety miles, though they should be watered daily, if possible; but in cold weather, or when not at work, they can remain much longer without any water. If not watered for three days, however, many suffer unless specially trained.' This is a very sensible view of the question, and shows that Sir Samuel Baker must have made a study of it; besides, there is no doubt his experiences were practical and varied, and that he was well qualified to judge. As will be seen later on, our opinions coincide more or less, except that I am opposed to training in any form, besides being quite Sir Samuel Baker positive that, when water is available, camels working regularly and steadily in a dry hot climate should be watered daily; and, as a rule, in the Nubian and Soudan deserts, even in winter, the sun is powerful.

Experiments and theories

I have tried all sorts of experiments when in charge of transport and in command of camel corps. I have watered camels once every day, and found that they always drank a small quantity, about four to five gallons. On alternate days they drank from five to six gallons. Every third day, especially with baggagers, I had a certain amount of difficulty in restraining them from getting at the water, which they rushed at only too eagerly. I am now speaking of the Soudan, when the weather was exceptionally dry and hot. On these occasions, which occurred on the march, carrying good average loads, they drank at a rough approximation at least ten gallons apiece. Some people have a theory, which I have also put into execution, that the camel only requires water every second day, ordinarily speaking, and that previous to a long march he should not be watered for three days, and then before starting allowed to drink to repletion. This latter portion of the theory is folly. After three days' abstinence he should not be permitted to drink much, say, not more than three or four gallons. Then send him to graze for a few hours, give him a feed of grain if you have it, and a few hours subsequent to this he may drink his fill; but whether on the march, or preparatory to one, it is fatal to let the camel drink on an empty stomach. He invariably over-drinks himself, gets off his feed, is shoved on and on, march, march, march, as if he was a cast-iron machine, consequently never recovers the effects, and most likely collapses entirely. Equally so on a full one. V.-S. Steel, speaking of watering camels after a long exhaustive march, or after unavoidable prolonged abstinence, says: 'With regard to water, it should not be given after a full meal, but is grateful ever to the wearied organ, rapidly restores the normal fluidity of the blood, which has been partially destroyed by abstinence, and with the above exception may be given whenever the animal feels inclined to drink it.' But if he had seen, as I have, the evil of watering camels on empty stomachs after prolonged abstinence and a long harassing march, he would agree with me, I feel sure, on this point. One instance I can recall, in the Bayuda desert, which occurred in January, after a march of 100 miles, across firm sand chiefly, and under a hot sun. It was on the afternoon of the fifth day that we arrived in Gakdool, and the animals had carried an average load of 400 pounds. I was busily engaged elsewhere, and before I could prevent it one division of about 150 camels had been allowed to drink their fill. Those I saw when I came up towards the finish were simply ravenous, and were emptying bucket after bucket. After a careful calculation I computed that on an average each camel drank from fifteen to twenty gallons. The second division, when its turn came, were only allowed four gallons per animal, and were then sent grazing, such as it was, for five or six hours. After this a small ration of grain (the only food we had, and that in very small quantities) was served out all round, and then the camels of the second division were permitted to drink as much as they liked. Next day the majority of the first division showed unmistakable

Watering on full and empty stomachs

signs of languor and heaviness, and many of them soon succumbed, none of them eventually escaping. This was due, I feel sure, to the overdrinking, coming as it did on the top of hard work and empty stomachs, and on an already enervated frame, and succeeded as it was by hard work minus food and water; while those of the other division had gained decidedly by the rest and treatment, and struggled on manfully to the end. This and other instances that came under my notice have convinced me that one of the results of making camels abstain from either food or water is that they will in either case gorge themselves to repletion; therefore, if you have been obliged from necessity to keep them on starvation diet, never give them the opportunity of doing so when you reach the land of plenty.

The best plan

Watering alternate days is not a bad idea in its way, but in my opinion, after giving every conceivable plan a trial, the safest way is to depend entirely on circumstances and conditions, and act accordingly. If water is procurable, whether on the march or at the halt, or even when remaining idle in cantonments, by all means water your camels once daily, the afternoon for choice. This I found was the best method, and when I had command of a camel corps in the Soudan it succeeded admirably. Whenever I went out on patrol, which was frequently, my camels used to cover on an average fifty miles a day in the desert without water, and with very little food, except a daily ration of 3 lb. of grain, and what they could pick up from the scanty herbage. This they kept up for three or four days, sometimes five and six, without being knocked up in the slightest, in the hot weather, too, in the country south of Wadi

Halfa, where at times I have known the thermometer to register 125° Fahr. I know that the desert tribes, when they allow their camels to graze in the larger oases for several months after the rains, water them regularly every day. For example, at Om Badr, in Darfur, 350 miles from Old Dongola, on the road to El Fasher, where there are said to be 500 wells, and where, in the ordinary course of events, 10,000 camels drink daily until the end of the dry season, when there is only enough water for 1,000; while about a similar number assemble at Gakdool, in the Bayuda desert.

Training mistake

Training a camel, so to speak, by only giving him water every second day, or keeping it from him for three days preparatory to an emergency, is simple nonsense, as I have previously remarked, for I maintain that the camel requires no special training. On account of his powers of abstinence there is no reason why he should be treated differently from other animals; and to me it seems opposed to common sense to deprive an animal simply because he has this power, altogether overlooking the fact that he only possesses it to a limited and not to an exaggerated extent as he is credited. This is a mistake, for a camel in watering and feeding, especially when marching and working regularly—except on an emergency when he is called upon to make a special effort—should be treated as an ordinary quadruped. Far from preparing him for an effort by training or treating him otherwise, this class of treatment slowly and gradually tells on him, and wears him out. Of this I feel certain. A special and systematic course of training, like that of the Oxford and Cambridge boat crews, or athletes in general have to undergo, is not the thing for the camel, and in the long run undermines his constitution, as it does that of the athlete. I am positive that the more you feed and water the camel during the ordinary routine, within bounds and not to excess, of course, the better fitted he will be on an emergency to abstain from food and water, and the longer will be his fast, than if he had previously undergone a rigorous system of training. I will go further, and say that he will be more capable of sustaining a greater number of these efforts, and that while he will live to do so your trained animal would have long since broken down and succumbed. It stands to reason that when you call on an animal to make such an extraordinary and sustained effort, the better his condition, the more likely he is to go through with it; and it is also within the bounds of common sense that his condition will be infinitely better if he has been well nourished previous to the trial than if he has been forced to abstain, because in the latter case you at once compel him to fall back on his reserve store, whereas in the former he will have to exhaust his daily supply. Besides, his stamina under these conditions is bound to be greater than that of an animal who has been constantly trained and kept down fine, undermined in fact.

Overtraining country breds

It is the same mistake that men with whom 'a little knowledge is a dangerous thing' make when in such countries as India and Egypt they take in hand the training of country-bred horses and ponies for racing. Their knowledge of the thoroughbred at home has probably been confined to seeing the 'Derby,' 'Goodwood,' or the 'Oaks;' perhaps they may have had the opportunity of going over one of the great training stables; so, with the dash of the sportsman inherent in most Englishmen, they enter their chargers, hacks, or polo ponies for some event, training them so fine that when the race comes off the poor beasts have not a run left in them. This is due to sheer ignorance of the fact that countrybreds cannot stand the training given to English thoroughbreds; not altogether because they are an entirely different class of animal, undersized and underbred compared with the latter (although they have more endurance and greater power of abstinence), but because as foals they have not been so well cared for and so well nourished, have less reserve to go upon—consequently it is a grave mistake to train this reserve away before the race. In other words, they are as a rule more or less in a state of training when regularly worked, and an extra strain reduces instead of improving them.

The assumption, too, that the camel has an extra stomach or stomachs, a natural provision for the storage of water, is, as we have seen, a misapplication of words; but he has rows of cells attached to the first, and also enclosed in the second compartment, which are set apart exclusively for this purpose. We know that he returns the partially masticated food from the second compartment to the mouth, which he chews at his own leisure, returning it to the fourth compartment, there to be digested. We also know that he can retain a certain quantity of water (about 1½ gallon) in the water cells, when full, by means of which he can on an emergency abstain from water for several days. If you keep him from water for a long time, and at the

Evils of starvation

same time starve him, or if you deprive him of one or other, it stands to reason that in the first instance he cannot chew the cud at all, and in either of the other cases he cannot chew it properly, for he cannot live for any length of time on food alone, and in the long run he must have water, with dry food especially, as the juices and secretions are not sufficient in themselves to keep the animal in health and strength. It must be remembered, however, that there are camels and camels, and that their powers of abstinence depend not entirely and exclusively on Nature's bounty, as has hitherto been the popular prevailing idea, but in a very great measure upon their breeding, and upon the country and climate they have been brought up in. Bisharin, Kabbabish, or Ababdeh camels, for example, that have been born and bred in their native deserts—great sandy waterless wastes—require less water and can endure without it for a longer period than camels of Lower Egypt or the Panjab, who under dissimilar conditions are accustomed to greener food and more water, consequently are much softer and less enduring.

Power of abstinence dependent on breeding

Virtues of water

Apart from this, however, there is more virtue in water than at first sight we would imagine. In the first place, it is a kind of food, and men and animals will exist on it alone for several days.

2. It is *par excellence* Nature's tonic, and as such it is absolutely a necessity to keep the body, and therefore the instinctive and reasoning faculties of animals, in a healthy, vigorous state, which would quickly become impaired without it.

3. Taken in reasonable quantities, inwardly and outwardly, it keeps the skin in an active and sanitary state.

4. Like a dust or thunderstorm it clears the system, cleansing and purging it of all impurities and secretions which if allowed to remain would generate disease.

5. It is an animal's only drink, and quenches his thirst effectually and naturally.

6. 'It is the medium by which the waste material of the body is carried away.'

7. 'It bathes every tissue, and dissolves and removes the products of tissue metamorphosis.'

8. 'It renews the system daily, acting as a rejuvenant.'

Taking all these points into consideration, it will be seen that, even making every allowance for the abstaining powers of a camel, water is really indispensable in order to preserve his condition, and eventually his life, and except on an emergency he ought not to be stinted.

Young herbage

It has also been stated that 'during the season, when fresh pasture is abundant, camels can go for weeks without water, provided they are not loaded or required to make extraordinary exertions. The juices of the plants which form their food are then sufficient to quench their thirst.' Here the writer is evidently not speaking from his own personal knowledge, and though he has got an inkling of the subject, he has either been led away by the verbose eloquence of a traveller, or has been carried away by his own vivid imagination. It needs no deep thought or knowledge to arrive at the fact that camels fed on green fodder require less water than when getting dry food, and that the more succulent the herbage, and the greater the moisture contained, the smaller the water supply they want. But, as I have just pointed out, the natives in the deserts, even after the rains, when the pasturage is fresh and green, water their camels daily, and this they do because they take a sound, practical view of the question, and consider that the moisture of the herbage is insufficient, and does not refresh the animal as a drink will, no matter how small. I should think, too, that in spite of the saliva and mucous secretion, which assist the camel in mastication, a certain amount of water is absolutely necessary to give the digestive organs a healthy, vigorous tone, as well as to enable them to carry out their functions with beneficial results.

There is no doubt that in the spring—which in the desert, practically speaking, follows the rains—when the herbage is young and succulent, or when, as often happens, a heavy dew has fallen, camels can graze in the early morning before the sun has dried it up, and that they can go without water for a longer period than in the dry season, when everything is parched and burnt up, but not for weeks and weeks. Lieut. Massoutier says that the camel can go twenty days without water, if *not* worked. This, from the point of view of a naturalist, is a most interesting fact. But even supposing he can, for sake of argument, looking at the matter in a purely practical light, what possible object can be gained by this enforced abstinence? None whatever that I can see, especially if the animals are not being put to any unnecessary exertion—running free, in fact. Or, if there is no necessity, and water happens to be plentiful, why deprive them? On the contrary, neither ourselves nor the animals are gainers, but distinctly losers, for this kind of treatment would very soon be responsible for a heavy death rate. And to do so, apart from the humanity of the thing, seems to me to be opposed to the commonest form of common sense—evidently a very rare quality nowadays!

How to let camels drink, and what quantity they generally absorb

The best plan is to leave it to nature—that is, to the animals themselves—as the natives do, and you will find that they will drink daily, a small quantity no doubt, but sufficient to answer the purpose, and to fulfil its legitimate functions, while it refreshes and satisfies the animal. There is no doubt, however, that when the grazing is fresh, as above described, marching under native management, where the camel is considered first and foremost, and everything has to give way to his convenience, he can make a greater effort, and carry on a few days longer, than when he is overdriven and stinted by us. Under such conditions he can abstain from eight to ten days, without much physical wear and tear, and without sowing the seeds of constitutional debility and premature decay. But four or five days' abstinence in the heat and on dry food is sufficient, if you do not wish subsequently to injure him, and eventually to cut short his life.

I have read somewhere that camels of the Arabian species will only drink five to six gallons at a time, which will last them for six days, while the Bactrian can take in only half that quantity. But in a hot climate, during steady work, my experience has been that even a camel belonging to the country can and will drink a great deal more than this. Therefore I should imagine that the Bactrian, or a camel of the

Arabian species born in a cold climate, being unaccustomed to great heat, would, if worked in a hot climate, drink twice as much as he would in his own country. So at least I have found. As to the amount, I have on several occasions seen camels drink as much as twenty gallons, after five to seven days' abstinence in great heat and when hard worked—and there was no restraining them; and after three or four days I have seen them stow away with ease from ten to fifteen gallons. As a matter of fact the amount a camel will drink depends in a great measure on the weather and the changes of temperature, and varies accordingly. The greater the heat, the greater the quantity of water they drink, and the more they require. But it also depends on the amount of work they are doing, and the quality as well as quantity of food they are getting. For if the former is severe, and the latter dry and deficient in bulk, their stomachs will have a natural craving for more water. And *vice versâ*, when the weather is cold, or if work is light, food green or plentiful, they can do with much less. Many natives, both in India and Afghanistan, have told me this, and the frequent evidence of my own senses has entirely confirmed it. V.-S. Steel, writing on this point, says: 'My experienced sarwān (a somewhat aged man, who had been with camels all his life) told me that in hot weather camels required watering every day; in cold they began to fail when without it for three days, and if denied it for five days they would die.'

The former portion of this statement is quite correct, but the latter, though right in its general principles, is a trifle overdrawn. Even in hot weather, I have time after time worked the same camels in the desert for four or five days at a stretch, without water and under a hot sun, with the best results; and as we have seen they will abstain up to ten days under good management and with green pasture. And if on such occasions you work them at night, and graze them by day, they will stand it well enough, and the after effects will be reduced to a minimum. As for a fit desert camel, even in the hottest weather, dying straight away after five days' abstinence, that is utter nonsense. At that rate I ought to have seen thousands die; though it is quite probable that they would do so subsequently, if further overtaxed and used as on service.

Daily watering when in work

Lieutenant Massoutier says that 'in summer, when working, a camel should have water every two or three days, and as a rule he should be watered whenever there is a favourable opportunity, for after long abstinence camels will rush to the water and soon foul it, and in such case they should always be watered two days running.' The fact of their fouling the water is after all a mere trifle which can be prevented in comparison to the really weighty one of daily watering, which Lieutenant Massoutier does not seem to clearly comprehend, or be decided about, although he recognises the value of frequent watering. The very fact of the intense eagerness and longing for water that camels display after a long fast clearly and intelligibly proves that they require it oftener, and that it is simply nature asserting itself. What stronger proof, therefore, can we have than this of the virtue of daily watering—the necessity, in fact, of leaving it to Nature herself?

L 2

Quality of water preferred

As to the quality of water preferred by camels, there is also much doubt and contradiction. On the one hand it is asserted that they are not very particular as to the water they drink. On the other, it is said that they prefer clean water, slightly salt. While a third authority maintains that they like still water; and curiously enough Aristotle, speaking on this point, says that they prefer troubled water. In fact he lays it down as a hard-and-fast rule that water should be made turbid before allowing them to drink. Here we have three opinions, all at variance with each other. Personally, I am inclined to the former up to a certain extent. The fact of the matter, however, is, that in this respect camels, like human beings, when suffering from thirst will drink anything, but as a rule they prefer clean still water. They will drink saline water; but this, I think, arises from the fact that they are usually obliged to put up with Hobson's choice, because the water in the deserts is often brackish. But if they are getting sufficient salt in or with their food, and they are given their choice between brackish water and sweet, they would drink the latter; though this, again, will depend very much on the locality they come from.

A camel in the cold season does not like cold running water, and if possible it is better to water him out of a hole or tank containing still water which has been exposed to the sun for a few hours. This is also purely a question of habit, and at all seasons a desert camel will prefer still water to running. This is not to be wondered at, for as a rule the so-called wells are nothing more or less than shallow holes—sometimes scarcely below the surface—scraped out of the sand.

To sum up, then: the entire question of watering the camel is only and purely a question of common sense after all, which should be left to each animal's individual discretion, subject to certain conditions which have been already pointed out—viz. not to let him drink on a full or empty stomach, for instance, or when heated, fatigued, and exhausted. It would be difficult, perhaps, on service to fulfil all these conditions, but if possible it is advisable to do so, because his life is so diametrically opposite to what he has been accustomed, so altered, in fact, as to exercise a marked effect on, if not to change, the nature of the animal. For in a state of nature, running as they do almost wild in the Nubian deserts, or in their normal condition under native management, camels will drink when they feel inclined, but will not indulge too freely, and do not therefore require supervision. General conclusions on watering

CHAPTER VII

FEEDING

The greatest care should be paid to this equally important branch of camel management, and, what is more, too much attention cannot be lavished on it. Do not lose sight of the fact that the organisation of the camel is delicate, and though by means of a limited power of abstinence he can do without food for a certain time, he is in the main, as regards both watering and feeding, very similar to other animals, and requires—more so when regularly worked—to be regularly fed.

Thrives best where bred

My experience has been that the camel thrives best in his own district, where he has been bred and accustomed to feed on certain kinds of food, and that if you take him into another climate and country under altered conditions of food he does not get on so well, and falls off in condition. If, for instance, you were to take special breeds of Indian camels, which feed principally on the leaves of certain trees—'pipal,' 'neem,' 'babul,' &c.—and place them in some of the deserts of the Nile, where only a few stunted bushes and shrubs grow—or, *vice versâ*, transfer the desert camel to India—you would find that they would not thrive. Of course I do not mean to imply that camels accustomed to leaves will not eat grass, chopped straw, or other fodder; all I say is that they do not relish, and as a rule will not eat, food which is entirely foreign to them, unless driven to it by hunger, when, like most quadrupeds, and bipeds for the matter of that, they will eat anything; but if given their choice they prefer, as a matter of course, food which is natural to them. A camel of any breed is on the whole a delicate feeder, and not easily pleased; a view, I see, which Lieutenant Massoutier also takes of the Algerian specimen.

We have already come to the decision that the camel is a very stupid animal, and requires to be taken to suitable grazing grounds, as not only is he unable to find them out for himself, but he is apt to be indiscreet, either by eating poisonous herbs, or by overeating himself when he gets into rich pastures. Unlike a horse he cannot control his appetite, and I have seen scores of them die in Afghanistan when they got into the large fields of beautiful clover that we marched through, from Candahar to Cabul, under Sir Donald Stewart, in 1880. It is, therefore, most expedient to watch them when grazing. Sir Samuel Baker, speaking of the camel, says that 'it is fond of luxurious living, and when it arrives in good pasture will eat to repletion; but when other animals starve it thrives on the ends of barren leafless twigs, the dried sticks of certain shrubs, and the tough dry paper-like substance of the dom palm, about as succulent as would be a green umbrella and a "Times."' The latter part of this statement I cannot altogether hold with. The camel will eat but he will not thrive on such food when he is doing hard and continuous work. Then, if the grazing is of this nature, you must supplement it with a ration of grain and chopped straw, hay, or other forage which is

Difference of treatment between natives and ourselves

available. The desert tribes, dependent as they are on camels for their very existence, consequently mindful of their interests and their animals, are very careful on this point, and even when carrying loads on the march they allow them to graze as they drive them along. Whereas in the service our drivers, unmindful and ignorant of the animal's peculiarities, and utterly oblivious of his welfare, will curl themselves under a bush and go to sleep, leaving them to eat whatever is in the way, ignorant and regardless of the fact that close by, on the opposite side of the watercourse perhaps, pasturage is plentiful and excellent. This shows that, unless you have trustworthy drivers, constant supervision is necessary; for never lose sight of the fact that the camel does not thrive on fodder which he has not been bred up on, but that if driven to it he will eat anything, even poisonous herbs; and, in spite of his size, and of the extra-abstaining capacity of his internal structure, his digestive organs are not proportionally strong—or perhaps I should say that when the animal is fatigued the stomach, which in its construction is purely muscular, becomes exhausted also, and its action is impaired, the third and fourth compartments especially failing in their digestive power. It stands to reason, therefore, that a large grain ration given when they are in this state is highly injurious, to say the least of it; but, all the same, I have seen this done time after time in Afghanistan, with fatal consequences —indigestion and colic, ending frequently in death. I have been present when several camels have been dissected, and the quantity of undigested barley found in their stomachs was more than enough to account for death. This is the stage when a few hours' grazing not only gives the wearied animals time to regain their energy, but time to restore the tired internal organs to their ordinary state of vigour, and to enable them to resume their normal functions; then, if water is available, let them have a small drink, and shortly after give them a small feed of grain. If there is no grazing, serve them out a small supply of chopped straw, but on no account grain. Should there be no chopped straw, allow them to rest for an hour or two, then a small drink, followed by a small ration of grain. And if these also are not to be had, as has often been the lot of the camel I have worked with, and this state of things goes on day after day, on the top of incessant toil and marching, it is needless for me to say what becomes of the poor creatures. The vultures and other carrion birds could tell, and the skeletons that invariably dot the track taken by a British force would in themselves furnish the enthusiastic inquirer with a history sad but more eminently eloquent than the concentrated essence of the descriptive powers of all the transport officers in existence, even did they wield the pen of a Kinglake or Napier. *Moral.*—Do not feed camels on grain if they have not been accustomed to it; and if they have, only on that particular grain, in small quantities and in the way I have described. And, above all, do not starve and overwork them.

Treatment in the Afghan campaign

During the Afghan campaign, 1878–80, firstly, because we were perpetually and continuously on the move, and had no time allowed for grazing; secondly, for the simple reason that no other food was procurable, we fed our camels on barley and 'bhoosa' (chopped straw), 10 lb. of the former and from 20 to 25 lb. of the latter daily, given in the evening when the day's work was over; more frequently than not the grain first, sometimes mixed together, the animal, as a matter of course, picking out the barley first. To my thinking a small ration early in the morning previous to marching is a good thing. Frequently, however, bhoosa was not to be had, and an additional ration of barley was served out, with most evil results, as already pointed out. The animals had been taken out of their element. They were, in fact, like fish out of water, being subjected to a mode of life and treatment they were altogether unaccustomed to—overweighted, overpaced, overworked, grazing done away with, and sometimes overfed on unsuitable food; while at others they got nothing at all to eat, because there were no rations to give them, though on occasions, had the authorities been reasonable, and consulted or even considered the transport, good pasturage would not have been passed by; but we were, as we invariably are, in too great a hurry to get on. As in Afghanistan, so in the Soudan. Seeing, as I have done, hundreds and thousands of camels die from sheer exhaustion, brought on by neglect and ill-treatment arising from downright stupidity, obstinacy, and ignorance, is enough to make one ashamed of having had any connection with the business. It is really too sickening to think that so great a loss of life should result from so trifling a cause—a cause so easily remediable, or removable, and, what is more, culpable, for nowadays stupidity and ignorance on such a subject as the proper treatment of the camel is distinctly deserving of severe censure.

There are occasions and emergencies—General Roberts's relief march to Candahar, or Sir Herbert Stewart's dash across the Bayuda desert to rescue Gordon—when you must push on at all hazards. Then in war, as in all speculations, it is, if not an absolute necessity, at least justifiable to sacrifice life. And when human lives are in jeopardy, to save them you must be prepared to do so at the cost of animal life, providing you are not utterly and cruelly reckless over it. In such cases, when you are constantly on the move and have no time, owing to the activity of the enemy or from other unforeseen difficulties, you cannot graze them (travelling, for example, across the desert from Korosko to Abu Hamad, which is bare sand and rock), you must give them rations. If obliged from necessity, and for **Rations** no other reason, to give them, always serve out a few handfuls of chaff all round at the end of the day's work, and water, blanket up (if cold or damp at night), and dole out the rest of the rations, the grain first, chaff afterwards, so that they can munch it during the first few hours, and chew the cud during the early hours of the morning. Sometimes both are issued together, but this is not a good plan; given separately is much better. For my own part I would sooner give a camel no grain at all than barley, which I believe is bad for them, **Grain, barley** except in very small quantities. It is heating and hard to digest, and not very nutritious. Crushed barley is not so bad; but how are you to crush it on service? Gram and dourra (a kind of millet) are both very good, and are, I consider, most suitable for the camel. He can get a grip of them and masticate them well. They are less heating and more nutritious than most grain.

The latter contains a large proportion of starch, and is considered more nourishing than wheat flour. A small quantity given daily is, so the Hadendowas say, of great use in preserving good condition in camels, and there is not the slightest doubt whatever that it keeps up the animal's strength very materially. In North Africa and Asia dried dates and beans are given to the camels, and are most excellent and fattening food, especially the former. The Russians in Central Asia, when they consider it necessary to keep up a camel's strength, give it a few handfuls of dry forage which, on the half loaf better than no bread principle, may be better than nothing, but, practically speaking, is useless, because dry forage should be given in quantities to do any good. As a substitute they give 3 lb. of meal mixed with 3 oz. of salt. This is far more nourishing, though here, again, the quantity is rather small. Kaffir corn and mealies in small quantities would do, I think, when working them hard; but do not forget when using the grain, even the best, to do so sparingly and with the utmost caution. The French in Algeria give emaciated camels from 4 to 6 lb. of oats per day; but the digestive organs of animals in such condition are not in proper working order, from a similar but stronger cause that affects those of animals which are in a state of exhaustion, and I think it very unwise to give them grain while they are in this condition. Turn them out to graze for a few days or weeks, according to the state they are in, as the natives do, until they have recovered themselves to a certain extent, and their internal organs have assumed a vigorous, healthy tone, then by all means give them a few pounds of grain daily, to put strength into them. I doubt, however, if oats, for the same reason as barley, are particularly suitable for camels.

Native food

In Arabia and in North Africa the natives are in the habit of crushing barley and dates, mixing them with a little camel's milk or water, and making them into small balls or cakes, which they give to their riding camels during and after a long hard ride. In India, and especially in the Panjab, barley flour is mixed with the melted fat of the Doomba sheep, in the proportion of three parts of flour to one of fat; also coarse wheat flour mixed with ghee (clarified butter), or with goor (coarse brown sugar) and ghee (in the same proportion), and made into balls, but given to animals in emergent cases only. The natives consider all three kinds very nourishing and more than equal to double the quantity of grain. I have heard it asserted that grain steeped in water is good for camels; but where, when, and how is it to be done on service, unless by the wave of a magic wand you could sink wells or cause rivers to flow in the desert?

Comparison between dry and soaked grain

Personally, I consider dry grain to be better, as the camel does not in the natural state of things, unless he is aged and his molars are decayed, require any artificial aid in the mastication of his food, his teeth being well fitted to crush, and his stomach being fully qualified to masticate it thoroughly, while the slime generated in the mouth materially assists it. If good grazing is procurable, 3 or 4 lb. a day of grain is ample; if indifferent, increase it to 6 lb.; should none be available, from 6 to 8 lb., but, if possible, do not exceed six, and

Alternative

avoid barley if you possibly can, unless it happens that the camels have been bred on it. Should the pasturage be really suitable and plentiful it is infinitely preferable to graze them only than to feed them on rations; but never graze them for less than six hours, and the more over that you can the better. In this case, unless the work is heavy and continuous, grain is unnecessary. In addition, six hours at least for rest and to enable them to chew the cud is also, I consider, most necessary in order to keep camels in really good condition. If there is no grazing and no grain, at least 70 lb. of chopped straw should be given daily, or with 4 lb. of grain from 50 to 60 lb. of straw, and with 6 lb. of grain 40 to 50 lb. of straw; for do not lose sight of the fact that, though grain is productive of muscle and stamina, a bulk of a less nutritious food is requisite to assist the grain in acquiring the desired effect, and without it the camel cannot keep in condition. It is advisable, especially when feeding camels on dry rations, to mix a little salt with the grain or straw—the former for choice—3 oz. three times a week, or, better still, about $1\frac{1}{2}$ to 2 oz. a day is the correct thing, and crushed rock salt is the best. As I have remarked, they will drink saline water, and when in want of salt it forms a substitute; but I am sure it is not so good for them as salt, and does not quite answer the same purpose, which, besides imparting a relish to the food and a tone to the system, assists the juices and fluids in accomplishing the work of digestion.

Some of the different trees, shrubs, grasses, &c.

If fed on dry or saline food, the camel naturally requires more water; *vice versâ*, when he is getting leaves and other green fodder which contain a certain amount of moisture, he requires less. Curious to say, too—and yet not curious, for it is only nature asserting itself—he is fond of green food, and having no power of discrimination or control he will, as I have previously remarked, especially if not watered, eat until he bursts when he gets into a field of clover, or lucerne, or other cereal. Leaves of all thorny trees and shrubs, saline and prickly grasses, are generally eaten by all camels, and preferred to any other by those accustomed to them, but even those who have not been take to them immediately. A small low shrub with tiny leaves and very long spiky thorns like the mimosa—a kind of camel thorn, I believe, and called 'agool' by the Arabs—which grows in Beloochistan, Sind, and on the banks of the Nile in Nubia and the Soudan, I have always found to be an especial favourite, and camels will eat it in preference to anything else. Another little shrub, very moist and juicy, small leaved, with tiny white flower, which grows in the valleys of the Nubian deserts green and fresh in April and May, is very much fancied. 'Camel thorn,' of which there are three varieties, I believe, in Egypt and the Soudan, is much sought after, also the leaves and branches of 'tamarisk' bushes; hence the necessity of his strong incisors, canines, and canine-like molars, which enable him to crush the twigs, &c. 'Mimosas,' and 'dwarf mimosas,' of which there are many thorny varieties, 'halfa' or 'alfa,' a long coarse grass they are partial to, and in the Soudan deserts 'sabas' and 'tress' grass, tufts of 'yellow grass,' and also a kind of coarse grass are, especially the two former, the chief food of camels, cattle, and goats. The leaves of 'sunt,' from which gum arabic is distilled, 'stunted acacias,' and 'dragon trees'; the 'nebbuk bushes' are, I believe, also eaten, also the leaves of the 'date' and 'dom palm,' and it is said that the camel will eat 'nettle,' 'thistle,' 'cassia,' 'wormwood,' and any kind of harsh prickly or dry hard vegetable. In the Sahara the following are the plants upon which he grazes—viz. 'getaf' bushes, which have a saltish taste and are much liked; 'rtem' a legumen, a great favourite; 'diel,' a bush which when it reaches the height of 1½ foot ceases to be eaten by camels, and is very common; 'sooid' a bush; 'drin,' 'alfa,' and 'boogriba' are all three grasses, the former growing on a sandy ground, the latter, which is very succulent, on a salt-impregnated soil. In India, 'babul,' 'neem,' 'pipal,' 'phulai,' 'kikar,' 'goolur,' 'jhand,' 'burgut,' 'behr,' 'goolali,' 'hees,' 'kurrul,' 'jaree,' 'jawassa,' 'lana,' 'kair,' 'karonda,' 'katila,' are the principal trees and shrubs which are commonly eaten, the leaves of the first three mentioned being considered the best. 'Mote,' 'khawid' when young, 'kassil,' 'sarson,' and 'tarameera' when in seed, are green crops which when in season the natives esteem most highly. The Bactrian species, in the intensely cold northern regions of Central Asia, are said to subsist on the leaves and twigs of 'willow' and 'birch,' and in winter merely on the dry leafless twigs which they can pick up.

When speaking of rations I omitted to state that, in feeding, always be most careful to see that the grain and straw are placed on a feeding-cloth, which ought to be supplied at the rate of one to every two camels. If this has been lost, make the driver use a sack, or a cloth or blanket of his own, and never, if you can help it, place the ration on the ground. In the first place you save a lot of the ration, a fourth or fifth perhaps, and eventually, possibly, the animal's life. By placing it on the ground they pick up sand and gravel, which after a time, hard work and exposure aiding it, produce sand colic and frequently death. At post-mortems held on them I have seen pounds of dirt and gravel taken out of their intestines.

System of feeding

V.-S. Steel is of opinion that the camel should be treated similarly to the horse, and fed frequently, and that he will thrive in like manner as that animal. As regards a horse, I believe most implicitly in this mode of treatment, but not so much a camel, though he certainly ought to have at least two feeds a day if he has been placed on a scale of rations. What I do believe in altogether is ample grazing, and ample time to allow them to chew the cud.

Advantage of grazing

One of the great advantages of grazing is that they obtain natural food, which is infinitely healthier and more suitable for them, besides the freedom from constraint and control which all animals, even the down-trodden camel, love. When, being free of all impedimenta, and out of the reach of brutality and cruelty, they can wander at will more or less, pick and choose where and when they like, stand here or kneel down there and ruminate; lie down, rest and chew the cud, maybe of morbid fancies, but more probably of some choice pickings that they have stumbled across; stretch themselves, and enjoy a good roll in some soft sandy spot; rub up against a rough prickly tree, a hard rugged boulder, or against one another, indulging in the luxury of a mutual and friendly scratch. Do just what they like, in fact, and feel in their own dense way that even their life is not altogether made up of hard knocks and blows and brutal drivers.

Relaxation

It is this utter relaxation which, even when there is no grazing, exercises a markedly beneficial effect on camels—a natural tonic which should be a part and parcel of their daily routine, and the total absence of which has an equally opposite and deleterious result, that accounts for the enormous percentage of sick, as well as the terrific death rate, among our camels on service. Too much stress cannot be laid on this vitally important point. If natural food is very plentiful, by all means make the drivers cut sufficient for the night's consumption, but never on any account for the day, because, for the reasons above given, it is infinitely better when halting to turn all camels out of camp to graze and rest, in preference to keeping them in. And if let alone they will get far more food and rest in this way, besides the advantages of freshness and choice; but a certain amount of quiet supervision is necessary to guard against the latter being indiscriminate and unwise.

If grazing practicable what to be done

In a campaign like the Nile, in which the line of communication was of unusual length, and passing as it did through a barren country, deficient in supplies and without natural resources, grazing was a most precarious means of subsistence. In such cases it should be supplemented by rations, though the enormous transport difficulties which supervene make it a question of extreme difficulty. Where, however, grazing is good it ought to be systematically carried out, except during an operation of exceptional danger, in the face of a bold and active enemy, where time is the all-important factor.

Should there be no grazing, a third feed of forage or straw should be given them, as a deficiency of bulk of proper food is too often overlooked; but here again the difficulty of transporting fodder in large quantities confronts us, and in the march from Korti to Metammeh was a complete failure, as the animals had to depend entirely, except for a very small grain ration for the first few days, on what they could pick up in the desert. As we marched every day from or before dawn to dark, and after it, and as at night they were all carefully secured, it is not a surprising fact that the poor brutes succumbed rapidly one after the other.

If no grazing, what to be done

It seems to be almost a universal idea amongst us, judging at all events from the rations we give on service, either on the march or in camp, that a camel when not grazing only requires about 20 lb. of forage in addition to grain, and not more than 25 to 30 lb. at the very outside without grain; and when he is doing no work we reduce his rations still more. But this is utterly inadequate, and as I have already pointed out he ought to get quite double that amount. There is some excuse on service when passing through a barren country, and when, owing to the almost insuperable difficulties of transport, forage is not procurable in sufficient quantities; but even when these do not stand in the way we stint our camels all the same.

Mistaken notions as to quantity of food

Even when he can get grazing, unless it is of the right sort and very plentiful, and he is allowed ample time to fill himself—for instance, if it is scanty and he only has three or four hours of it—he ought to get a certain amount of forage. It is no wonder that on service our losses in camel-flesh are so abnormally heavy and disproportionate, because, apart from other causes, we so frequently overfeed them with grain to make up for deficiency of forage; and even when we have sufficient forage we underfeed them with it—it being in reality not only a necessary of life, but an absolute necessity to keep life together, especially when we are taxing that life to the utmost.

Curiously enough we seem to lose sight of the fact that the abstaining powers of the camel, though dual, are unequal, and that he cannot endure hunger as well as he does thirst. Or is it simply ignorance with most of us? Or yet, again, is it mere thoughtlessness, or an utter indifference and disregard for the poor brute's life? I am pleased to say that on this point Lieut. Massoutier is of the same opinion as myself, and he recommends that a camel should get 30 to 40 kilos. of forage daily, and at least three or four hours' grazing a day. And he goes on to say that 'a camel can go from four to five days' journey with grazing alone, but it is better then to supplement it by grain, and it is necessary afterwards to give him one or two days' rest in a good pasturage.' An average specimen of an ordinary breed will do this, whereas one of a good breed will carry on easily for double that time, and in their own deserts, if the grazing is good and plentiful, for longer, provided water is frequently obtainable—say, every alternate day at the least. The whole question, in fact, is distinctly conditional, and on these two conditions—i.e. an abundance of natural food and water—they could in proper hands work and subsist for weeks. But if the

What work a camel can do with grazing, and how to supplement his green food work is hard a supplementary grain ration is all the better, and the more needful to sustain and support the stamina; it must, however, be grain to which they have been accustomed. A day's rest in a good pasture, at the rate of every fourth day on a long and trying march, and once a week on shorter journeys, is an absolute essential to maintain condition; what is more, in the end a saving in time and money is effected, because the animals do not get knocked up, and march all the quicker for it, and there is less loss of life among them. On the termination of the former they ought to be turned out for several days, say, from a week to a fortnight, altogether dependent on the length of march, the amount of work done, and the condition they arrive in.

When camels are subsisting on dry rations only, and the grazing is either *nil* or scanty, it is imperatively essential to give them green food, such as clover, lucerne, or the ordinary grasses, in order to cleanse and purify their systems, and to keep them free from scorbutic and other skin affections—in fact, to preserve their condition. One good feed, or about four hours' grazing daily, or every alternate day at the least, is sufficient to effect this.

When they should not graze

I have already alluded in chapter iii. to a statement by Lieut. Massoutier as to 'the refusal of camels to eat camel thorn when saturated with moisture; and for the reason that it is injurious to them when in this state, they should not be sent out to graze while the dew is on the ground.' The former part of this we have discussed. The latter, as to the liability to injury, we will now go into. On this point I think he is so far right, that camels, being of an organisation that is delicate and extremely susceptible to catarrh, may catch cold at such an early hour of the morning, and so sow the seeds of some pulmonary affection; though Lieut. Massoutier would seem to imply the likelihood of an internal organic complaint through the mere eating of moistened herbage. That this effect might be produced if the herbage were soddened, and noxious gases so generated that would interfere with the ordinary routine and the systematic action of the different compartments of the stomach, which after constant recurrence would set up internal inflammation and impair such action, I can easily understand. For my part I am averse to giving them grain or other food which has been soaked as baneful on this account, though cleansing and damping it is, I consider, a good and wise precaution. I can, however, hardly think that dew would penetrate into the leaves of camel thorn or other plants sufficiently to sodden them, or to sodden them to such an extent as to create any deleterious gas. I have seen animals die presumably from this cause, but I have always doubted, and still doubt, that it was the real cause. I can readily understand animals that are regularly and continuously sent out to graze when the dew is on the ground, or fed on soddened food, developing a disease of those organs which assist in assimilating the food, somewhat in the way above mentioned, and eventually dying from it, but not otherwise. I have also seen camels die in Afghanistan, which the natives told me was due to poisonous insects in the grass, but which in all probability arose from poisonous weeds, and in some instances from overeating pure and simple.

Horse sickness and its probable causes

While on this topic I do not think it will be out of place to allude to the widespread theory regarding horse sickness in South Africa, which is, that it arises from eating moistened grass, and it is the rule out there not to graze horses while the dew is on the ground. This deadly disease is prevalent from the Cape up to the Zambesi, and from being comparatively mild in the southern parts increases in intensity the further north you go, the basin of the Crocodile river, and the region lying between it and the Zambesi, being by far the deadliest. When I was at Macloutsie and Tuli in 1890–91, the horses of the Bechuanaland Border Police and of the British South Africa Company's Police suffered very heavily, losing about ninety-seven per cent. from this cursed malady, which in its destructive deadliness always reminded me of that awful and mysterious scourge which is so fatal to humanity in the East, and which so far, like itself, has baffled and defied science.

I always took the greatest care of my horses, and the greatest interest in watching each individual case, and in doing all that it was possible to do for them. I saw some hundreds die, sometimes at the rate of eleven a week, and one conclusion I came to, rightly or wrongly I will not presume to say, was that these deaths had nothing to do with grazing in the early morning, but that the infection was, like cholera, in the air, and inhaled whether a horse was in the stable or not. My orders on the subject were stringent, and were, I know, strictly carried out, and the horses never went out grazing until the sun had been up long enough to evaporate the dew. Yet the mortality among them was terrific, and, as stated, about three per cent. only recovered. Some of them, apparently well to all outward appearances, were suddenly seized with the most violent symptoms, and died within two hours. Others fought against it with tremendous pluck, and without even a groan or a murmur, for twenty-four to thirty-six hours. Others, again, gave in to it in less than half the time, their groans and agonies being almost human, and realistically heartrending. While only two or three struggled heroically, but in a dazed, stunned kind of way, and held out for four or five days before submitting to the inevitable. Horses that had never been out of the stable except for exercise in the afternoon, and that had been fed on bran, mealies, and forage, were attacked in the same way, and succumbed quite as rapidly. In all cases of post-mortem, and we had a good many, all of which I attended, the lungs were entirely diseased and perforated, and in many instances they were rotten.

In the low-lying veldt, and in all depressions and valleys, those especially watered by a river, heavy morning mists, which hung low, were a noticeable feature, more so in the cold and dry seasons, and it seemed to me that horses who were exposed to them inhaled a malaria which got into the system and attacked the lungs, doing its work insidiously and without detection from lack of outward and visible signs—the first external signs being languor and heaviness, followed quickly, sometimes instantaneously, by feverish symptoms which rapidly increased, along with a yellowish frothy discharge from the nostrils, and in some cases a swelling of the head—and before a remedy, much less a cure, could be effected, the poor creature was dead. In a few words, the impression left on my mind is that it is a combination of low fever and lung complications suppressed internally, which, when the mischief is done, and it is too late, breaks out externally. The secret, I fully believe, lies in a nutshell, and if the internal mischief could be detected at the outset, or within a few hours of it, taken in time, in fact, a remedy if not a cure will be found to nip it in the bud, and so save the valuable life of many a noble animal. This is merely a suggestion I throw out, for in the face of scientific research I would not presume to assert an opinion; but if nothing else, it appears to me a more plausible, if not more reliable, cause than that which is generally advanced.

The fact that the severity of the sickness is far more intense in the uncivilised and wild portions than in those parts which have been some time occupied, and that it is also so in the lowlands in comparison to the highlands, is food for reflection, and appears to substantiate the air and malarial theory to an appreciable extent. For it is generally recognised that malaria disappears, or diminishes very considerably, before civilisation, and this takes place when a wild country has been occupied for some time, and when the bush has been cleared away, the undergrowth burnt, and the soil turned up; provided, of course, that it is a reasonable level above the sea, say, at least, from 1,500 to 1,800 feet, and not a swamp or marsh, or low-lying alluvial deposit.

Say, however, for argument's sake, that disease ending in death can be caused simply by eating moistened

Why Massoutier's views as to moistened grass are untenable

herbage or poisonous grasses; (1) why should some animals escape altogether? (2) why should others get it and recover? (3) and why should the effect be quicker on some than others—except perhaps from superiority of stamina and constitution? And why should a like proportion of animals who are never exposed to this risk get the same symptoms, present the same organic appearance, and die, in fact, of exactly the same disease as those who have run all risks? With regard to the air theory the first three questions might likewise be asked; but the answers are beyond me, except to conclude from the terrific mortality that we had at Macloutsie and Tuli that the germs of the disease were in the air, and to leave to great and glorious science to produce the solution of the mystery from the womb of futurity.

Summing up

To sum up, then, in a few words. You cannot be too particular in feeding camels, nor can you pay less attention to them, if you want to get good work out of them under exceptional circumstances, than you do to cavalry and artillery horses. Do not overfeed them, especially with grain, and do not vary the rations, as they not only lose condition whether their ration is increased or decreased, but in the former case it often engenders disease which proves fatal. Above all things be rational, and do not starve them on the principle that they are ruminants possessing special powers of abstinence. Even this class of animal cannot ruminate on nothing, and it is a positive fact that in the Bayuda desert I did not see five camels in a thousand chewing the cud. Poor brutes! it would have been precious hard for them to do so on starvation diet and empty stomachs, for even a camel must feed regularly, and have food inside him before he can chew the cud.

I might write a great deal more on these exceptionally valuable subjects, but I could do no good. Nothing more that I could say would add greater weight to what I have already said, or express it more forcibly. If I have at all events succeeded in impressing on you the vital importance of watering and feeding camels during ordinary times so as to better fit them to cope with an emergency, as also the common-sense view that they only require to be treated as ordinary quadrupeds, I have gained my object, and will proceed with the next chapter.

CHAPTER VIII

LOADING

In a transport sense this is also a subject of very great weight—I am not attempting a pun—but as a matter of fact it is, as a great many of the ailments from which camels suffer are caused purely and simply by bad and careless packing.

Loading a pack animal seems, so some people think, a very simple arrangement, but like many things in this world of ours it is not so easy as it looks, and to be well done it requires a great deal of patience, practice, and experience. Men who have been accustomed to camels all their lives, bred up with them from their youth, are naturally the best. I do not mean those who only breed them, but those whose animals are constantly employed carrying goods—such as the Hadendowas, Kababish, Bisharin in Egypt, the Brahuis in Beloochistan, and the various tribes in Sind, Panjab, and Afghanistan—men of a country, in fact, whose only means of communication across their sandy, waterless deserts is by camel.

The secret of loading

Careless loading, more frequently than people imagine, causes sore backs and sore sides. The great secret in loading a camel—or any animal for the matter of that—is to balance the load evenly. If this is done no saddle girth is required. The Kababish—a tribe in Upper

Nubia who were employed by the military authorities in the desert march in 1885 under Sir Herbert Stewart to carry goods from Korti to Gakdool—loaded their camels perfectly and altogether by balance, without the use of girths; and another great advantage we derived by hiring camels from them was that they only had one driver to every ten camels.

Size and weight of loads

All loading should be done by balance, consequently all goods for military purposes ought to be made of a certain size, shape, and weight, if possible. No load in the shape of bale, box, or package should ever exceed 80 lb. as a maximum (something that one man can move about easily), or 50 lb. as a minimum; nor should they measure over 3 feet in length, 1½ foot in breadth, and 2 feet in depth. With these sizes and weights loading is made much easier and simpler. Heavier or bulkier weights and longer measurements only impede the movements of the camel, and turn loading into a labour of pain. It is a needless infliction of cruelty, for boxes, bales, &c., could easily be constructed of a size and shape suitable to pack-animals —camels, mules, donkeys, &c. Some authorities on transport consider that the camel is well adapted for carrying long articles, such as 'scaling ladders,' 'pontoons,' 'large double-pole tents,' 'baking-ovens,' &c. Of course, with the exception of the elephant, he is better adapted than any other pack-animal, because he is bigger and up to more weight; but even when well loaded, things like these, especially 'large tents' and 'pontoons,' are apt to bruise and damage him in the neck, shoulders, and hindquarters. Unless unavoidable, owing to the nature of the country, wheeled transport should be used in preference for this class of stores. Cases and casks, or any globular or oval-shaped packages, are exceedingly bad loads for camels, as they are very difficult to adjust and impossible to steady.

Mule loads Mule loads should not exceed in length 2 feet, breadth 1 foot, depth $1\frac{1}{2}$ foot; and for donkeys smaller dimensions if possible.

How to place a load Loads should be placed so as not to be either too high up over the animal's back, or too low down on his sides, but should rest high on the ribs, as they prevent freedom of action. Of the two extremes, however, it is better to have loads too high than too low on this very account. I have often seen clumsy misshapen loads badly slung, and so low that every step the unfortunate camel took—or, to speak more correctly, tried to take—he not only barked his legs very badly, but, owing to the presence of the load in such a low and faulty position, he was quite unable to take a full and free stride. This—apart from the nasty bruises, which in a hot climate especially quickly develop into sores, or if on the bone lead to lameness—wearies and harasses the poor beast so much that, if allowed to continue, loss of condition would ensue. The driver who loads in this brutal careless way ought to be severely flogged, and the officer in charge of the convoy who allows it should be suspended until he learns to be more thoughtful and considerate.

Do not place too heavy or too bulky a load on an animal's back. Not only does it crush and damage the saddle, but in the long run it injures the animal. It is wiser not to put any weight at all on the top or centre of the back. Never choose a stony spot, if you can avoid it, for loading purposes, but always pick out the softest place, so as to save the animal's legs, the knees especially, from being cut and injured by the rocks and stones.

It is easy enough to load without nets, provided the drivers are handy, and know how to use the rope and tie knots. In distributing goods, the first thing a transport officer should see to is an equal distribution of goods according to the weight-carrying capacity of each animal; next, that each load is divided equally into two parts, both in weight and dimensions. Each half should then be secured to the longitudinal ribs of the saddle, and their upper ends ought to be fastened by the ropes which hang over the clutches, so that there should be as little pressure on the ribs as possible, and thus protect the animal's flanks and spine from injury. The loads should be so packed and fastened that they can be placed on and taken off the animal without untying the rope. There is a good deal of art in this, as the load requires to be well and evenly adjusted, and balanced to a nicety. The rope holding it together should also be distributed over the load at equal distances, otherwise a just and even balance would not be obtained. The Aden drivers I had at Suakim in 1884 were very smart at this. With inexperienced drivers, such as a transport officer invariably has on all our expeditions, or with fatigue parties of soldiers, it is advisable to use nets, especially on service where time is all important, for (1) a great deal of time and trouble is saved, (2) the loads and the animals get less knocked about, and (3) the daily loading and unloading is made so much simpler and easier; all the

Loading with rope

Better to use nets

more so when you have to contend against impossibilities, with only careless ignorant men to assist you. Suleetahs are better than nets in wet weather, but (1) are heavier, and (2) wear out quicker. In these cases particularly always be most careful to look to the girthing of the saddles. This is a frequent source of sore backs and sides, and in addition a source of extra trouble and work. If the girths are loose, and the camel badly loaded, the odds are that before he gets a few hundred yards from the camp, saddle, load, and all will come off, not, however, before it has given him a rub or two. Even with the Aden drivers above alluded to I had the greatest bother on this very account. In the cold of the early mornings they were so torpid that, good drivers as they were, a great deal of supervision was required to get them to girth up the saddles properly. But this is nothing when you are accustomed to it.

Fatigue parties

With soldier fatigue parties one's whole time is taken up in showing them what to do, and how to load. They know nothing about a camel and care less, though on him depends everything—all their creature comforts, food, clothing, and shelter. They are more or less afraid of him, and when they get the chance will ill-treat him. As to when he gets to his destination and how, whether whole or battered and bruised, they are quite callous. Even if it so happens that the selfsame soldiers are going to accompany the convoy they take little more trouble, and then only, probably, if the stores in question belong to their own particular corps or company. They do not know how to load, either from ignorance of the bad effects, or callousness, or both, and so long as they get on somewhere and anyhow they are perfectly happy. To start with, then, your fatigue arrives—a discontented, grumbling lot, totally ignorant of the work they are about to do. They begin by throwing the loads on anyhow and everywhere. As a rule it is all the same to them, for they are not going with the convoy. They know nothing and, what is more, they care still less about a nice and equal balance of the load. Their only way—method it cannot be called—consists in chucking on the first thing that comes to hand, regardless as to how it is rolled or packed and fastened on. I have frequently seen a load at least 50 lb. heavier on one side than on the other; consequently, all one's time is taken up in supervising and instructing these men how to load, and it is hours before the convoy is ready to start. This is no exaggeration, and only transport officers who like myself have tramped thousands of miles and carried tons of stores can realise what it is to deal with Tommy Atkins on active service, especially if he has never been to India. Only when I have been without drivers and in a state of utter helplessness have I ever tried to make any use of them, but even when I have been short-handed I have entirely dispensed with their services from choice. You may lay it down as an axiom that loading camels with fatigue parties of soldiers is a most pernicious system, and one to be avoided, unless the authorities take the matter in hand, and set to work seriously to initiate a system of instruction in this branch of camel management, which, like every other question in connection with it, requires a thoroughly systematic and practical course of training; and until our men are taught to handle animals that they will have to deal with on active service they cannot be taught how to load them, and cannot be expected to learn intuitively, as it takes a great many years of solid experience to get accustomed to and become intimately acquainted with the camel, and his peculiarities and peccadilloes.

Arrangement of loads

A transport officer, if at all concerned about his beasts, should superintend the packing of each separate load; but when there are a great number, and you are working against time—as you invariably are—this is almost impossible, much as you would like to. When you are looking after several hundreds, though you may exert yourself to the utmost, you individually cannot be here, there, and everywhere. While you are seeing to some in one place, others in another spot have been loaded, and you are obliged, so atrociously have the loads been put on, to unload, and make the men reload under your personal supervision. This has happened to me times without number, and the only way out of the difficulty, if you have had timely warning—and if your sole mainstay is a fatigue party—is first to take over the stores and arrange them separately by loads for each animal, or settle with the Commissariat, Ordnance, or other officer to whom they belong to have them so arranged. Too much trouble cannot be taken in having all loads ready and placed in proper position—in rear of each animal—so that if you are loading at night you know at once where to get them, and so avoid confusion and save time. The British soldier—in fact, all soldiers—hate fatigue work, especially that of loading up animals, and of all animals the camel. An Egyptian battalion which was at Suakim in 1884, which was employed solely on fatigue work, was just the same. I always had a party of these men to assist me in loading my water convoy. Egyptian-like, they were extremely noisy and lazy, and were more in the way than anything else, so I used generally to get rid of them, and do the work entirely with my Aden drivers.

No. 3 Auxiliary Transport Company in the Nile campaign of 1884–85 was a good instance of this, and I have seen them take a whole day loading their camels, a task that experienced drivers would have done in a fourth of the time. On more than one occasion I was obliged to assist them with men of my Transport Company, or they would never have got off the ground. It was exactly the same with No. 5 Auxiliary in 1882, but then I had the assistance of a handful of men who knew something about mules, otherwise we should have still been stuck in the sand between Tel el Mahouta and Kassassin. Even in the Afghan campaign of 1878–80, and in other smaller expeditions, the want of knowledge of loading shown both by British and native soldiers was lamentable.

Naturally enough, the whole security of a load, and to a certain extent that of the animal, depends upon the adjustment of the load, which itself, as a matter of course, depends entirely on balance. If badly slung the load will come off constantly, and damage itself, or, what is even worse, it will either hang so loosely, sit so unevenly, or shift and sway about so awkwardly, as to impede and harass the animal in its movements, as well as to bruise his sides and legs, as already pointed out. Too much care, therefore, cannot be given to the correct adjustment of loads prior to

Adjustment of load

leaving camp. In fact, no animal should be allowed to leave the ground until its load is properly adjusted, and as each section is loaded up the conductor in charge ought to file his animals past the officer commanding the company, so that all mistakes can be rectified before a convoy starts.

Inspection after starting a mistake

The system of inspection after starting is not a good one, because conductors and drivers, once on the road, generally shove on as fast as they can; and the latter, regardless of consequences, thoughtful only of themselves, and utterly improvident of the animals, will give you the slip and push on, oblivious of loads and animals, nor will they attempt to remedy matters until either the former falls off or the latter falls down. Besides, once camels get on the move, it is wiser to let them keep moving; and there is greater economy of time, and a greater certainty of good work, in the way that I have suggested. Such at least was my experience.

What to be done in case of shifting of load on the march

Should a load become disarranged on the march, do not wait until it inflicts a bruise on the animal, or until it comes off, as is the general way with drivers; or if it has got loose and is shifting about, do not try and fix it up while the animal is moving, by tightening a rope, or by shoving the load up or down, or moving it backwards and forwards. This is sheer waste of time and labour. Take the camel out of the line or drove *at once*, so as not to impede or check the progress of the remainder, and have the load taken off and readjusted once and for all. It is very curious how a load which has been faultily put on at the start will keep coming off constantly during the march, causing unnecessary fatigue and injury to the unfortunate animal, and most unnecessary trouble to the men. And yet, so perverse and contradictory are the ways of humanity, that unless you stand over the latter, and insist on the load being fastened correctly, it will not be done. I have frequently seen the same load come off six or seven times in a short march. With professional and experienced drivers fatigue parties are, I am thoroughly convinced—as I have more than once pointed out—a mistake, even when you are short-handed. It is better, and at the finish quicker, to do without them, and intrust the loading to men who understand it, who ought to be made to feel the responsibility, and who will on this account naturally take an interest in a proper adjustment, more especially if the animals belong to them.

Necessity of fastening load securely before starting

In such case, instead of the drivers in each section loading separately and independently, it is better to combine them by sections, and load up each section collectively. This not only is a superior plan in every way, but is system as opposed to chaos, engenders a healthy spirit of emulation or rivalry between sections which is productive of eminently excellent results—great economy of valuable time, and of the powers of the animals; while loading individually and in driblets, without any organization, in a happy-go-lucky, haphazard way, means excessive standing about, which fatigues the animals before they start on a march, and in the end altogether wears them out.

As a rule, nothing on earth will induce a camel to rise if he feels that his load is too heavy for him, or altogether beyond his strength, and if he is at all young

Camel's objection to overloading

he will give tongue to a great extent if you try and force him to get up, in fact, at the bare imposition of the load. An older camel will be much quieter over it, but will persistently refuse to budge. This is put down to obstinacy, but I question if instinct has not something to say to it; and this is about the only case, I think, in which a camel does show that he has just a spark of some form of intelligence in him; and it is man who displays the obstinacy, when he forces the poor brute to stagger along overloaded, until he falls down, never to get up again.

A camel who is young and restive, or one who is vicious or in a state of 'mast,' will not always remain down for the imposition of a load, but becomes fractious and restive, and will frequently jump up. In such cases it is as well to tie their fore-legs together, and if they happen to be in a biting humour it is perhaps advisable to stand over or in front of them with a stick. Do not, however, give a stick to a driver unless you are by to see he does not ill-use the animal.

Training to carry

The training of a camel as a beast of burden or as a riding animal usually commences at a very early age, and is accomplished very gradually and very systematically. The first step taken is when he is a few weeks old, while the bone is yet soft and pliable and his limbs supple, his legs are bent under his belly and he is taught to kneel down and rise up only. When he has thoroughly mastered this, and by the time he has grown older and stronger, in his second year, the saddle is put on him and he is taught to do the same thing. In his third year, when his bones are getting more set, very light loads are put on him, and he is further instructed to kneel down and rise up. In his fourth year the weight of the load is increased until he gets accustomed to it, and so on gradually until he is five years old (though I am sorry to say that the rule is often broken through), when he reaches the maximum weight and thoroughly understands what is required of him. The course is now finished, and he is considered fit for work. The riding camel is broken in somewhat similarly, except that when he becomes used to the imposition of a light weight he is ridden instead. Sometimes the Arabs work them when only four years old, and in our expeditions numbers of two- and three-year olds have been sacrificed; but to be on the safe side, and as a wise and just measure, no camel should carry a load until he is at least five years old.

Keeping loaded camels standing

Before concluding this chapter there is one very great evil which I must call attention to, an evil due entirely to want of system, and which has hitherto been responsible for injury to numberless camels, besides helping along with other causes to kill many; and that is, the evil of keeping loaded camels standing for hours at a stretch in the cold of the early morning prior to a march, or on the road owing to a block. The first of these is easily avoidable by making divisions, brigades, and regiments load and start at different hours, according to their precedence of march, instead of all loading and falling in at the same time, which is invariably done. The second cannot always be avoided, even under the best management and with the greatest care, because, should a force moving in several lines, as it would across a plain, be suddenly confronted by a narrow defile, a block is bound to ensue; and the only plan to adopt in this case is to make the animals in the rear kneel until it comes to their turn to proceed, as this, to a certain extent, takes the dead weight off their backs and limbs, and eases them.

Massoutier's objection to camels kneeling

Lieut. Massoutier takes exception to this, and says that camels should never be allowed to kneel *en route* unless the convoy is attacked, as this position with their burdens only fatigues and injures them. That he is quite right no one will deny, and on service, if within the bounds of human possibility, it should be avoided. But occasions and circumstances, such as mentioned, will crop up over which we have no control; and when it comes to a question of standing or kneeling, it is simply a choice of the lesser evil to make them kneel. Of course, if the nature of the road is known, and the fact of the existence of narrow defiles and such obstacles, the order of march can accordingly be daily arranged to meet such exigencies by making the transport move on a narrow or broader front.

When I was Brigade Baggage-master from Cabul to Peshawur, and had the arranging and disposing of several thousand camels, we never got off the camp ground in a morning under four hours, and when, as in the Jagdallack and Khyber passes, we were cramped for space and had to move on a narrow front, usually single file, it took a long weary seven hours or more before all were on the move. I know that I was always one of the first in the morning to be on the move, and invariably the last to arrive in the camp in the evening, or, as often happened, in the pitchy darkness of the night.

NOTE.—Please observe that when I speak of *drivers*, not only in this chapter, but all through the work, I allude to the class of men we are in the habit of getting on service—utterly inexperienced, worthless ne'er-do-weels, usually unemployed loafers attracted by the high wages; and when I refer to 'professional' drivers, I mean men who are either owners and breeders of camels, or servants to such, men who have tended camels from their youth up, and who have been accustomed to them from their earliest infancy.

CHAPTER IX

MARCHING AND CARRYING POWER

Here we have another matter of vital importance in connection with camel transport, and it is hard to say whether it or the questions previously discussed of 'feeding,' 'watering' and 'loading' are of greater importance. In reality they one and all so hinge upon each other, and the evils which arise from neglect of them are so evenly balanced and so comparatively serious, that they deserve an equal amount of attention.

Like the others, the marching and carrying powers of the camel have been grossly exaggerated and misrepresented; although he can carry a good load and march well, especially on sandy soil and over loose shingle, yet he must receive great care and attention. It is a popular error to imagine that the baggager can travel the long distances and work for the long hours—i.e. sixteen hours daily—that people who are ignorant of him say he can. Camels when worked regularly—like all other animals—require feeding (grazing particularly) and rest, and twenty miles a day (perhaps twenty-five in a push) is a good average. Of course, I am speaking now of long distances. For short journeys —say, up, to 250 perhaps 300 miles—animals in the best of condition, and at their normal pace, can work sixteen hours a day, but except in cases of necessity it is advisable not to force them beyond this, unless you wish to injure them. After work of this kind they should be turned out to graze, and have a complete rest for a week to ten days, or longer, according to the state they arrive in. Ensor says that 'the camel is essentially a traveller, and rest for him is an abnormal condition,' and with the former portion of this statement I quite agree. There are no better roadsters in their own respective lines than the baggager and Sawari. In proper hands the former will plod, the latter swing, along day after day, week after week, and month after month; but they must have food and they must have rest. The Kababish—to whom I have more than once alluded—when conveying our stores from Korti to Gakdool, a distance of 100 miles, used to get to the latter place on the fifth day, and the average weight of their loads was 300 lb. They always drove their camels like a flock of sheep, spread well out over the desert, grazing them as they went—hence paucity of drivers; and it was only on these conditions—that they should be left entirely to themselves, without European supervision—that they undertook to hire out their animals. In open country the Bisharin and other nomadic tribes also drive their camels in line, and not in single file, and allow them to pick up what they can as they stalk along; and the average distance at which their caravans travel is twenty miles a day, dependent altogether on circumstances, the nature of the grazing and water supply being considered first and foremost, so that one march might be thirty miles long and another only ten. The Arab tribes in Algeria, and the

French also, I believe, drive their camels, and let them graze as they march along, covering usually twenty miles a day. At this rate they do about one and a half to two and a half miles an hour, and at the end of the march have nearly eaten their fill. The practice that we have on service, of tying from four to six camels in a string, and sometimes as many as sixteen, in Indian file, tail to headstall, or to the load, and sometimes most cruelly to the nose rope, is most iniquitous and cruel into the bargain. I have seen many poor wretched brutes who, through debility or from some internal disease, could hardly crawl, dragged along until the rope snapped, and they have fallen to the ground from sheer weakness. If you do happen to get a camel of this kind or a slow lazy one in front of a string—in the former case, when he has crawled along until he has dropped from exhaustion, there is a temporary block and stoppage; and in the latter case, unless you put him behind, the pace is considerably diminished. Besides this, many is the load I have seen dragged off, because the camel in the rear hung back, while the one in the front to which it was tied kept on advancing steadily. This is all the more astonishing, because on the north-west frontier of India, and in other parts as well, also in Beloochistan and Afghanistan, every camel country in fact, the natives always march their camels in droves—a plan which, as far as the animals are concerned, is indubitably the easiest and best.

Comparison between line and Indian file

From a military point of view there are objections to this, as I have heard it asserted that camels which have once been accustomed to move in strings, if

Objections to droves of camels confuted

suddenly driven would take a long time to get over the feeling of strangeness at being perfectly free, and their natural tendency would be to crowd together and knock off their loads. This argument is soon dismissed. As just remarked, the training of most breeds of baggagers previous to falling into our hands is to move in droves, and if we only had the sense to continue the system, and place them in competent hands, no such *dénouement* would ever take place. Another objection is that, in case of attack, camels tied in strings are more quickly formed up than a driven convoy. I have never seen the experiment tried, but, with proper drivers, I altogether question it; as a matter of fact, I believe that driven camels could be formed into a compact mass and made to kneel in much less time than those tied in strings—of course, always provided they are trained animals in the hands of trained men. If, however, they are tied in strings, not more than three at the most should be tied together, as this is the greatest number that one man can properly and easily manage. More even uniformity and quickness of pace is thus obtained; there is less chance of the disarrangement, and consequent packing and unpacking, of loads; less lagging and dragging on the part of camels; and less injury is inflicted on their nostrils, which are frequently torn to pieces owing to the iniquity of this barbarous practice, and on account of the general insufficiency and utter negligence and apathy of our drivers. Besides, when a difficult place confronts you, the animals are more quickly and easily untied, with less stoppage to the convoy, and therefore with a saving of time. I need

How they should be attached

hardly point out that the advantages gained by tying a few in a string, as compared with a lot, sink into insignificance besides those of the driving system, and that these remarks apply to it, only with far greater force and emphasis.

What to do in difficult places

In all difficult places, such as a steep ascent or declivity, or a very narrow rocky defile, camels, if tied in strings, must be untied, and led one by one until the obstacle is surmounted or passed; and in a place of this kind, the narrower the defile, the greater must be your care to avoid a block, which only leads to unnecessary delay and confusion, and this is bound to ensue if you fail to untie your camels. This is another strong argument in favour of driving them, for a great saving of time and trouble is effected in not having to constantly tie and untie them when moving over hilly and broken country. Last, but by no means least, the animals have greater freedom, are less harassed and fatigued, can pick up a certain amount of food on the road, require fewer drivers—half the number, in fact—and altogether are more manageable and more easily supervised.

Moral

After due and deliberate consideration, I have arrived at the conclusion that driving is infinitely preferable to leading camels, not only on account of the advantages already enumerated, but because the immense importance, in a transport sense, of having fewer followers to feed, and in a military sense to protect, cannot be overlooked. And if the ills of the animal and his general welfare all round are matters of indifference to us, and if the other advantages to be gained will not move us to adopt the better system, surely this reason in itself should be a more than sufficient inducement.

Natural working hours of camels

Eight working hours in twenty-four, and at the outside certainly not more than ten, are sufficient for camels carrying fair average loads, in the pink of condition and well looked after, for they require at least eight hours' grazing and six hours' rest. This applies equally to riding camels, who should not be made to carry more than 250 lb. including rider, and who with this weight, and properly ridden and husbanded, will travel from fifty to sixty miles a day for a week, and forty for a fortnight to three weeks; while with 300 lb. they can keep up an average of thirty miles a day for a long distance. A camel for a long journey is far less fatiguing than a horse, once you get accustomed to his peculiar swinging mode of progression. As a rule, if pressed to do more than eight hours' riding on a long rough journey, unless you ride at night, he does not get sufficient time to graze, as of course when you are on the move he gets nothing, except a mouthful snatched now and then, and he requires six hours' grazing at least. If possible, he should be fed morning and evening. On service of course he must be tied up at night, and even in time of peace during cold weather he ought to be brought in if grazing, and blanketed up.

Paces of baggagers

The baggager is a slow walker, his average pace in a long journey is two and a half miles per hour, and under favourable conditions, especially when marching at night, or in the cool of the evening, and over firm sand, he can easily increase it to two and three-quarter miles; and in my experience I have known him at times to do three, and even over three miles, when Mr.

Wiseacre has had the handling of him. If you can avoid it, never work them in any weather between 10 A.M. and 4 P.M., more so in a hot climate when the heat is excessive, as even camels of a hot country always march better at night. These hours should be devoted to grazing. The ordinary Sawari can walk from two and a half to three miles an hour; jog—his best and easiest pace—from five to six miles an hour easily, while a good one will cover six and seven; but you must keep him up to the mark (for he and the baggager are naturally lazy) by occasionally tickling him with a 'korbaz' (a whip of hippopotamus hide). He can run from eight to ten miles an hour, but it is not his natural pace, and he cannot keep it up for long, and even when you are accustomed to it it shakes and jars you tremendously. 'Jogging' is no doubt the best pace for long and continuous journeys.

How to obtain an even pace

The slowest camel should invariably be placed in front of a convoy, so as to regulate the pace, and to arrive at and maintain a more or less even rate of progression. This will not be difficult, as camels are essentially lazy, and will not go any faster than required. Whereas if the faster walkers are leading, it becomes a necessity to drive on the slower ones to make them keep up. So it is that many good camels who happen to be temporarily debilitated or sorefooted are overdriven, until they break down completely. This cannot be prevented unless actually under the eye of some responsible officer. Besides, a certain amount of urging is at times indispensable, for without it there is sure to be a great deal of straggling, which creates large gaps in, and doubles or trebles the length of, the convoy, thereby adding considerably to the duties and responsibilities of its escort in protecting it.

Riding camels of good breeds undoubtedly have great speed and endurance, and are said to do 100 miles and even more in a day. Burckhardt, in his work on Nubia, relates an instance of an Egyptian camel which travelled 115 miles in eleven hours, besides being carried twice over the Nile, an operation which occupied about twenty minutes each time. I can quite believe that an exceptional camel would do this, for I have known even average specimens cover forty-five to fifty miles in six hours, and ninety to ninety-five miles in twelve to thirteen hours, without being specially pushed or pressed. The great feature about either class of camel is, that so long as you do not drive them beyond their normal pace, they can keep it up for hours at a stretch, eight to ten in the day, and they can maintain this day by day (as we have seen) for an indefinite period; but in a long journey it is always wiser to halt every fifth or seventh day, even if you have to increase the daily distance, and always select a place where there is good pasturage for the halt. In fact, make your halts subservient to the grazing, and not merely to routine; for it is little use stopping at a bare sterile spot where the animals can get nothing to eat, and it is far wiser to overstep the limit, go a longer distance and make forced marches in order to arrive at good pasture, rather than keep up a fixed routine at the risk of starving your animals. It is more or less a case of, in the choice of two evils, choose the lesser. Naturally, in a hostile country, where grazing is not always practicable, you are obliged to

Paces of riding camels

act by routine; but if possible, so long as proper and reasonable precautions are taken to prevent the animals being stampeded and raided, even at the risk of a fight, graze your camels when and where you can, for do not lose sight of the fact that they will not thrive without it, and in the finish you will get far more out of them. Everything naturally depends on the nature of the country. In countries where grazing and water are plentiful march camels regular distances, but if these are at irregular intervals, then march accordingly; but the general average should not exceed twenty to twenty-five miles a day, according to (1) the length of the journey, (2) the weight and nature of the loads, (3) scarcity or abundance of fodder and water, (4) intensity of heat or cold; in a few words, in proportion to the difficulties of the route, and the climatic and botanic conditions in general. Everything must give way to the camel, like the shoe that is made to fit the foot, and not the foot that is tortured to fit the shoe; make your marches to suit your camel, and do not make them to suit your own convenience, or because those demi-gods Routine and Regularity say that you must. When your animals are concerned never let that bugbear of the British officer, fear of responsibility, stand in your way. By taking care of your camels you are indirectly caring for and thinking of your men; and if you do your duty conscientiously, always act fearlessly on your own responsibility.

Transport officer's duties before starting

It may be assumed, without even a shadow of doubt, that when a convoy is about to march the chief problem that the transport officer in charge has to solve is his best plan of action as to mode of procedure, so as, first of all, to assure the safety of the convoy; second, to arrive at this without unduly fatiguing or starving his animals; and to do this he must take into consideration the general conditions above given.

Everything in the first place naturally depends entirely on these, and on circumstances generally—such as the character of the enemy, the nature of the country, and the condition of his animals; so that in arranging his convoy and its order of march he would, as a matter of course, weigh one with the other.

How to march in open country

In open country it is always advisable to march on as broad a front as possible, and it is preferable to have camels spread well out, or in several short lines, than to have them in a few long unwieldy lines, which lead to greater stretching out and straggling. In this way they can be kept more in hand, and better under the transport officer's own eye. And, believe me, the real secret of success in transport is *personal supervision*, which must be constant and conscientious; and the steadier the constancy, and the stronger the conscience, the greater the success. In this way, too, he can deal with the pace, and so prevent his animals being unnecessarily harassed; in fact, he can cope with every point and any emergency. And on no account whatever should a transport officer leave his convoy except for a strictly legitimate purpose, and especially to take part in or watch a fight, as is too often the case, to the utter neglect of his own duties. I have seen this occur on service with very bad results, and it is a practice which should be promptly put down by the authorities, and yet, with our present system, it is not to be wondered at. If the country is hilly, and he is obliged to move in one line, he must keep moving up and down constantly to see that his orders are being strictly carried out.

General remarks on proper system for convoys

To define a proper system, on certain lines and by hard-and-fast rules, as to the actual conduct of a convoy, does not come within the scope of this work, but the rules I have laid down as to the treatment and management of camels generally will apply. Always bearing in mind that, when on the march, conditions and circumstances *must* be considered prior to forming a conclusion or deciding on a definite plan. This duty is a most important one, demanding the greatest activity, vigilance, and experience, and requiring a thorough conscientiousness, determination, and a fixed tenacity of will and purpose on the part of a transport officer. And he must never allow circumstances or conditions to depress or dispirit him, but take as his guiding principle, and place before him as a magnetic axiom, the mottoes of 'Never despair!' 'Courage, and forward!' Nor must he ever forget that the *mainspring* of an army is mobility, which is entirely dependent on its transport; and that the general efficiency of this vital portion of the machine hinges on the individual efficiency of each unit, which in its turn depends on his own personal exertions.

Proper time to march

It is, as a rule, wiser to march camels, baggagers especially, by night, because (1) they have more time, all day in fact, to graze; (2) march quicker than under a hot sun; (3) lose less tissue; (4) are not so much fatigued, as the sun takes it out of them; (5) minimises the chances of exposure, and reduces the liability of sowing the seeds of various pulmonary diseases when the nights are cold or damp.

Marching by night, except when in actual contact with the enemy, is as a rule quite feasible, especially on lines of communication; such, for instance, as we had on the Nile from Wady Halfa to Korti, where, for all practical purposes, with an almost interminable and impassable desert on both banks of the river, we were as safe as if in Hyde Park. It is advisable in more ways than one when, as occurred in that campaign, the animals were totally unprovided with covering or clothing. Then, marching in the desert, where at times the cold is intense from 2 A.M. up to sunrise—the coldest hours in the twenty-four—the exercise keeps them warm, they are less exposed, if at all, and run far smaller, if any, risks.

Even desert camels, who can stand heat better than those bred in more civilised and cultivated districts, walk and work better by night. In fact it is, when feasible, preferable to do so with all breeds and classes of camels, even at the risk of giving a certain amount of discomfort to the men; for in reality it is an immense economy in the end, not only in saving further and greater discomfort both to men and animals, but in saving the lives of numbers of valuable animals, or, in the way which the ratepayer looks at it, large sums of money.

In the Afghan campaign of 1878–79–80, marching from Sukkur to Candahar, when my company was escort to an elephant 40-pounder battery; and again from Candahar to Cabul; and, lastly, from Cabul to Peshawur, a tramp of twelve hours, especially on the former march, was nothing. Frequently we were fourteen and fifteen hours on the move, a couple of times over twenty, and once twenty-three. All this time the wretched camels, half frozen and half starved, had been staggering and standing under heavy loads without a check; and in the same campaign—owing to the desertion of the drivers—I have seen from ten to twelve camels tied in a string, the consequences being frequently very disastrous. At times, when I think over all I have gone through, or rather what the unfortunate camels have undergone under my own eyes, the suffering and torture that they have been put to, unwittingly maybe, and yet from sheer ignorance and thoughtlessness—while I have looked on, doing my best to alleviate their troubles, I can conscientiously say, but owing to the want of a proper system utterly powerless to avoid or remove them—I can hardly realise that I have witnessed what I have.

Treatment on military expeditions

Treated as he is on military expeditions the camel has no chance given him to show of what stuff he is made—the endurance and stamina he really has if given a fair trial. In fact, to find out his real worth, to see him in his true colours, you must see him working in his own country under men who live by him. In the commercial caravans which travel between Suakim and Berber, Korosko and Abu Hamed, also in Afghanistan and India, &c., &c., his true value is tested, for he is in the hands of those who value and appreciate him—if for nothing else from a pecuniary point of view, for all their wealth lies in their camels—consequently, he is under proper management.

Advantages of commercial caravans

Their convoys certainly have many advantages, which are almost, but I will not say altogether, unattainable in a military train. They have above all things the choice (1) of any route, therefore choose the easiest; (2) of halting at the time and place most suitable and convenient to rest and feed their animals; (3) and they have better opportunities of procuring grain or forage, if necessary owing to an insufficiency or want of pasture. On the other hand, a military train, for various reasons, due probably to the tactics of the enemy, has no choice in the matter, but is compelled by necessity to cross an arid waterless desert, as in the march from Korti to Metammeh, or march through barren mountainous country, as we did in Afghanistan, or when, in order to outflank and get in rear of the enemy, a change of base is indispensable, as in the Egyptian War of 1882. The loads, too, are usually clumsy and unwieldy and excessively hurtful to the poor brutes, who are generally overloaded, underfed, and rarely, if ever, get any rest or grazing. That a great many of these defects can be remedied by system I need hardly say, sometimes even to the choice of routes, as recent experience has demonstrated; and that a comparison between the native system and our own in the management of a convoy cannot fail to show up our shortcomings and mistakes, if it will not teach us wholesome and profitable lessons.

The greatest care is necessary, even with the caravans; for the journey from Suakim to Berber, owing to the scarcity of food and water, is a very trying one; and that from Korosko to Abu Hamed is most severe, the distance being 230 miles over the worst desert conceivable, with next to nothing to eat, and only one well on the whole road, about half-way. The heat, too, is terrific during the greater part of the year, and the mortality among the animals is very great, thereby increasing the difficulty of transit. The Afghans manage their 'Kafilas,' or convoys, somewhat differently from the Bedawins, though they both act on the same guiding principle of subordinating everything to the camel. They manage to escape the winter by travelling in autumn, and returning to their own country in the early spring. They have no fixed time for marching, and no settled marches. Everything—time, place, distance—has to give way to the camel. They very naturally halt at the best grazing places, sometimes for a day or more, and will then march from 30 to 40 miles, perhaps, to another oasis they know of; but this is, of course, in a bare desert where there is no grazing, and then they let the animal travel his own pace. If the days are too hot they march at night, and *vice versâ* if the nights are too cold they march by day. Like the Arabs, Egyptians, Panjabis, Beloochis, &c., they are acquainted with the habits and diseases of the camel, and if he falls ill they know how to treat him, which I am sorry to say is more than we do. Camels do not thrive unless regularly grazed, so are better adapted for trading than military purposes. I allude to baggagers especially, as Sawaris are distinctly suitable. I ought to have said that the Afghans do not march their camels the forty miles in one stretch, which would take them from sixteen to eighteen hours, unless they are obliged to do so through sheer necessity; but halt, unload, and rest them for a few hours, generally about half-way. Their system of making everything subordinate to the camel reaches as near perfection as it can, and in this way and no other it is wonderful how much can be got out of him.

Asiatics and the inhabitants of northern Africa get far more out of a camel than we do; in fact, there is no comparison, because not only do they depend on him for a living, but for their lives; consequently they take care of him, and do not override, overdrive, or overpace him. Better far to get 1,000 miles out of him in 80 to 100 days, in good condition at the finish, than 1,000 miles in forty to fifty days, with a total and irrecoverable wreck, the probability being that you do not get through that distance. Overweighting and overpacing mean slow but certain death to the camel. Some wiseacres imagine from his size that he is up to much greater weight than he can really carry. Looking to his points to see if he is up to a certain weight is a matter that never strikes them. Possibly they are not aware that he has any points. He is a great, tall, rawboned, apparently powerful-looking animal. He is already well loaded—say 400 lb. There are no spare animals available, and our wiseacres wish to push on to a station in front. Get there they must, by hook or crook. They are suffering from a disease most common on service—the 'get-to-the-front fever,' so an extra 100 or 150 lb. is shoved on to the wretched animal. On they must go. What do they care if this overweighting eventually kills the poor brute or not, so long as he struggles along and gets them to their destination? Care? Why, not a rap as to the animal's patient suffering; no thought of it ever enters their heads for a moment. Shove on the weight, crush his spirits, let him suffer, kill him! After all, he is only a camel, they say, and what do a few extra deaths matter?

I am not now speaking so much from a humanitarian

point of view as from that of a transport officer. You do not as a rule place too heavy a weight on a horse; why, then, should you overweight a camel? There are occasions of emergency and necessity, precipitated, no doubt, from want of ordinary preparations and precautions, when a British general cannot help himself—the march across the Bayuda desert in January 1885 for Gordon Pasha's relief being an instance. Then the poor animals were starved for want of food and water, and overweighted for want of spare animals. 'Needs must when the devil drives,' but on ordinary occasions this state of things need not exist. These same wiseacres that we have been speaking about overpace their already overladen animals; as frequently as not breaking down, and in the end reaching their destination not nearly so quickly as they would have done had they gone the right way to work. Naturally not. Overweighting and overpacing are errors opposed to common sense, and in connection with transport little judgment is required to tell you that they are the most glaring you could commit. Overdone meat—anything overdone, in fact—is spoilt. Overdone camels are broken down and rendered useless, or are killed in the attempt.

Mistaken notions with regard to camels

The fact is, the idea seems to be inherent amongst us, but I am glad to say fast exploding, that the camel is a cast-iron animal, capable of any weight, able to stand any hardships and fatigue, and that without food and water, on air alone in fact. There was a time when he was shrouded in mystery, and as a consequence was a much exaggerated, overrated animal, but that time is passed. He is no longer a mystery, or ought not to be, as the chances in recent years, within the last fifteen notably, to study him and learn his ways and peculiarities have been innumerable. On the contrary, those who have studied him and know him best, who have marched and ridden with him under all conditions—heat and cold, wet and dry, plenty and starvation, adverse and favourable—will tell you that, in proportion to his bulk, he is not up to great weight, and that he is very delicate, easily liable to cold (unless Bactrian, and born in a cold climate, and then great heat will affect him), and unable to stand excessive heat; and that, taken altogether, he is not nearly so strong or so hardy as was formerly supposed. But do not misunderstand me, and do not misconstrue my meaning, and run away with the idea that I am depreciating him. On the contrary, no one more fully appreciates the full worth of a camel, and no one, I think, knows it better than I do; and so I repeat that he is not the infallible wonder that he has been represented; but all the same, in proper hands, he is perfectly invaluable, and can perform and endure what no other animal can.

Camels should be loaded, not evenly, but according to their strength, power of carriage, and endurance. Breadth, not height, is the surest sign of these powers. Thus a camel may be tall and big, but deficient in muscle, bone, and stamina as compared with a shorter or smaller one who is thick-set and deep. It is these short, muscular, deep camels that are the best; yet, because he is tall and big, a greater weight is shoved on him, and sooner or later he collapses. Camels, like horses, should be specified as only up to a certain

Judgment of the weight of loads

Best weight-carriers

weight. With a proper system of transport this would be feasible enough; but under existing conditions, battling against time, as our transport on service always does, it would be rather difficult. Still, it is marvellous what can be done when the shoulder is put manfully to the wheel. I think I am right in saying that Sir Charles Napier did it in Sind. When he formed his camel and land transport corps, the weight each camel could carry was ticketed on his neck. What he did then we surely could do now.

Weight-carrying capacity

It is quite a mistake to think that the baggager can carry the enormous weights attributed to him. The opinions that existed—pretty universal they were too—as to his weight-carrying capacity were simply erroneous and absurd, and even nowadays great ignorance prevails on this point. I have heard it stated verbally, and I have seen it in standard works of reference, that he can carry from 1,000 to 1,500 lb., and with this 'mere nothing' on his back march daily from thirty to forty miles day after day. I could quote several instances, but one will serve my purpose well enough. Dallas—where he got his information from I do not know, but he does not speak from personal experience—says: 'Large powerful camels will carry 1,500 lb. for three or four miles, and these will travel for several days with a load of 1,000 lb. Those coming to Egypt from the interior of Africa rarely carry more than 5 cwt. With such loads as these they can travel thirty miles a day.' Granted that a camel will carry 1,500 lb. for a few miles, for all practical purposes there is little use in this, and if you insist upon his doing three or four miles a day with this weight the mere infliction of it will tell on him in the end. I have, for the matter of that, seen a porter in Egypt staggering under 1,000 to 1,200 lb. for a few yards. The same argument, but in a greater degree, applies to the camel carrying 1,000 lb. for several days; and even 560 lb. for an extremely long hard journey like that from the interior of Africa, across those immense wastes, to Egypt is not to be despised. It is positively ludicrous, and I should like to give some of these wiseacres a turn at tail-twisting a camel under the same conditions as we had in Afghanistan from 1878–80, or up the Nile in 1884–5. Never again would they venture to make such appalling statements, and never again, if I mistake not, would they volunteer for transport work on service. There are times when, on good roads, with abundance of food, &c.—in fact, under the most favourable circumstances—for a short journey, that a camel will carry a considerable weight. I have seen 600 lb. and more carried in the Panjab; and in Egypt the El Arish camel, used by the Egyptian Artillery, and Delta camels generally, take about the same weight. The Bactrian species are up to greater weight than the Arabian, and those of Turkestan, of this species, when in good condition and of average strength, carry up to 550 lb. for long journeys. I remember reading some years ago a translation from the Russian, on their expeditions in the Khivan and Khirgiz steppes, where the writer speaks of the camels which are found in the latter carrying from 480 to 880 lbs., according to the time of the year; but as many of his remarks regarding the camel—he was writing from a military point of view—were distinctly of the Brobdingnagian order, and as incorrect as they could be, I am disinclined to believe the latter part of his statement. Even in the hands of those who know him, for long journeys and continuous hard work, no camel in the world will carry over 600 lb. With the stamp of animal that we invariably have in our little wars, 300 to 350 lb. should be the limit. Good camels, well cared for and looked after, will take 400 lb.; but only in cases of exceptional emergency, or unless their ultimate fate is a matter of indifference, would it be wise to place more than this on the very best weight-carriers.

Average weight of loads

It is impossible to lay down a fixed average load for a convoy, as one camel may be able to carry only 300 lb., and another may take 500 lb. It is as well for transport purposes to divide them into two classes—viz. 'the strong' and 'the weak'; the former will carry from 400 to 450 lb., the latter from 300 to 350 lb., though, as I have said before, it would be better to find out each individual animal's strength and capacity. The weight of loads ought to vary considerably, and should depend entirely on (1) length of march, (2) nature of country, and (3) the nature of hardships and deprivations that the camel will have to endure. A good transport officer will, therefore, before fixing his loads, take these points into consideration, and he will also base his calculations on scarcity of food and water, and the severity of the climate. Naturally, the longer the march, and the severer the conditions, the smaller the weight of the loads, and *vice versâ*.

Muscular and nervous deficiency in hind-quarters

The camel, even a denizen of a mountainous country, is a bad climber, due to want of power behind, and it needs but a glance to detect the marked disparity there is between the muscular developments of his fore and hind quarters, the latter being very deficient—as well as in the nervous supply—anatomists will tell you. For this reason, also, he is unable to jump, and at his best jumbles over a tiny obstacle in the clumsiest way possible. Hence it is that in the Bolan, Kurram, and Khyber passes a far greater proportion of camels succumbed at the foot of all the ascents than down hill or along the general level of the road —a loss of life which frequently might have been avoided by an occasional judicious halt and rest at the base of the hills or rising ground.

Precaution to be taken when marching in mountainous country

If marching in a mountainous country, it is a wise precaution to halt for a few minutes only on the top of a rise, or at the base of an incline, so as to give the camels time to regain their wind, and to pull themselves together. But on no account stop half way up or down an incline, no matter how slight. In fact, avoid halts in a day's march, and the fewer you have the better. If possible, and there is nothing to prevent it, it is better still to keep camels always on the move in a tolerably level or slightly undulating country from one camp to the other. For, as already pointed out in chapter viii., both standing and kneeling under loads is a pernicious and injurious habit.

It has been asserted that the camel travels equally well either up or down hill, if taken slowly—which is decidedly a matter of difficulty going down—and if the incline is not very steep. This is not so. In fact a really steep slope is out of the question, and even a moderate one is difficult. For the matter of that all animals—the camel most certainly—ascend a hill far better than they can descend. The pressure, as we know, is much greater on their shoulders and forelegs—on the knees and hocks especially—in going down than up, because all the weight is thrown on to them. Therefore they are far more apt to stumble or come down, as the downward progression has an accelerating tendency; the hind legs, especially in a camel, seem to give way, bend right under, and simply drag along after the others. The pace, in fact, is insensibly increased to a trot, which a camel seemingly cannot check, partially due no doubt to the weakness of his hind-quarters; and the steeper the descent, the more jerky and unsteady it becomes, until the load is very soon disarranged, and thrown on to the animal's neck, or comes off altogether. Small short-limbed animals are best for hill work, and the long-legged camel is not at home in mountains; a level or gently undulating surface is best suited to him.

Their behaviour on sandy or stony and boggy ground

Over sand, loose shingle, stony ground, if the stones are not too large and jagged, he can move well. In wet and slippery, soft and boggy ground he is more or less useless, becomes nervous and anxious, and seems to lose all confidence in himself. His feet appear to lose all hold of the former, and he slips and slides about; while in the latter he sinks down according to the yielding nature of the soil, loses his head, flounders, falls, and probably ruptures, or if overweighted disjoints his hips, or splits himself up. With the riding camels I had in the Soudan several instances occurred in rough broken ground of animals having their shoulders put out of joint or broken by stepping suddenly and sharply on a stone, usually when going down hill; and when

On rough broken ground

scouting in the desert I lost several in this way, usually through careless and reckless riding. Should the ground be at all cut up by watercourses or ravines (which are slippery) his fears add to his already increased exertion. Numbers have thus laid down their loads and their lives at places such as these. Ravines, water-courses, and marshes

If the ground you are moving over is clayey or rocky, it is advisable not to march during rain or immediately after, for reasons already given. Should it, however, be a case of absolute necessity to march, it is better for the animals to do so during the rain than subsequently, because there will be less chance of their catching cold, and getting rheumatism or other diseases, as the exercise will keep them warm. Naturally the officer in charge would select the driest and best route available, and one over rocks and stones would at such a time be much more desirable than across clay or mud. Clayey and rocky ground

At Trinkitat, however, in 1884, we had a nasty marsh to cross, luckily no distance from the camp, over which the sappers had improvised a kind of fascine roadway, which only increased the camels' difficulties tenfold, and which after the first essay we carefully avoided. Many a camel and many a load was lost in it, or said to be at all events. The beauty of the whole thing was, that when we had struggled through it by dint of extra elbow-grease and strong adjectives, our intelligent Intelligence Department discovered that there was a good road round the dread morass very little longer than the short cut.

The camel, though it is not generally known, is a strong swimmer, and I have seen him swim across the Strong swimmer

Nile at Wady Halfa, where the stream is very broad and the current powerful, and also in the harbour at Suakim; so that most ordinary rivers, except in the first rush of flood, would be no serious obstacle to him. He can ford a river well, even if deep, so long as it is not rapid, and should the bottom of the ford be shifting sand the passage of a number of camels is said to make it hard and firm. Of course, in both the above instances, as well as when ferrying them across, unload and unsaddle them.

Good traveller

To sum up, then: in spite of the gross exaggerations and misstatements regarding the marching and carrying powers of the camel, it will be seen that for speed and endurance the Sawari and the baggager, according to their respective classes, and under certain conditions, cannot be surpassed. I have made many quick rides with the former and many good marches with the latter; but I cannot do better than quote one of the late General Gordon's, who to this day is remembered by the Bedawins in the Soudan for his fast performances, and that was his last memorable ride from Korosko to Abu Hamed, across 230 to 260 miles of the very worst desert in North Africa, when, in company with Colonel H. D. Stewart, of the 11th Hussars, he accomplished it in fifty-two hours' riding all told, continuing the journey to Berber, another 143 miles, in twenty-four hours, or from 373 to 403 miles, including halts, in nine days. As an example of what the Bactrian species can do, I cannot give a better instance of great hardiness and endurance than the exodus of the Kalmucks in January 1771 from Russia, during the reign of the Empress Catherine. In all about 600,000 souls were concerned, and in the first seven days, on camels, horses, and waggons, they got over 300 miles, in dry but cold weather. Many of the cattle succumbed. Close to Djem they were stopped ten days by snow, and had to fight a force of Cossacks, who occupied the defile. Defeating them they had to press on quickly, as Catherine had sent an army after them. They now killed and salted all the remaining cattle, and left behind all the incapable women and children, besides all aged and sick. The winter increased in severity, and though they burned all their saddles and waggons hundreds were frozen at every encampment. In the beginning of June spring alleviated their troubles, and they crossed the Torgai, which flows into the Lake Aksakal to N.N.E. of Lake Aral. In 150 days they had covered 2,100 miles, and lost 250,000 souls, whilst of all their animals the camels alone remained. Here the Russians, reinforced by Bashkirs and Khirgiz, hereditary enemies of the Kalmucks, overtook them, so they continued their retreat, only reaching the frontier of China in September. Thus in eight months they had accomplished a distance of one-eighth of the earth's circumference in a straight line. I am indebted to Quatrefages' able work on 'Human Species' for this interesting fact. Of course we are unable to draw any comparison between the powers of the camel and the other animals (which the Kalmucks purposely destroyed); nor do we know the number of casualties that occurred among the former, and the proportion that accomplished this ever-memorable march; but the bare fact that even some survived is in itself sufficient proof of the stamina of the Bactrian species, under the severest conditions and the most trying circumstances.

CHAPTER X

AILMENTS, CAUSES AND REMEDIES

I do not for one moment pretend that I am well versed in all or nearly all the ills to which camel-flesh is heir, for the very good reason that I do not know them all; but I will do my best, and attempt to describe those that are most common, and that have come, or have been brought, under my notice at different times in various expeditions that I have been in, under varied climatic and other conditions. It would be perhaps as well to point out, however, that I bring no professional or technical knowledge to bear on the subject. What is written here was picked up chiefly from natives of India and Egypt—for I never lost an opportunity of learning all I could from them—also from some veterinary surgeons who, like myself, took an interest in and had a fellow-feeling for the poor ill-used camel. Like everything else about a camel, the greatest possible ignorance has prevailed among us regarding the diseases that he suffers from. Recent years, however—in the Afghan campaign notably—much information on this point has been brought to light, through the observation of certain veterinary surgeons and transport officers keener than the majority, but principally from native sources. These tribes in India, Afghanistan, Arabia, Egypt, &c., naturally, as I have more than once remarked with reference to the management of the camel, know infinitely more about his complaints and their remedies than we do.

The following are some of the ordinary complaints, viz. :—

1. Galls, saddle.
   (a) „ crupper.
   (b) „ tail.
   (c) „ head.
2. Eating away of nose.
3. Blood-poisoning.
4. Blotches.
5. Deep tumours.
6. Cold (catarrh).
   (a) Rheumatism.
7. Sore throat.
8. Pneumonia.
9. Cold struck.
10. Heat struck.
11. Taplarga
12. Colic.
13. Itch.
14. Mange.
15. Diarrhœa.
16. Dysentery.
17. Debility.
18. Exhaustion.
19. Guffa.
20. Swelling and inflammation of the feet.
    (a) Sore feet.
21. Wearing away of the soles of the feet.
22. Zaharbahad.
23. Rupture and disjointing of hips.
24. Dislocation of the shoulder.

It goes without saying that galls are more numerous than anything, especially amongst baggagers, and I tried to point out in chapter vii. that this was one of the evils of bad loading and inattention generally to the fitting and girthing of saddles; but there are other causes as well, which we will now discuss.

1. *Saddle galls* are commoner and of a more serious nature than other galls, for in the first place they give greater pain, and in the second they frequently end in loss of health and condition when, as I have seen, camels, heavily and badly weighted, are marched day after day long distances and abnormally long hours without proper medical treatment of any kind, but with Saddle galls

a lavish amount of ill-treatment. The pain and irritation the poor beasts must have suffered from the rubbing of atrociously made saddles and badly balanced loads, to say nothing of the worry from flies, dust, &c., and of the extremes now of heat, now of cold, can be better imagined than described. The parts which are usually galled are the hips, hump, sides of chest, withers, and loins, but of these the latter, I think, suffer the most. The causes may be summed up as follows :—

(1) Ill-fitting and badly constructed saddles.

(2) The rough and wretched material with which the pads or panels were lined.

(3) Likewise the miserable stuffing or padding of the panels—generally chopped straw—which worked into a fine dust and oozed through in a very few days.

(4) The framework roughly and loosely put together, so much so that it was hard work trying to keep the saddles from falling to pieces.

(5) Constant and unavoidable changes from transfers and deaths.

(6) No time for refitting or repairing saddles.

(7) Ignorance, inexperience, and carelessness in loading.

The misfit of the saddles, as will be seen from the above, was due entirely to defective construction and inferior material. When on the top of this patent 'sore-maker' a heavy load was shoved on anyhow, without the slightest regard to balance or adjustment—in most cases too heavy in proportion to age, size, and strength of the animal—can it be wondered at that 'sore backs' were the result? The inexperience and ignorance of the Europeans in charge and of the drivers—who, in addition, were brutally cruel whenever they got the chance—was appalling; and in Afghanistan, but notably in Suakim in 1884, and up the Nile in 1884–85, these latter were the most incompetent useless brutes—men who had never handled a camel in their lives. At Suakim, had it not been for my handful of Aden drivers, I do not know what I should have done. At Tel-el-Kebir, in 1882, I was with an Auxiliary Transport Company, and we had over 200 drivers, the scum and riff-raff of Malta—men who were perfectly at home in or on the water, but who had never seen a mule in their lives—the most villainous and ruffianly crew that I have ever had dealings with, utterly worthless and lazy. What can you expect with such material, and what transport officer in the world, even were he endowed with the patience of Job, the strength of Hercules, and the conscience of—well, the most conscientious man in existence, could do justice to the animals and ensure them proper treatment? Even were he to devote night as well as day to it, he could not do it.

The casualties that arose in Afghanistan from the same causes, want of skill and attention in loading and in fitting saddles, were something enormous. I regret that I cannot go into detail, as I have no statistics by me, but a couple of examples will, I think, suffice. At Sibi, which was on the line of communications between Jacobabad and Candahar, out of some 10,000 to 11,000 camels 5,000, or about 50 per cent., had sore backs. At the Peiwar Kotal, after an inspection of 5,750 baggagers, 2,330, or over 40 per cent., were also inefficient.

Of the more recent Nile expeditions I can give some

fuller particulars. No. 3 Transport Company, which returned to Korti from the front (Gakdool, I think) about the middle of February 1885, was inspected by Veterinary-Surgeon Smith. He found a very great proportion suffering from saddle galls so severe as to incapacitate them from work of any kind for a very long period, probably from six months to one year. Many, also, were so worn out and debilitated as to be, in his opinion, beyond recovery, while he reported that the company was utterly unfit for further transport work for some time. A day or two after this V.-S. Burt inspected the camels of No. 9 Company. He reported that they were in such a terribly emaciated condition, and were suffering from such extremely severe galls, as to render them totally unfit for further service. He also examined those of the Remount Depôt, and came to the conclusion that many would not be fit for work in a month and a half or two months. That in his opinion they were more likely to improve under treatment in the depôt than by turning them out to graze, as had been decided upon. It is a curious fact that the camels belonging to these desert tribes get no medical treatment—or rather I should say that the natives use no medicines as we understand them, externally or internally—hot irons and a few crude appliances being what they chiefly resort to, and yet their camels recover. It was also curious that the Kababish camels employed by us were remarkably free from galls, sore backs, &c.; and yet not curious, for herein lay the secret—they loaded properly and purely by balance, they did not let a camel go on until he was overdone, but took him in time and gave him complete rest. When an animal gets knocked up from some cause over which they have no control, if in the desert, they leave him, on the off chance of his picking up. The Light Camel Regiment—320 strong—arrived at Korti on February 6. With but a few exceptions V.-S. Burt pronounced them to be in very low condition, with every appearance of having been overridden. With the exception of a few 'sore backs' they were, on the whole, free from disease, and had every indication of having been as well looked after as circumstances had permitted. Out of 540 baggagers that were at Korti a large proportion were suffering from saddle galls of the worst description, rendering them quite unfit for use. Many of these galls were extensive and very deep, in many instances penetrating right through the skin, exposing the bone beneath. In addition to this their condition was so low as to be bordering on exhaustion, their strength and endurance having been too severely tested. Loss of tissue consequent on continuous hard work with insufficient nourishment had reduced them to a state of attenuation and weakness. Curiously enough, the general health of these camels, in spite of their poor condition and the severity of their galls, was good, and they were singularly free from any organic disease.

(*a*) *Crupper galls* are caused by rope cruppers, which are useless and unnecessary. Crupper galls

(*b*) *Tail galls* are another result of this absurd appendage. It is supposed to steady the saddle, also to save trouble to the driver, who, instead of leading his own string of animals, ties his leading camel on to the string in front of him, because if tied to the tail the rope is always slipping off. This rope can be done Tail galls away with, for, as a matter of fact, it adds little or nothing to the steadiness of the saddle.

(c) *Head galls* are caused by the iron jag and chain belonging to the head-collar squeezing and cutting the sides of the lower jaw, while rope head-collars bruise and cut the bones of the nose. The treatment for galls among the Bedawins of Egypt and the Soudan, though barbarous, is no doubt effective. The sore is burnt with a hot iron, and then rubbed over with camel's urine or pigeon dung. It must on no account be exposed to the sun, and washing it with water is not allowed, as constant washing will bring on inflammation.

One of the best treatments for all sores and galls is to dress them with Dougal's or Cooper's sheep dip. Every wound which is raw should be first of all washed, cleansed, and dried before applying the mixture with a paint brush. This must be done morning and evening. To get it ready for application, melt 1 lb. in a quart of hot water, and wait until it cools and partly solidifies. If the wounds are slight, wash them morning and evening with a solution of half an ounce of alum dissolved in one quart of water. The great object is to keep off flies, so as so prevent maggots, and keep the wound quite healthy, and so hurry on the healing process. Kerosine or paraffin oil, carbolic acid and tar were frequently used in Afghanistan, and though rough and ready were most effective. Turpentine is also an excellent thing.

Eating away of the nose

2. *Eating away of the nose* is due to the fly-blows deposited in the nostril, which turn into maggots that eat into the flesh. It is also frequently aggravated by a too constant recourse to the nose peg and cord,

which in the hands of brutal drivers is entirely abused, and pieces of the nostrils are actually torn away by violence and nasty sores formed. The natives in India have a remedy which if applied twice daily will cure a bad case in a few days. Its component parts are—

	Tolas
'Akh' leaves	6
'Bilawa' (a medicinal plant)	10
'Tara meera tel' (oil made from a herb)	20
'Tootia' (blue vitriol or tutty)	20

Maggots will appear in any wound that has been neglected, and in a remarkably short space of time, and the utmost care should be exercised in dressing a wound regularly twice a day, so as to keep out the fly-blows. If they do get in, spirits of turpentine should be squirted into the wound, or a piece of tow dipped in it and placed on the wound.

Camels have sometimes also a running from the nose, not due to catarrh, but whether from the same cause as the above I cannot say. Arabs and Moors brand the nose cross-wise with a hot iron. I have found alum and a wet rag dipped in salt water very efficacious for sores of all kinds when, as I have been oftener than not, in charge of convoys on the march without medicines or appliances of any sort, and without the slightest chance of getting them. A dollop of Nile mud proved a most useful and excellent remedy: after having first washed and cleaned the sore, it was allowed to harden, and of course the animal carried neither saddle nor load. I will not assert positively that it had any curative properties, though it certainly not only kept the sores very fresh and healthy, but the flies from settling on them, and, what is more, they were not long in healing. The idea was purely experimental on my part—what in the appropriate language of Mr. Burnand would be called a happy thought—and suggested itself one day when I was at my wits' end to know what to do; the sweetness and softness of the Nile water decided me, for I felt that the mud deposited by the water, containing as it does any amount of vegetable matter, would do no harm, even if it did no good. Since writing this I came across the following in 'Chambers's Journal' for August 1892, which I quote with interest:—'In the course of a discussion which took place recently after the reading of a paper at the Society of Arts, Mr. J. Hughes referred to the composition of Nile mud, the fertilising value of which has always been regarded as being great. Samples of this mud he had, some years ago, had occasion to analyse, and he found two special points about it which were not generally known—one of these was that the water was remarkably soft, and the other that it contained a considerable amount of "nitric acid." The mud, in fact, was a complete manure, containing all the essentials for the food of plants in a very fine form, which alone was a great advantage.' The first of these points I learned ten years ago, after constant external and internal use of Nile water; the second I am glad to learn, it accounts entirely for the healing of the sores.

Blood-poisoning

3. *Blood-poisoning* is as a rule the result of working animals with bad unhealthy sores and galls, though of course, so professional men have informed me, this is not the only cause. I am not exaggerating in the least when I say that I have seen scores and scores of unfortunate creatures with sores bigger than a saucer,

and oftener nearer the size of a soup-plate, and so deep that one could have thrust both fists into them; and to make matters worse they were simply alive with maggots. In fact, they were so rotten and stinking that it was impossible to approach within fifty yards of them.

4. *Blotches*, which are of two kinds, red and black, are said by the Egyptians and Arabs of Algeria to be from the bite of a poisonous fly—perhaps the 'tsetse'? —in the Upper Nile regions, and on the borders of Abyssinia. They have two treatments. Should it be of a mild type, olive oil, mixed with tobacco, is given internally; in more serious cases the hair immediately round the blotch is shaved off, and a red-hot iron applied to the exposed flesh. **Blotches**

Lieut. Massoutier, in speaking of camel diseases, alludes to the 'debab' fly as being one of the most formidable enemies that is to be found in Algeria, the bite of which is so poisonous as to cause great suffering, and frequently death within twenty-four hours.

5. *Deep tumours* are found in the breast and belly, and are a source of anxiety, owing to the uncertainty as to how they will burst, externally or internally. If the former, the camel will recover, and the natives do not treat them specially for it. If the latter, death ensues. **Deep tumours**

6. *Cold* (*catarrh*) naturally is more prevalent in winter, or in wet, inclement, or changeable weather. In the Bolan Pass, and in Afghanistan, where the cold was simply intense, the camels from the hot plains of Sind and the Panjab suffered terribly, and, to make matters worse, the extremes of temperature were so marked, very often as much as 50° between day and night. This **Colds**

enormous difference was observable in the deserts and up the banks of the Nile, and in both campaigns was one of the principal predisposing causes of disease. From the beginning of November to the end of February was the worst period. In a great many instances the *colds* were so severe that the animals were greatly weakened and debilitated, and in some cases I believe that pneumonia was the result. Frequent variations of climate, extremes of temperature, continued exposure, unavoidable hardships, and want of proper clothing at night did more mischief even than the saddle galls. Out of over 300 camels I had with me marching from Wady Halfa to Korti, a great number were suffering from colds in some shape or other, eyes watering and noses running being common symptoms. Every precaution that was possible under the circumstances was taken; but as we were unprovided with blankets, and the nights, as previously remarked, became colder than the day by 40° to 50°, there was nothing to do but grin and bear it. Talk of the policeman's lot being an unhappy one, with many apologies to Mr. Gilbert, but his experience of the transport officer and his woes must be altogether *nil.* Coughs were also pretty common, and in some cases were concomitant to the colds. A good remedy is about an ounce of turpentine mixed with three or four beaten-up eggs, which should be repeated daily until the cough is better. The animal ought to be well blanketed and put under shelter if possible. A diet of soft crushed nourishing food is highly necessary, especially if the cough is severe. There is no doubt that in a complaint like catarrh 'prevention is better than cure,' and the best, in fact the only, way out of difficulty is to take care of your animals, especially in a climate where the extremes of temperature between day and night are very marked. Blankets are a necessity, and in the wet or snow place a mat or a piece of felt underneath for them to lie on.

(*a*) *Rheumatism* was another malady derivable from the same causes, but principally from excessive exposure in wet weather and constant chills, and the remarks as to prevention and cure apply to it equally. **Rheumatism**

One ounce of nitrate of potash, mixed in a pint of water, or with 1 lb. of flour or powdered grain, made into a ball or cake, and given morning and night, is considered efficacious. It is also good for a cold.

7. *Sore throats*, due to the same causes as catarrh, were pretty rife in both the wars just alluded to, and in a large number of cases the camels were affected so severely as to render them unfit for work for some days, with proper treatment of course; but as they were invariably worked, there is no need to wonder at the great mortality. During a temporary halt on the Nile —at Ambigol, I think—to clear away a block of stores, we had another transport company besides mine, but through sore throats and catarrh generally the majority of the camels were for some time unable to work. **Sore throats**

8. *Pneumonia* frequently followed catarrh, especially when the animal, instead of receiving care and medical treatment, was worked as if nothing was wrong with it; and the causes were the same as in catarrh, except that they were aggravated by extra work and exposure, whereas, on the first symptoms, rest and protection from cold would have been the only sure means of prevention. The symptoms are indicated by feverish- **Pneumonia**

ness and general debility, the nostrils and linings of the mouth become dry, and blood occasionally exudes from the former; coughing, heaviness, languor, constipation, loss of appetite, and consequent suspension of rumination, while the urine gets thicker and darker. V.-S. Steel, in describing the symptoms, mentions among others that the cough is only occasional; loss of appetite sometimes complete, at others partial; likewise as regards the bowels, in some cases there is constipation, in others the reverse; the urine is not only dark but has an increased ammoniacal colour; and he goes on to say that 'there will be no perceptible respiratory difficulty or disturbance, neither, so far as my observation goes, is much information to be derived from auscultation (listening to the respiratory sounds by the application of the ear to the chest), still less by percussion (or tapping the parietes of the chest). These three latter statements are most irregular facts, difficult to theorise upon, but probably the pneumogastric nerve again offers a solution of the mystery. It is said that this nerve originates at a greater distance from the brain than in shorter-necked animals, consequently, being less intimately connected with the nervous centre, the sympathy of the lungs with general nervous disturbance may be diminished.' At the advent of this disease he advocates rest and protection from cold as being specially necessary, and the following treatment as appropriate:—

	Tolas
Henbane (hyoscamus)	6
Dhatura (datura or thorn-apple)	1
Turmeric	24
Mustard seed	24

Make into eighteen balls, and give one two or three times daily.

The appetite may be tempted by offering a variety of food frequently, and plain gram is often particularly relished. The Indian remedy is :—

	Tolas
'Kala ziree' (cumin seed, *Cuminum cyminum*) . .	4
'Lassan' (borage, bugloss)	10
'Metee' (a very active vegetable poison) . . .	1
Salt	2

9. *Cold struck* is a complaint which the natives of India say is due to a sudden chill, got when the camel is in a state of great heat, and which often knocks him completely over and renders him incapable of action. It no doubt happens towards the evening, when the animal arrives in camp after a hot march, is unloaded, unsaddled, and suddenly exposed to a cold wind before he has cooled or has been blanketed up, or, as generally happens, there being no blankets, he remains all night exposed to the cold and damp night air. My orders, and I always saw them carried out, were to unload, but not unsaddle for an hour, or until the animal had quite cooled down. When I was unprovided with blankets I used to cover their loins with grain cloths and bags, and I have also kept on the saddles when the cold was very great. Cold struck

One of the Indian remedies is :—

'Goor' (coarse brown sugar)	1 lb.
'Mitha tel' (sweet oil)	2 quarts
'Mal kangni' (staff tree, *Celastrus*)	1 lb.

10. *Heat struck*, called by natives of India 'sargaya,' is confined to the hot weather. The hair loses its crispness and, in the tail especially, will come out if touched. This is ascribed to want of water, overwork, and exposure to the sun. Death often results. Heat struck

The natives pour green oil and salt mixed (steeped all night) down the affected camel's throat in the morning. If oil is not procurable, 'ardawa' is often used in place of it, about 1 lb. at a time.

Taplarja

11. *Taplarja* is the name given to a disease by the natives of India, the symptoms of which are constant shivering and falling to the ground—a kind of fever and ague, I should imagine, due to chill and damp. There is a word in Hindustani called 'Tap-i-larza,' which means an ague, and which I believe is the correct one, the other being a vulgar corruption. If the animal is not dead within a few hours the chances are in favour of his recovering in two or three days' time. Camel breeders attribute it to a certain wind, and their remedy is to brand the sufferer with three straight parallel lines on his head and on both flanks; but with what effect I am unable to say, though they have great faith in its efficacy.

Colic

12. *Colic.*—Colic, as I remarked in chapter iii., usually arises from overeating green food, and also from overdrinking; undigested barley, also sand and gravel, being likewise responsible for it. In two words, from improper feeding, and occasionally from internal chill. A camel so afflicted rolls on the ground in great pain, and when from the effects of green fodder or undigested grain, the body swells up. The Arabs treat this in the same way as they do blotches, shaving off a long narrow strip of hair on the belly, and branding it with a red-hot iron. The best plan is to lay a couple of blankets over and one under the animal, so as to keep it warm, and give it two quarts of linseed oil in one dose.

13. *Itch.*—Itch arises from neglect in management and dirt and filth generally. Irregularity in watering and feeding, change of food, insufficiency of green, and superabundance of dry food particularly, assisting materially. The skin becomes intensely dry and scaly and blackish in appearance; the animal rubs itself against everything it comes into contact with, and scratches the irritated parts with teeth and hind feet. What is left of the hair should be shaved off, and tar, neat or mixed with grease, rubbed into the affected parts daily, and this operation should be repeated three or four times. Being contagious, affected animals, it is almost needless to remark, should be immediately isolated. Itch

Another application which the Panjabis use is the following :—

'Gaud hak' (brimstone)	1 lb.
'Sarson ka tel' (oil of a species of mustard) .	2 quarts
'Chok' (orris or iris roots)	1 lb.

This is made into a liniment, and rubbed well into the skin. Sometimes the oil made from a herb called 'Tara meera' is substituted for mustard oil.

14. *Mange.*—Mange is derived from the same causes as itch, more or less, and presents like symptoms, except, I believe, that the skin in the latter disease is infected by parasites. The affected parts should be clipped very closely, or, better still, clip the animal all over, and common butter, grease of any kind, or other vegetable oil rubbed into them, while the camels ought to get plenty of green food. This is also a contagious disease, which, like itch, spreads very rapidly, and requires immediate isolation. It is very prevalent Mange

among camels that are suffering from debility brought on by overwork and starvation. Another good remedy is to mix sweet or train oil with a fourth part of its weight of sulphur and rub it well into the affected parts; this should be left on for two or three days, and then washed off with soap and water. When the skin is dry give a second application, and if necessary a third; but in slight cases two are usually enough. A camel badly affected requires half a gallon of oil and 1 lb. of sulphur for each application.

Both were very common in Afghanistan and Suakim, as I well know to my cost. I do not recollect it being so prevalent up the Nile; but many camels, V.-S. Phillips told me, suffered from a skin disease which was neither itch nor mange, and, if I remember rightly, was not contagious. It was also due to change of diet, constant use of dry food, grain especially, want of time for natural mastication and digestion, and an inadequate supply of water. And it was his opinion that this withholding of water for days, which was frequently done, as I have before pointed out, owing to the mistaken impression prevailing that it is necessary to do this in order to prepare the camel for desert marching, was utter nonsense. Entire change of diet and general management were, he said, the chief factors in the production of this disease, which I imagine is the same as that which V.-S. Steel, in writing on camels in the Afghan war, speaks of as 'scurvy.' He writes: 'Mr. Kettlewell suggests that the chronic diseases of the lungs might be of a scorbutic (scurvy) character, the result of the depraved and impure blood through a deficiency of vegetable acids. A reference to the nature of scurvy in the human subject favours the notion; so may our camels have suffered similarly at Suakim and up the Nile.' The conclusions that V.-S. Steel and Kettlewell have arrived at are the same that I have formed after a long and varied experience. And I am quite convinced that an overabundance of dry food —especially grain and chaff—an insufficient supply of water, and a long continued deprivation of green food will induce scurvy in the camel as it will in other animals, and on the same principles as it does in man.

15. *Diarrhœa* was very common in all the expeditions I have been in. It frequently if not always accompanied cold and debility, and resulted from catarrh and exposure when in poor and weak condition. Too much grain, especially barley, often aggravated it, acting on the already weakened digestive organs. It is often brought on by excess in drinking very saline water or of eating green fodder; and excessive work, overpacing especially, is often responsible for it. **Diarrhœa**

Two drachms of opium powder, mixed with two quarts of rice jelly (made from boiled rice), should be given morning and evening until the purging stops; and the animal should of course be warmly clad at night, and during the day if cold.

16. *Dysentery*, due to the same conditions as the above, but aggravated, also, from drinking bad or swampy water. The excrement is slimy, sometimes bloody, and the smell very strong; urine highly coloured and little of it. The camel becomes very restless, getting up and lying down all the time, and he is terribly pulled down. V.-S. Steel recommends a quart of castor oil, to be repeated once or oftener according to **Dysentery**

the appearance of the evacuations, continuing it when these are slimy. If the purging is not checked, take

	Tolas
Opium	1
Hemp resin (bhang)	4
Turmeric	24

Divide into eight doses, and give one every eight hours until the purging diminishes.

And he goes on to say: 'I cannot speak myself from experience of the efficacy of these medicines, but should think the prescription for dysentery the most promising; possibly alum, 4 to 8 tolas twice daily, might be some service.' I feel sure of this, as I have found it of great use both externally and internally. One of the remedies in the North-west of India is:—

'Sarson ka tel' (mustard oil)	1 quart
Crushed 'haldi' (turmeric, *Curcuma longa*) .	1 lb.
'Ata' (flour)	1 lb.

These are mixed into a paste, and made into balls, and given morning and evening until the purging is stopped.

Another form of treatment is to commence with 2 quarts of linseed or castor oil, and then the following—1 drachm of opium powder, ½ scruple of calomel, mixed together in 1 quart of rice jelly. Give this three times a day, keep the animal warm, and continue until there is a distinct decrease in the purging.

Debility

17. *Debility* was as prevalent as galls and catarrhs in all our expeditions, and due to 'overwork' generally, overweighting, overpacing, and overmarching; in other words, insufficiency of food in general, but want of grazing in particular; and last, but not least, want of water.

18. *Exhaustion* is more or less the last stage, and was commonly the sequence of debility, diarrhœa, and dysentery. In most instances, once it sets in death quickly follows. I have spoken more fully on it in chapter v. Exhaustion

19. *Guffa.*—The first time I came in contact with this form of disease was on my way up the Nile, and from what I could make of it the symptoms seemed to me to be very similar to an acute attack of colic. My knowledge of Arabic then was very limited, and I never could clearly understand whether the natives said that it arose from eating a poisonous herb or from the bite of a poisonous fly. Some natives at Abu Fatmeh told me that it was brought on by marching too quickly in a hot sun (overpacing, in other words) or from cold, the two extremes in fact. Symptoms—violent pain in stomach, slight running from eye and nose, fœtid breath. Remedy—ground dourra mixed with 'hameera' (yeast), or the stalks of 'loobieh' (beans). This sickness, as we have previously seen, is put down by some Arabs to the tsetse fly. It seems doubtful whether the camel is impervious to the sting of this fly or not, though I am inclined to think that it is. Livingstone, in his 'Last Journeys,' says 'that the camel did not seem to feel the fly, but that in one that died in shiverings and convulsions, though the symptoms were not like those observed in horses and oxen, yet the blood had an arterial appearance similar to that in other animals killed by the fly.' The Rev. C. J. Wilson, in his 'Uganda and the Egyptian Soudan,' writing on transport in Central Africa, states: 'The presence of the tsetse fly prevents the employment of the system of bullock waggons in vogue in South Africa, and renders Gaffa

the use of pack-horses impossible. The country is quite unsuited for camels, even if they are proof against the tsetse, which they are not. In all probability,' he adds, 'the tsetse will disappear as the country becomes more opened up, and the wild animals upon which it feeds become extinct.' When the Nile campaign was over I remember reading a book, the name of which and of the author I have forgotten. However, I was greatly interested in the following extract, which I give:—'There is a disease very common among camels, which the natives call "guffa." We were not able to make out clearly what it was; some of the Arabs declared it was catching, others that it was not, but all said that a number of animals that we had brought from the "At bara" were suffering from it when they were bought. Whenever we had to complain of any of the drivers having allowed a camel to run down through negligence, as we thought, the excuse was that it was suffering from this complaint. It was certainly in a miserably poor condition, and at the time appeared to have a fit or convulsion of some kind. It rolled on the ground, apparently in great agony, and was only induced to get up after much difficulty. Somehow or other we got there in a day's march, but it was never afterwards good for much. Some of the natives said that this disease was caused by the bite of the tsetse fly.'

This does not throw much light on nor does it elucidate the question, as there seemed to be the same want of clearness as to the disease and its cause that I felt; and from the writer's own words the natives seemed to have taken advantage of his inexperience, and were evidently making convenient use of this 'guffa' by imposing on him. Still it is interesting as showing that such a disease does really exist.

Swelling and inflammation of the feet

20. *Swelling and inflammation of the feet.*—This is due to constant and excessive exposure to rain and snow. As a rule a dry climate is essential for breeds of the Arabian species, though with great care they will stand moisture. Camels of the Bactrian species are of course better adapted for damp, because they are accustomed to it, and, as we have seen, the pads of their feet are harder.

Sore feet

(*a*) *Sore feet.*—Camels that have walked a long time or a long distance over stony or rocky ground frequently suffer from tender soles and get knocked up, and if not looked after they often go lame. A strong coating of tar constantly applied, and rest, of course, are the best remedies.

Wearing away of soles of the feet

21. *Wearing away of the soles of the feet* is caused by excessive and continuous wear and tear, especially over broken stony ground, and as a rule occurs in old camels. I have seen some instances of it myself, where the cushioned pad has been almost worn away to the quick, rather more in the fore than in the hind feet, which are less used, I suppose, and which the natives protect with straps of leather. Gilmour, in his 'Mongolia,' mentions that the soles of camels' feet wear into the quick, and that they have often to be patched by thongs drawn through the callosities.

In both these cases, in wet sloppy, or rough rocky ground, the advisability of making an easily fitting leathern buskin to fit over the foot is obvious, so as to protect the lower pads—in the former case from being cut by sharp jagged stones, and in the latter—the upper portions as well—from getting chapped and swollen. The simpler its construction the better, allowing plenty of ventilation and free play to the foot. It deserves attention, and need only be used when employing camels in extreme cases. It is worthy of note that our old friend Aristotle mentions that the soldiers when in military expeditions put shoes on their camels' feet, because they were fleshy, in other words tender.

Zahar-bahad

22. *Zaharbahad* is a kind of dropsy, or poorness and thinness of the blood, produced by overwork and absence of proper food. I have seen some cases in Egypt, but I believe I have more than once confounded this with the swelling brought on by moisture. V.-S. Steel, speaking of it, says: 'A dropsical affection (Zahar-bahd), I am informed, is a frequent result of the debility produced by hardship and exposure, and was particularly prevalent during the siege of Delhi; but I can safely assert that it was not a prominent malady in Afghanistan.'

Rupture and disjointed hips

23. *Rupture and disjointed hips.*—This occurs when they get on to wet, slippery, or soft marshy ground, and often down a steep, slimy slope. If they are overweighted and in a weak state, as they invariably are on service, an accident of this nature is nearly sure to happen. The extreme length of their hind legs and the weakness of their hind quarters no doubt accentuate the risk.

24. *Dislocation of the shoulder.*—This I have seen happen to riding camels in rough broken ground stepping suddenly and awkwardly on a stone, or by making a false step, and frequently was due to carelessness and recklessness on the part of the riders in not guiding them properly. At other times it was

purely accidental. A good number were lost like this in the Soudan. The only thing to do on service is to shoot the poor creatures, and put them out of their pain. In some cases the shoulder not only slipped, but got broken. While on this topic I should like to say a few words, as I have seen such cruel and unnecessary bungling both in Afghanistan and Egypt over shooting camels, as many as six revolver bullets in succession emptied into the poor beast's head without having the desired effect. One shot right behind the ear is sufficient, and is the only place that will kill him.

It will be seen by a careful perusal of the above that, apart from saddle galls, which primarily incapacitated, but eventually (aided by neglect, exposure, and starvation) killed a large percentage of camels in Afghanistan and Egypt, dysentery, diarrhœa, debility and pulmonary affections created great havoc amongst them. It is very hard to say which of them created most; the latter did a vast deal of mischief, but my experience was that general debility—the predisposing causes of which we have gone into, which were due to want of proper supervision, and to the ignorance, cruelty, and neglect of the hired drivers—accounted for most of all. I cannot conclude without quoting *in extenso* what V.-S. Steel says on post-mortem examinations: 'These revealed, in every case that came under my notice, pulmonary disease in almost all its varieties at Quetta, where the first were made; acute congestion and inflammation of the lungs were evidently the cause of death, and such was the case in all instances during the inclement weather on the way up to Candahar. On the homeward journey, when the atmosphere was more genial, it was chronic results which proved fatal. These chronic affections may be familiarly understood by the term consumption—not that the subjects showed the true lesions of phthisis, as it is medically called, but certainly corresponding with the more extended meaning of the word, as a "wasting away." Dense deposits, called tubercles, were found; abscesses in the substance of the lungs, named "vomica"; condensation, producing a liver-like appearance, denominated "hepatisation"; many parasites of the order classed Hydatids; and the caseous degeneration of blood, constituting a kind of embolism, were here located. An examination of the digestive organs did not indicate structural derangement, but while the rumen was filled with ingesta, the second and third stomachs, together with the intestines, were remarkably empty; showing that the food had collected in the first stomach, but that general debility and interference with natural functions had prevented its being carried further on for the purpose of being properly digested and prepared for the assimilation. In one case only did I find that the liver participated; in that one, however, tubercles existed, which would be the result of disordered circulation.

'The deductions to be drawn from the foregoing are that the want of nutrition produced debility, and such deterioration of blood as to prevent the lungs—which, it has been explained, are so intimately associated with the circulation—performing their office properly, the result ultimately being absolute disorganisation of those organs themselves. In addition to this the paralysed condition of the digestive organs had been sympathised with by the respiratory, as we have seen they are capable of doing through their connection by means of the pneumogastric system of nerves. Practically, want of proper food, accompanied by exposure, so debilitated the camels as to predispose them to disease, and the severe cold, together with trying changes of atmosphere, excited disease of the lungs of an *acute* or quickly killing character; latterly the continued want of proper nutrition, although not associated with extreme exposure, induced *chronic* or more lingering disorder, which in many camels, although they were for a time equal to a certain amount of exertion, caused death when they were called upon for extra efforts, and the rate of mortality amongst them, exactly corresponding to the length of the marches, confirms the idea. . . . One remarkable result of my post-mortem investigation was that the pleura, or covering of the lungs and chest, was in no instance involved. In most animals this membrane is nearly always included when the lungs themselves are attacked, and in this particular instance, where the chest was so specially exposed, it could hardly have been anticipated that it could have escaped; but such appears to be a *peculiarity* in the camel, for my personal observation was immediately endorsed on my mentioning the fact to Mr. Kettlewell, who had himself noticed the apparent anomaly. It will be gathered from the foregoing that disease of the lungs, then, was pre-eminently the most fatal; that some died of dysentery, which is a known accompaniment of scurvy, I do not doubt, as I observed many camels during life much emaciated from that cause, and I heard that in the Northern Army many succumbed to the premature birth of calves, an accident which we can perceive to be the result of debility.'

Prevention better than cure

Many of these ailments—galls, sores of every kind, colds, and skin diseases especially—might easily be prevented if greater care and attention were displayed in the treatment of the animals, and may safely be put down to ignorance, carelessness, and mismanagement. For their sake and our own let us devoutly hope that a new era is about to dawn. As a great proportion of these arise from the same or nearly the same cause, and as the majority of them drift into debility, and finally collapse, it ought to be easy enough to grapple with them. And so it would, if we were only a little more rational in our treatment, and were we to exercise a greater amount of common sense than we do.

Stomach and skin responsible for many ailments

First step towards prevention

The stomach is originally responsible for most indispositions, and the skin, which, as we have seen, is badly ventilated, is an apt assistant, aggravating and predisposing to congestion. The first thing to do, then, on the prevention principle is to treat the stomach and skin in an ordinarily sensible manner. Give the first mentioned the food which is adapted to it, along with a supply of water sufficient to aid assimilation, at the same time to purify and invigorate the system. Cleanse the second, both externally and internally, so as to ensure all the ventilation possible; the former by careful grooming, the latter through green soft diet and condition balls.

The second

The next thing to do when an animal shows any signs of ailing is to take it in hand at once, and not to wait until he has developed a disease, or until he is in the past-cure stage, when it is too late; and the treatment which ought to follow is, as a matter of course, 'rest' and 'diet.' Rest first, because nothing ought to prevent it from being given. Diet second, as it may not always be procurable, though every effort should be made to procure it. Neither of these, with a proper system, are in reality so very formidable an undertaking as they appear to be. To meet the former a larger percentage of spare animals is necessary in every transport unit, as well as at certain fixed depôts, placed on lines of communication. To provide the latter, the Commissariat should make special arrangements for sending it up to the front, if not procurable on the spot or in the vicinity. Rest

Good wholesome soft farinaceous and green food, something nutritious and fattening, will usually answer the purpose, such as wheat or other flour, meal, rice jelly, ground gram, dates, beans, &c., and clover or lucerne in moderate quantities. Always bearing in mind to give them, if possible, what is adapted to them, and what, as a rule, they have been accustomed to. This is another strong argument in favour of the Government breeding its own camels, ensuring, as it would, unity, uniformity, and economy of system, by the production of one class of Sawaris, and one of baggagers, bred up on certain diet. It being quite impossible in buying or hiring a large number of camels to get sufficient of the same breed. Diet

This dieting, in skin diseases especially, and rest, will do more for them than all the drugs and medicines in the world, except, of course, in cases of lung and other specific complaints. While all wounds should also be dressed and treated, cleanliness being as indispensable for a camel as for any other animal—a fact we do not seem to recognise, or which, owing to our natural antipathy to the unfortunate creature, we altogether ignore.

Lastly, when a camel is convalescent, he ought to be turned out to graze in good green pasture, until he has completely recovered his strength and condition.

But we can never expect such results until we have a permanent and practical system. And this will never be until all ranks of the Transport, from highest to lowest, have an intimate and thoroughly practical knowledge of the animal. While officers and warrant officers, as a special qualification, should go through a veterinary course. The benefits that such a system would confer on the animal would be enormous; while the efficiency and economy that would accrue to the service and State would be almost impossible to realise.

CHAPTER XI

EQUIPMENT

Like everything else in connection with our camel transport on service the gear has always been as bad as it could possibly be. No greater evil can be well devised than a badly-fitting saddle, for, as we saw in chapter ix., it was on account of the utter rottenness of the saddlery that such a large proportion of camels both in Afghanistan and Egypt got galls, which when taken in time only temporarily incapacitated them, but which ruined them for good and all when worked as they invariably were. As we have already read in the same chapter that the saddles served out to the transport service not only fitted badly, but were so defective in the construction of their framework, as well as in that of the pads and padding, which were of the poorest and worst material, it is quite needless to go over the same ground. It is simply iniquitous, however, that such should have been the case, looking at it from a humane as well as from a transport officer's point of view, and it is high time that a move were made in the right direction, and a pattern saddle fixed upon and kept in stock.

The saddles used by us in Afghanistan, as previously pointed out, were bad, but not quite so bad as those we had up the Nile, which were continually falling to

Saddles on service

pieces, and it took us all our spare time—and there was very little or none of that—to keep the frameworks together by lashing the uprights with tarred yarn, while we patched the panels as best we could—a piece of grain bag generally, for we had no proper material—and stuffed them with chopped straw, the only and the worst thing we could get. Dried grass, cut into lengths of twelve to fifteen inches, can also be used as stuffing; but it is little if any better, and we were unable to get it. Whenever we halted for the day, I always made a saddler-corporal, assisted by some of the drivers, repair, and if possible refit, all the saddles he could; but as a rule—except when we marched at night—we had precious little daylight to work in. It was uphill work besides, as the saddlery was so utterly rotten that, on the very same principle of putting new wine into old bottles, it was really useless trying to mend it, and heart-breaking into the bargain. When I first took over the saddles at Assouan all the framework had to be lashed together, all the panels stuffed, and the majority of them had to be cut down and shortened because they were too long—in fact, every single saddle had to be altered in some way or other, and when we had finished very little, if any, of the original ones was left. It would have been wiser and more economical to have supplied me with new saddles, and in the end time and money—both valuable items—would have been saved. Another instance of one of the many aggravating minor obstacles which a transport officer has to contend against. During the Nile Expedition I took over at Assouan some 350 camels, with which I was to carry forage for a portion of the Light Camel Regiment as far as

Wadi Halfa. Needless to say I found the equipment in a most deplorable condition, the framework of the saddles being simply in pieces. As we were to start in a few days I lost no time in going over to the Ordnance officer with rather a formidable requisition for various articles (tarred yarn especially, to lash the frameworks together). I had already drawn a certain amount, but found that it was insufficient, as I had not anticipated getting such hopeless gear. The Ordnance officer, who was very young and inexperienced, informed me that I had drawn enough, and refused point-blank to give me any more. I promptly rode off to the Brigadier-General in command, explained matters to him, and returned in a few hours armed with his authority to draw whatever I considered requisite for the overhauling of my equipment.

A good pack-saddle necessary

What is wanted among various other things to make transport efficient is a good pack-saddle, and without it your animals must deteriorate into an effete and debilitated lot, not worth the cost of maintenance. As has been pointed out over and over again, this want has made itself felt in all our expeditions, and has always been one of the principal sources of mischief. Too much attention cannot be paid to this, for it is self-evident that the better your equipment, the more durable it will be, and the better condition will your animals maintain—the latter, in fact, being to a great extent a result of the former. This can be very easily procured, and there would be no difficulty in making a pattern saddle. The framework should be made of a light durable wood, strongly put together. The panel ought to be lined with a tough but not too coarse and not too porous material—say felt—and stuffed with tow or some such fibre which would not easily pulverise like straw. One of the chief points in a good saddle is to make the frame so that it will not rest on the hump or spine, and press too much on the ribs. This is easily done by making the frame light and compact, with a well-padded panel, so that when the load is placed on the saddle there should be a plentiful supply of ventilation, with a free current of air passing right through. This framework and saddle, with ropes for securing them to the animal, should not weigh more than 40 to 45 lb. The ropes belonging to the saddle are the girths, crupper, and neck band; while for other purposes there is a leading-rope, headstall, nose-string, and net or bag to carry loads in, and a blanket, which is indispensable when the nights are cold. Hobbles are sometimes used to secure camels with, instead of tying the fore legs with ropes. These in all weigh another 40 lb., which gives a total weight of 80 to 85 lb., which is quite enough when you consider that he will have to carry a load of from 300 to 400 lb. maybe. Some transport authorities state that the weight of the saddle complete (items as above given) should be 114 lb. This I totally disagree with, as I think it is far too heavy. A mat, cloth, or hide, for feeding purposes, is also necessary. 'Paulins or coverings to protect the loads should be provided to the transport, in the proportion of one to two pack animals. The size for two camel loads should be about 8 ft. by 6 ft. Better far, however, if these were put over the camels. The saddles of the 'kootchie' pattern, used by some of the Pathan tribes in Afghanistan, were far superior all round, but in strength and lightness particularly, to the wretched things we had.

The Bedawins and desert tribes in Egypt, Nubia, and the Soudan use a saddle for riding purposes which is called 'makhloofa.' It is rather small and light (I have forgotten the weight, I am sorry to say), but well and strongly made. A sheepskin is generally placed for the rider to sit upon. It is fairly comfortable, and plenty of things can be fastened to it, such as saddle-bags, water-skins, *tentes d'abri*, guns, and a few days' rations. In India and Afghanistan one very similar to this is used by the natives. I do not think the native saddle can be much improved on as regards the principle on which it is built; but, of course, the means of putting the framework together, in addition to the quality of the wood and the material composing the pads and stuffing, can with advantage be superior. **Makhloofa**

It stands to reason that in this, as in the case of the boats used on the Nile, long centuries of experience have taught the natives the most suitable form to adopt. Blindly conservative and opposed to reform as they usually are, there are, for all that, certain lessons that we can learn from them—and we should never be above learning them. The French in Algeria, it seems, invented a pack saddle; but after a short trial it was found to be unsatisfactory and inferior to the Arab pattern, so was abolished and replaced by the latter, which had hitherto always been in use.

The saddles that were used in the Egyptian army were the same as those which were supplied to the 'Heavy,' 'Light,' 'Guards,' and Mounted Infantry Corps in the Nile Expedition. I do not recollect their weight, but they struck me as being rather too heavy. They might have been lightened with advantage, without in **Mounted Infantry pattern** any way interfering with their efficiency. The pommel was far too high, and I know cases where men have been suddenly shot forward and thrown against it, or when thrown off a camel did not quite clear it, who were badly ruptured. These saddles were too concave in shape, which made them rather uncomfortable in a long, quick ride; but on the whole they were tolerably good, though there was room for the improvements above suggested. Personally, I have made some long and rapid rides in them, and have little to complain of. Stirrups were used with them. This, I think, apart from a military sense, was a great boon, as it enabled you when your legs got stiff in one position to change to another in more ways than on the 'makhloofa,' for on a long journey sitting cross-legged, or allowing them to hang without anything to rest on, was at times very tiring. Yet I have known many Europeans who have preferred to ride in the latter. I cannot resist from mentioning here a trifling incident that occurred to me in connection with this self-same saddle when I was up the Nile. A young officer, who shall be nameless, with a very grave face informed me of the recent *invention* of this saddle, with which, it appears, he had had something to do. The look of gravity rapidly changed to one of blank astonishment when I replied that he may have improved on the native pattern, which I thought was doubtful, but that the inventor had lived some few thousand years ago, probably in Arabia, somewhere about the time that Nimrod the mighty hunter flourished.

Spare equipment and material

Every transport company ought to be a complete unit in itself, and furnished with a certain percentage of spare equipment and spare material, in order to grapple with the constant effects produced by wear and tear, and to admit of the repairing and refitting of saddlery being thoroughly carried out. To do this, a proper supply of saddles and carpenter's tools should be issued, and competent men placed in charge of them. Rope should be given freely, and without stint. The inconvenience which I have frequently seen on service from lack of this most useful and necessary article has been woful. No unit, however small, should move without a certain proportion of useful medicaments. Medicine-chests ought to be made of a size and capacity to suit the requirements of a section of 100 camels, and should be in charge of the conductor, who ought to be duly qualified to treat a sick animal. Oil and tar in reasonable quantities are indispensable, while branding irons and shears are always handy.

Carriage of sick and wounded

With regard to the carriage of sick and wounded, special arrangements should be made, and camels for the purpose ought to be very carefully selected for their (1) strength, (2) steadiness, (3) staidness, (4) age. The older and staider the better, and the heavier in build the steadier they are in their movements. Worn out and effete camels should on no account be used—as we did in the Bayuda desert, where the camels were so exhausted and fatigued that they fell down from utter weakness, while they were made to get up and were dragged on behind the stronger ones, in fact driven on by sheer brute force. Judging by my own experience on that occasion, the agonies suffered by the poor unfortunate sick and wounded men must have been very terrible. Against the actual means of carrying sick and wounded I have nothing to say, except that the arm-chairs could be made a little more comfortable, and ought to be constructed so that the sufferer should be protected from the cold at nights, which in Afghanistan and the Soudan was very intense, and added to the misery and pain, which was quite enough in itself. This could be easily done by strapping a waterproof rug round it. As to the hammock, there are three points deserving of attention: (1) the way in which they are secured to the saddle; (2) the angle at which they are slung; and, last but not least, (3) the adjustment and balance. All three want looking to and putting to rights; and when this is properly done the motion will be diminished, and the patient will subsequently suffer less. The balance particularly requires to be preserved, because without it it would be impossible to secure the first two points, and if on one side a man happens to be much heavier than the other—and you cannot get two men of equal weight—the difference ought to be made up by artificial means. I can speak feelingly, because on one occasion, for a journey of 200 miles, my companion was a far heavier man, and while he was close to the ground I was right up on the animal's back. That we both suffered extremely I need scarcely say. These are, however, questions that strictly concern the broader subject of transport, so I will say no more about them.

Precautions as to saddles

Each camel should be served out with a saddle fitted and stuffed especially to suit it, and to avoid mistakes its own number should be stamped on the saddle. The greatest care should be paid to this to prevent drivers from changing saddles, because the size and shape of the humps are so different that what will fit one animal will not another. Too much attention cannot be devoted to the constant repairing and refitting of equipment, but more especially to the stuffing of saddles, and particularly in the case of thin and debilitated animals, who are specially liable to galls and sores.

As soon as a camel is galled, on the principle that 'a stitch in time saves nine,' he should be unloaded and unsaddled, and his load transferred to a spare animal. If in a case of necessity you are obliged to go on using him, remove a certain amount of the stuffing by unstitching the lining, or if this is scanty, move it to either side and keep it in its place by a few stitches, so as to leave a hollow over the sore, and so avoid pressure on it. Do not on any account allow a hole to be cut in the pad, as I have frequently seen done on service; for besides spoiling the pad permanently, unless the hole has been cut large enough and very carefully, its rough and jagged edges will help to irritate the sore, as also to enlarge it, or possibly cause a fresh one.

Stuffing saddles

In stuffing saddles it is very advisable not to go to extremes. With an insufficiency of stuffing the weight of the load is apt to bring so much pressure on the framework as to make it felt through the pads, and so produce friction. On the other hand, do not overstuff them, because when too thick the pads will not conform to the shape of the back, become clumsy and lumpy, and galls are the result. The pads ought never to be allowed to take the shape of the back, but should in the first instance be stuffed to fit accordingly.

Nose-peg and crupper

I am utterly opposed to the use of the nose-peg and crupper. The former as being useless, and simply an instrument of torture in the hands of cruel lazy drivers, which can be entirely dispensed with, especially when camels are driven, as they should be, instead of led in strings, as they are. I am, of course, speaking of baggagers, as they are more or less indispensable with Sawaris; but they should be only used when absolutely necessary, and then sparingly and judiciously, and only trustworthy men should be allowed to use them, for much injury can be inflicted on the nostrils when used to excess.

The crupper is invariably made of thin hard rope, which causes a wound under the tail—a wound which only helps to irritate an animal which is already sufficiently irritated by other sores, and the accompanying worries of flies, dirt, and the painful friction of saddles, loads, and ropes. It is, I consider, a totally unnecessary infliction of cruelty, because with a proper adjustment of saddle and load it is not required, except perhaps in a very hilly country. If used in such case, it should be made of webbing, tape, or some such soft substance. If this is not procurable, and in any case, a piece of soft rag should be wrapped round the part that fits under the tail, which ought to be washed daily, as well as changed frequently, to prevent it getting too hard.

Why drivers should not do repairs

On no account should hired drivers be allowed to repair saddlery, as this class are usually utterly ignorant of the smallest details, and their work would be very badly and carelessly done. Consequently the results would be extremely defective, and highly injurious to the animals. Any individuals showing special aptitude and smartness for the work might be allowed to assist, but only under supervision. This work should really be done by a special staff of saddlers, under the constant and immediate superintendence of sectional and divisional commanders, in addition to the officer in command, and the vital importance of it cannot be overestimated.

Drivers should be responsible for gear

Under a permanent system with professional drivers each man ought to be held responsible for the gear belonging to his camels, as well as for the proper care of it; but even then supervision is necessary. Such men will naturally take a certain amount of pride in looking after both animals and equipment, because they would thoroughly understand that the fitness of the former depended entirely on the excellence of the latter, while on both depended their own welfare, besides the general efficiency of their own particular section, division, and company directly, and of the service at large indirectly. These, at least, are the principles that should be imbued into all ranks, for without them you cannot expect to arrive at that pitch of excellence which is absolutely essential to success. Hired drivers should also be made responsible for their animals and equipment, under exacting and constant supervision; but while trying to get all you can out of them, expect as little as possible, and do not let your expectations run away with your judgment.

CHAPTER XII

MANAGEMENT

UNDER this heading every single subject in connection with a camel should be included as a matter of course, but those on 'watering,' 'feeding,' loading,' 'marching and carrying power,' 'ailments, causes and remedies,' and 'equipment' are so very important, and I had so much to say about each of them, that I thought it better to treat them separately. Of course, as I have lost no opportunity of pointing out all through these pages, it is by general management and supervision only that full value can be obtained from a camel. Hence the superiority of the natives over us. It is on this, and this alone, embracing as it does every point in connection with the camel, that the efficiency of transport can be maintained; and this result depends entirely on the formation of a system, so thorough in every detail, and so essentially practical in every respect—based, in fact, on practice and experience, as to attain as near perfection as possible. And until such a system is introduced as a permanency, and a special class of men trained for it, so long will our transport remain as it always has been, and as it still is—inefficient, and utterly unable to grapple with a sudden crisis, because it is built on a foundation which is faulty and unpractical, and which is entirely incapable of expansion.

The question of drivers, at least so far as we are concerned, is certainly one of the most, if not the most important in the organisation of camel transport, so much, if not all, depending on their treatment and management of the animals, which in a very great measure rests with them. **Drivers**

To ensure this it is absolutely necessary to raise and maintain a large body of thoroughly trained men in peace time, so as to have an efficient and reliable nucleus, upon which you can at once set to work when it is requisite to expand the transport. In order to arrive at this high state of efficiency, drivers should be regularly organised and administered under strict discipline and on good, liberal terms, so as to secure the right class of men. **Organisation**

With such a system, and on these premisses only, provided they belong to a warlike race—which should be a *sine quâ non*—would it be wise or desirable to give them a military training. Under existing conditions, with hired drivers, it would be madness even to think of it. In Candahar, where we armed our camp followers, several instances occurred in which the Afghans first took their swords away from them, and then added insult to injury by killing them. The same thing also happened in the Bolan Pass with the Bombay transport drivers, who were ruthlessly murdered by the Murrees. On the other hand, in Sir Charles Napier's Camel and Baggage Corps, the system answered most admirably, and the corps were quite independent of military escorts, grazing guards, and fatigue parties, as they performed these duties for themselves. One driver was appointed to each camel, drilled, armed, and trained as a soldier; but of course they belonged to fighting tribes, such as the Beloochis, Pathans, &c. These or the Panjabis, Hadendowas, and Somalis would all do well in this respect, and they are excellent camel men as well.

Military organisation the best for transport

There can scarcely be any doubt, I should say, both from a transport and military point of view, as to the question of a military organisation being the best for any transport. At the same time, in the education of all ranks, the ruling and vital principle of the system must be transport first, military training second—merely a supplementary and secondary adjunct, which secures independence from military escorts and guards, adds to its own strength in case of attack, as also to that of the fighting force, which can thus be kept intact, and which it would otherwise sap and weaken. The fact that it is essentially a working (and not a fighting) corps cannot be too strongly impressed on all ranks. For 'aping' is not only a sign of the times, but has become a perfect craze, which has grown contagious, and which has caught on in many of the departments in our army.

Owners as drivers

As a general rule, camel breeders and owners will *not* act as drivers. This applies equally to mules and other animals; so that when we require a large number of drivers we are perforce—having none of our own—obliged to hire anybody we can get hold of, and pay him highly into the bargain. This in itself ought to be a sufficient motive for a sweeping reform in the transport system; for it stands to reason that with hired drivers a transport cannot maintain efficiency, it being a well-known fact that it is next to impossible to get the right stamp of men; and the sooner we recognise the fact that good drivers are essentially a necessity the better. There can be no question about this. To look after camels you require men who have owned, bred, and driven camels all their lives—who know their ways, habits and characteristics most thoroughly, and who understand all their peculiarities and peccadilloes.

Hired drivers as a general rule are utterly worthless scamps, whose sole knowledge of a camel is to have seen him stalk through the streets of a town of which they are the refuse. Or it may be, as sometimes happens, that they have been forced to serve against their will; but whether or no, as a body they are careless, callous, and cruel, know nothing about their animals, care still less, and illtreat them on every possible occasion. They have no sympathy with or feeling for your cause, and no interest in the animals; consequently you have no hold on them—they desert and leave you in the lurch as soon as they have made enough money, or when they reach the confines of their own country, or, in fact, whenever they get a good opportunity. This requires looking into, as of course the well-being of the animals depends in a very great measure, if not entirely, on those who are immediately entrusted with them. Of course, a good transport officer can knock some work out of the most useless and unwilling drivers; but such work after all is very imperfect and unsatisfactory compared with the amount obtained willingly from competent men, an eighth of which is preferable to a whole of the former; to say nothing of the extra exertion requisite on the part of the transport officer to get even

Unfitness of hired drivers

this iota, which harasses and fatigues him to a great extent, especially when he requires most of his time, energy, and capacity for other and more important purposes.

The way to deal with natives

In dealing with natives, above all things, firmness and fairness are essential. Once show that you are undecided, or hesitate in the smallest way, and it is all up with you. Always pay the men yourself; see personally that they get their rations, clothes, and everything that they are entitled to. Show them that you take an interest in them. On the other hand, be very severe and strict; punish them promptly for any violation or dereliction of duty. Do not try to reason with them, or do not appeal to their feelings—the class of men we have on service do not as a general rule possess any. If necessary, however, the only way to appeal to them is by a flogging, which is the only appeal they understand. Fining is inadequate, and often no infliction whatever, because such unprincipled loafers as we get do not appreciate the true value of money, and as frequently as not it is a matter of indifference to them. Do not bully them, and, above all, do not be changeable and uncertain to them, but let your guiding principle be decision. No one that has not actually gone through the mill can conceive any idea, much less form an opinion, of the difficulties in this one branch alone that a transport officer has to contend against, the tact he requires, and the delicate way in which he should handle these men (1) to get any work out of them, (2) to prevent desertion. All the obstacle races ever run have been child's play to it. I could fill pages on this point alone, but I think I have said enough for our purpose.

The first thing to see to in the formation of a transport train is to divide it into proper units for purposes of discipline and interior economy, each unit to be complete in itself, and commanded by an efficient officer, assisted by efficient subordinates. A company of camel transport should not consist of more than 800 camels, as this is quite enough for one officer to look after properly. It should be divided into two divisions of 400 each, the right and the left, and further subdivided into four sections, Nos. 1 to 4 belonging to the right division, and Nos. 5 to 8 to the left. Each division to be commanded by a subaltern, each section by a conductor; all officers and conductors to be well mounted on smart, handy ponies, the former to have two, the latter one apiece. No other Europeans to be allowed, except, perhaps, an officer to assist the officer in command of the company. Each divisional officer to be held responsible to the commanding officer for his animals and equipment; each sectional commander to be held responsible to the divisional officer; so as to have each section a complete unit, and a chain of responsibility running right through. Officers and conductors (who should be warrant officers) to be specially selected for their knowledge of animals, smartness, and for special fitness qualifying them for transport work; and they should previously undergo a systematic and practical training, and pass a thoroughly practical examination before taking up the active duties of transport. **Formation of a company**

This is not a work on transport, still I have sketched a bare outline of what I consider a transport company should be, as I wish to point out that this is absolutely necessary, for without a regular system, and with inef- **Inefficiency the result of want of system** ficient subordinates, instead of management you obtain mismanagement, and as a natural sequence the animals suffer severely, and in no time are worked to death, or are reduced to a state of utter helplessness. Without a system you must expect to have inefficient officers and useless drivers, and with these latter you cannot expect to get anything else but indifferent work out of your animals. An officer may be as smart, active, and conscientious as possible, and he may work like a slave; but if he is ignorant of transport work and of camels and their ways, and equally so as to the management of natives, it is terribly uphill work; and should he happen to be a determined, zealous fellow, just as he has licked his rabble into shape and knocked a little method into them the campaign is over, if it has not ended long since, and the transport is no longer required. I use the words licking and knocking—vulgar though they be—intentionally, as it is the only way in which a transport officer on service can infuse or impart any system—zeal or liking for the work he never can—into the class of men that he has to deal with. In each of the expeditions that I have served I flatter myself that before I had been long in contact with my drivers I had managed to imbue a certain sense of awe into them which was productive of good results—work; but were I to relate how I set about to obtain these results, Exeter Hall would look aghast.

General inexperience

Situated as we are at present no transport company should consist of more than 400 camels, as this is quite enough for an inexperienced man to look after. I have nothing to say against the individual officers of our Army Service Corps, but in the days when the same department was called the Commissariat and Transport Corps, not so many years ago, during one of the numerous expeditions in Egypt—the senior officer in charge of supplies and transport to the field force, assisted by several of his own department, had to organise a camel train. Neither he nor any of his assistants had the slightest idea how to do so, for they were entirely ignorant, even in the most rudimentary way, of the camel and its capacity, and of the necessary equipment required. I will not say how he obtained it, but in the end things came right somehow. The senior got a C.B., and most of his assistants promotion or a special mention in the 'Gazette.' On another occasion one of these officers, who during his entire service had been in a Commissariat office, was placed in charge of 800 camels. Needless to say that he was quite helpless, but further comment is unnecessary. The blame does not rest with the officers of this department, who do not go to India, where they might learn the rudiments of their profession, or where at all events, if they so chose, they might pick up a little knowledge of the camel, and who have no other means of learning. It is only within the last ten years that Egypt has been open to them, but after all this has not been a large experience, and only a small proportion of them have had it. I do not wish to draw any invidious comparisons between our English and Indian Transport Departments, for the latter is by no means a model of perfection that is worthy of imitation, as a knowledge of our recent frontier expeditions has taught us, but I merely wished to point out that in India an officer has more opportunities placed in his way of learning, not only about a camel, but every description of animal, and if he is keen and observant he has only himself to blame if he does not learn something. No, the fault lies with the system, and not with the individual; and one of the most glaring imperfections in our army is this temporary transport hurriedly raised to meet an emergency, and the most noticeable fault in this temporary transport is the inexperience of the officers and the utter worthlessness, ignorance, and incapacity of the drivers that are invariably employed.

Afghan reminiscences

The driver question in Afghanistan was one strong enough to appal the heart of the stoutest transport officer. On the march up to Candahar we had few if any drivers, as they deserted between Jacobabad and Quetta, before we got into the enemy's country, and the soldiers had to be told off to act as such. One extract from my Afghan diary will throw a light on the miserable state of affairs: 'I was on rear guard to-day (December 20, 1878) and had to leave 161 bags of Commissariat stores on the ground from want of transport, many of the drivers having deserted and (to make matters worse) taken their camels, which were hired, with them. This is a very common trick of the Sind (Sarwans) drivers, who go back to Jacobabad by a circuitous route—so, at least, it is said—and in many instances are re-engaged by the Commissariat.' In the march from Cabul to Peshawur, after General Roberts had marched to the relief of Candahar, and Abdur Rahman had been placed upon the throne, my drivers were all Pathans from the surrounding districts. Fearing desertion I was determined to circumvent them, so, prior to our march, I had them all collected and fallen in. One by one, assisted by my men, we stripped them perfectly naked, and took away all the money that each man had in his possession. We were obliged to undertake this operation, repulsively filthy as it was (and the Afghan is the dirtiest brute on record), for they are all such thieves, and, having the greatest mistrust for one another, hide away their valuables in the most extraordinary places. The amount taken from each man was duly entered to his credit, and I informed them that on arrival at Peshawur, but not before, the money would be returned to them. Not a man deserted (for the Afghan is most avaricious, and loves the chink of money), while other corps suffered greatly. My drivers, if anything, were rather pleased than otherwise over the result of my manœuvre, for the Afghans have a keen sense of humour, and appreciated the fact of my having outwitted them.

Intermixture of Europeans and natives a mistake

Up the Nile, also, the drivers we got at Assouan, Dongola, and all along the river, were not camel drivers, and many of them were old decrepit men and mere boys. The handful of Aden boys that I had at Suakim, as previously mentioned, were excellent, so also were those and some Somalis that I had up the Nile; but unfortunately there were too few of them. The former were quieter and easier to manage than the latter; but on the whole I would sooner have the Somalis by themselves, without any soldier supervision. No; Thomas Atkins—though a most estimable person, for whom I have great respect—in his management, or rather mismanagement, of the native is a failure. He does not know how to treat him. At one moment he is too friendly, the next he will kick and cuff him. The

Somalis would not stand this. At first there were one or two rows, but things soon found their own level without very much interference from or reference to me, and Tommy, when he found that the Somalis were only too ready to return the compliment with a heavy knobkeri, let them alone. This mixture of European subordinates with native drivers is a great evil, and one to which I am very strongly opposed.

Another objection

Another great objection to employing soldiers with hastily improvised transport is, that to enable them to carry out their work of supervision they ought to be mounted. If not mounted you get little or no work out of them, in fact they are more in the way than not. No allowance is made for this, and, whether permitted or not, they mount the laden camels; but this is not all. The drivers also mount, while those who are placed over them for supervision, especially if no officer is by, take no notice of this infringement; and so matters go on, drifting into a go easy, take-my-chance method. Everyone rides; in fact, they all do as much as they like, except when the convoy is in charge of an officer, and they happen to be directly under his eye. Do not forget that a convoy unavoidably opens out and straggles to a great extent, so that the officer cannot be everywhere.

Soldier supervision a mistake

The conclusion, after varied experience, that one naturally arrives at is, that for work of supervision over natives the British soldier is useless (even when commanded by a zealous, conscientious officer), because he himself, besides ignorance and inexperience of the work, requires constant supervision. One half your time is taken up in superintending his movements and actions, the other half in watching the natives. Your energies, powerful though they be, cannot cope with impossibilities, and you have not sufficient time to devote to your camels because soldiers and drivers occupy it all day.

On the march all drivers and soldiers should be made to walk. The addition to the load on a camel of 100 lb. and upwards makes all the difference. In 999 cases out of 1,000 he is already overweighted, or carrying all he can. The immediate result of this overweight is that he cannot walk up to his usual pace. He is then driven and urged on to keep up with those not so handicapped. Result No. 2 is that he is overpaced. Result No. 3 is rapid loss of appetite, consequently of condition. Finale, total collapse and breakdown. Breeders and owners never ride their camels when laden, not to my knowledge at least. They usually have a few empty ones that they keep for emergencies, which they use when tired. This question of drivers is a sore topic with me, and one on which I could fill pages; but that would not answer my present purpose. All I have tried to do is to convince the reader that it is one of the existing evils in our very faulty system of transport, and if I have done that I am satisfied.

Laden camels should not be ridden

As I have previously remarked, we can learn many lessons from the French in their management of camel convoys in Algeria, and this is one. In the pamphlet by Lieut. Massoutier that I have so often alluded to all through this work, he states that no soldiers, &c., of the Commissariat or Ordnance Staff are allowed near the camels for fear they should overdrive them in order to arrive in camp early, while no camp followers of any description are ever allowed near the baggage columns; and striking or ill-treatment of camels or their drivers is strictly forbidden. No further explanation is needed, but let us read, mark, and inwardly digest these golden maxims.

Spare camels

This brings us to another very weighty matter—namely, that of spare camels; and herein to a great extent lies the very marrow of a transport system on service—viz. a sufficient percentage of spare animals, 20 per cent. if possible, but certainly not less than 10. Every unit ought to be complete in this respect, and in the field and on the march this percentage should be kept up. These units should be fed from a reserve accompanying the force, otherwise those already loaded will be called upon to do more than they can, and a breakdown will be the result. Many are the collapses that could have been avoided had there been a reserve. All other branches of the military machine have a reserve, why not the transport? Why not indeed? With an inefficient transport a force is cramped and slow in its movements, and mobility, one of the main characteristics, almost the essence, of a good army is out of the question.

Spare camels are also most useful when, as often happens, the drivers get footsore, knocked up, or fall sick. There is no help for it in the present state of things but to place them on a laden camel, as convoys on lines of communication are always without ambulance conveyance, medical aid, or comforts. Once or twice between Assouan and Halfa, had it not been for the river, I would have been placed in rather an awkward position by men falling ill. I had no medicines, and they were unable to march, so I was obliged to place them on 'dahabeeyahs' (Nile boats), which were on their way to the front with stores. Spare camels are a necessity, and no convoy should be without them. They should never be used on any pretext whatsoever, not even by the officer in command, for any purpose but the legitimate one—the relief of sick animals or men; but for the latter there ought, of course, to be a separate percentage of sick carriage. It is an absolute impossibility to keep up the efficiency of a transport unit if deficient in this respect. The number of points that are inevitable in order to preserve a state of efficiency are so numerous and so self-evident that to advocate and lay stress on them appears to me like the reiteration of some well-known truism, and yet, though they are facts well known, and the truth of which are recognised, no steps are taken to improve or remedy them; and so we drift and drift until the next war breaks out, when (with the regularity of a recurring decimal) we commit the same blunders, rehearse the same farce, and repeat the same errors that practical men have pointed out and condemned on previous occasions; and this absence of a proper percentage of spare animals is one of the most important, and one of the chief causes of all our transport breakdowns. As a matter of fact, in nearly all of our expeditions we first of all start with too small a number of animals, already overladen; so that, though there may have been a small percentage of spare ones, practically speaking there are none, because these few are very soon utilised owing to casualties which are hastened by (1) an insufficiency of animals, (2) overloading. This was notably so in the Nile campaign 1884–5, so much so that all the camels belonging to the first line of transport were worked off their legs on the line of communication up to the very day they were required for their supreme effort across the Bayuda desert. On these lines it follows that before we are half way through a campaign the main body of our camels is so debilitated and crippled that, even granting that a good start has been made, the reserve—which is seldom or ever more than a nominal one—has been long since merged into the first line.

This question of general management cannot be too strongly impressed on a transport officer and his subordinates, and the greater care and attention that he and those under him pay to these points that we have all along discussed, the more efficient will his transport become. In fact, a high state of efficiency cannot be otherwise attained. Whenever it was my lot on service —which it frequently was—to tail-twist the ill-used camel, I drew up certain rules and regulations for the guidance of my subordinates, and I did my best to see that they were carried out—circumstances permitting, of course, for I always recognised the fact that on service, owing to its exigencies, one cannot always stick blindly to any specified line of conduct. Circumstances alter cases. This, also, I tried to impress on the conductors in charge of sections, so that when they were by themselves on convoy duty they should know how to act and carry out my orders as closely as they could. The following, as well as I can remember, was a general outline of their duties—viz. :—

Orders to conductors

1. Give the camels a small feed prior to starting in early morning—one hour at least before loading.

2. See that the drivers beat and brush out the pads, and shake the saddles before putting them on.

3. That each saddle is properly girthed.

4. Personally superintend the loading of each camel.

5. See that each load is properly balanced and adjusted before starting.

6. Load each animal according to his age, strength, and size.

7. March with and superintend his section on the march. Keep sharp look-out after drivers, and permit no irregularities.

8. Allow no one to ride a laden camel.

9. If on convoy work never keep his animals unnecessarily standing under loads, but keep them moving, and get to destination as quickly as possible without overdriving.

10. On arrival at destination unload at once.

11. Not to unsaddle for at least one hour, or until camels have cooled down. This is to apply day or night. Turn saddles upside down to expose inside of pads to sun and air until dry. Examine them, and see that all necessary repairs are made. Inspect animals—treat sick, and dress all sores, galls, &c.

12. Rub down, especially round the hump and ribs—the parts covered by saddle. (Rough brush good for this, if not available use hands or straw. I have seen a brick used.)

13. Give small feed (if no grazing), then water when

water is procurable, preferably in the evening. Be present at all feeds and waterings.

14. Always march by night (enemy permitting) when the weather is hot, and even when it is cold, if not too cold.

15. If there is grazing, graze between 10 A.M. and 4 P.M. If not, and you have been marching by night, give feed.

16. When brought in from grazing secure them in rows, backs to the wind, or in an oval, as there is less chance of their straying. Near forelegs to be tied, or hobbled.

17. Blanket them. If there are none and the cold is intense put on saddles, and when they have finished feeding throw feeding-cloth over their rumps.

18. If giving grain rations give feed when blanketed. One feeding-cloth to two camels. In case of vicious camel feed him by himself.

19. In dealing with natives never take the law into your own hands, but report the circumstances.

20. If possible, halt for the day every fourth day, or once a week at all events.

21. Have an inspection of all equipment once a week, or oftener if possible.

22. Look especially to the stuffing of the pads and the fitting of the framework.

23. Repair and fit equipment on every available opportunity.

24. Nurse his camels to the utmost, and should he detect any signs of a camel beginning to fail or fall sick, unload at once, and transfer load to a spare animal.

25. Never carry stores without a way-bill, and before starting take stock of their condition, and check one with the other, to see they correspond.

26. On arrival at destination act similarly, and get a receipt for your stores prior to handing them over.

27. Personally supervise *every duty* in connection with your animals, because on the thoroughness of this depends their welfare.

28. Keep a diary, and enter daily the performance of all duties, all casualties, changes, accidents, &c. Everything that occurs in fact.

When in cantonments, or in a standing camp, too much care cannot be taken as to its site and position, nor can too much attention be paid to the drainage and general sanitary conditions. A well-sheltered place is the best at any season of the year, and in a hot climate a *tope* of trees is the most suitable in every way. Always utilise any walls or banks that may be convenient, and whenever and wherever you can shelter your animals from damp and cold winds. The ground you select should be dry or sandy, and as level as possible, with a very gentle slope. **Selection of site for a camp**

Certainly in camp, and on the march when possible, each transport unit should have a sick line. The most suitable spot ought to be selected on the lee side of the camp, in the most sheltered place, and on the softest and most comfortable ground. In a standing camp rough sheds should be improvised, especially when there is no natural shade to protect the animals from the glare and heat of the sun. And all available means should be adopted to keep the flies off and the dirt from all open sores and wounds. **Sick lines**

Special selection of orderlies

Men ought to be specially selected for their knowledge of the animal, and of its ailments and their treatment, and they should be told off as special orderlies, their sole duty being to look after the sick. The camels ought not to be mixed up, but kept together by sections and divisions, and a proportion of orderlies from each of these should doctor their own animals. A smart headman should be placed over them, who would be indirectly responsible for the drugs and medicines; but with Orientals it is wiser to keep certain of these—such as opium, for instance—under lock and key, or they will make away with it. Sectional and divisional officers would naturally superintend their own animals, but the whole should be under the immediate supervision of the officer commanding the company.

Supervision of officers

Selection of sick

As a rule, only animals that are unfit to carry loads and saddles should be sent over to the sick lines, and such camels, besides medical treatment, ought, as a matter of fact, to be placed on special diet, as pointed out in chapter x.

Manner of treating a sick camel

In reality, however, what a sick camel—one, I mean, that is totally incapacitated from carrying a load owing to galls or sickness—wants more than anything else is complete rest, and as soon as he is growing convalescent entire freedom and good grazing. Nature is the best doctor, and effects a sounder and speedier cure, provided that you do not leave it to her when it is too late. As soon as the animal is in a convalescent state he should be turned out for days, weeks, or months, according to circumstances and the severity of his illness, until he thoroughly recovers and regains his strength.

Sick and remount depôts.

To provide for this on service sick or remount depôts should be placed at certain intervals on the lines of communication, naturally dependent on their length and on the nature of the country. Here all sick camels should be left, and replaced by fresh ones. Those only very slightly and temporarily indisposed need not be left, but any that show signs of staleness or debility, and all those with fresh rubs and galls, are better left to recoup. For it is in this way the mischief is done, and by working these animals the debility increases and the rubs develop daily; they gradually grow weaker, and finally succumb. Taken in time, with rest and good diet, they recover in a few days—pick up their strength and renew a fresh lease of life, in fact. These depôts should be well stocked with a large surplus of working animals, so as to replace the sick; and if properly worked, they would, I feel sure, be an immense economy. For it is better in the beginning to purchase double the number of camels than to try and do the work with less than half, all of which we kill and replace, until in the end we have purchased far more than we would have been obliged to had we commenced with the requisite number.

How a camel that has been idle should be treated

A camel that has been resting in camp without work, owing to weakness, sickness, or other cause, or that has been allowed to run loose for some time, naturally loses condition and becomes soft, especially about the hump and ribs. Such animal should be put to work very gradually and systematically, as it is more liable to galls and to breakdown, and until its condition has distinctly improved it should only carry light loads and make short marches, both of which can be increased by stages in comparison with its improvement in condition.

How one that is weak

A camel that is at all sick or weakly from debility or other causes ought at once to be transferred to the sick lines, or, if not bad enough for this, should be kept apart and fed separately, as he does not get a chance with strong healthy ones. In fact, if it were feasible, it would be very much better to separate all camels when feeding them on grain or green fodder. For they are naturally greedy, and will bolt any food which pleases them, or when they are hungry, swallowing it without proper mastication, and they will regularly race each other to see who will eat the most. On these occasions slow eaters and weakly ones fare very badly, and those who are next to bullies—among whom camels, like humanity, have a goodly proportion—get simply nothing but bites. *Moral.*—Bullies should be isolated.

How generally

A camel should never be worked either on an empty or on a full stomach. One is nearly as bad as the other. In the former case a feed should be given them in ample time to allow for rumination, and if time is limited, let the feed be a small one. In the latter instance they ought not to be worked until at least four hours after, so as to give them time to chew the cud and digest the food.

Sleeping capacity

A camel is not a heavy sleeper, and he can apparently do with very little sleep, but what he cannot dispense with, and what in fact he undoubtedly requires, is rest, as well as a certain amount of time in which to chew the cud. For this purpose, and to preserve their condition, camels should be left alone for at least six hours, and no one should be allowed to go near or disturb them in the early part of the night. This rule needs to be strictly enforced, as drivers are late sleepers and inclined to be noisy.

Dead camels, how to be treated

In a standing camp, when a camel dies the body ought to be removed at least one mile from its precincts, to leeward of the prevailing wind, and when the hide has been removed the carcase should either be burnt or buried. On the march, before abandoning a camel a transport officer should make certain that he is done to a turn, and cannot be brought on. If there is any hope of his ultimate recovery, and he cannot find an asylum for the poor brute on the road, he should take what steps he can to provide a certain amount of food and shelter if possible. Above all, he must take all precautions while life is still in them to prevent drivers and others from killing and flaying them for their skins, which they are sure to do when compensation is given for an animal.

Precautions to be taken before abandoning

How camels should be placed

Camels should invariably be placed with their backs to the wind, as they are less exposed, and their chests and loins are better protected. For this reason, arranging them in parallel lines facing one way is undoubtedly the best method, because it has the additional advantage of occupying less space. If, however, the camels have been accustomed to camp in circles, it is wiser to leave existing arrangements alone, so long as they do not interfere with other conditions. Hired drivers prefer this way, because it saves them trouble, and in cold weather they sleep inside the rings ; but owners usually prefer the former plan. An oval is better than a circle, because it also economises space, and the animals who face the wind are rather more protected than in an open ring. But from a transport as well as military standpoint the first-mentioned arrangement is the best, and should always be used.

Space occupied

One camel, in its natural state, occupies about 25 square feet; when laden with a small compact load, 55 square feet, and with a bulky load 75 square feet. A circle with a radius of 11 yards, or a square 22 yards square, will hold fifty camels.

Separation of sexes

It is, as a rule, considered advisable, both in camp and on the line of march, to separate the females from the males, and put them as far away from out of sight and smell of each other as possible. But as a matter of fact, the simplest and most practical way is to isolate an animal when he is vicious or 'mast.' Native camel owners by no means stick rigidly to this rule as far as I know.

Grazing guard

Camels when out grazing anywhere, and at any time, ought to be in charge of a grazing guard. As this is only a precautionary measure to ensure their safety, and to procure the best pasture available, the drivers should be placed under a sectional officer, whose duty it should be to select the most suitable grazing ground in the locality, acting, of course, in accordance with the general instructions issued by the commander of the force. And a divisional officer should visit and inspect the guard at least once a day, to see that all orders have been carried out.

Stable hours

There should be regular stable hours with camels for feeding and grooming as with cavalry horses, and the greatest care and attention should be given to both. For with the useless and scoundrelly class of drivers that we invariably have, the strictest supervision is absolutely necessary—at the former time to prevent robbery of rations, and to see that each animal gets his full allowance; at the latter to ensure a thorough cleaning of animals and equipment. All hands should be present under sectional and divisional officers.

'Particular attention should be paid to the grooming' of camels, and every opportunity that I got on service I always made my men give them a good rubbing down on the hump and back. After devoting a great deal of thought to the question, I have come to the conclusion that the grooming of a camel should be quite as elaborate as that of a horse. And, if anything, it should be more careful. Apart from all other reasons of cleansing from dirt, parasites, &c., I consider it is all the more important in the case of a camel, on account of the deficiency in its skin of perspiratory follicles and ducts, about which I spoke in chapter i. After what I said there I need hardly point out the absolute necessity of keeping the skin as clean as possible, so as to give it every chance of having the pores open and in a state of action, thereby ensuring the health and fitness of the animal. To obtain this a certain amount of friction is necessary, besides giving the animals immense relief and diminishing the chances of sore backs. Therefore, two hours daily devoted to this cannot be more practically and usefully employed. Grooming

For the mane a large wooden comb is useful. For the body a rough brush, a wisp of grass or straw, or a bundle of twigs, will remove the dirt, while a piece of coarse sacking or other rough material will do to rub him down with for a final polish.

A camel is generally infested with ticks and lice, Vermin

unless he is thoroughly well looked after and kept clean. Even then he will pick them up when grazing in the bush. These parasites, the former especially, not only worry and annoy the poor animal, but if left long enough on him will perceptibly reduce his condition, and, in addition to the irritation which they cause, are often the indirect means of producing sores, as the animal will rub and scratch himself against any obstacle to relieve the itching. To prevent this daily grooming is an absolute necessity. Should a camel be badly covered with these parasites, take him away from camp, shear his coat as close as possible, pull and scrape off all you can, and rub his body over with paraffin or carbolic oil.

Remedy

When nothing else has been available, I have often used a powerful infusion of the strongest tobacco, and found it efficacious both for horses and camels; or, if you can get soft soap, the two together make a good mixture. Put ½ lb. of cut cavendish or twist into 2 quarts of boiling water, and let it stand until cool. Also put 2 lb. of soft soap in 2 gallons of water, and stir it up into a solution. Then mix them well, and apply with a medium brush, rubbing it well into the skin. Cover up the animal with a rug until dry, wash off the mixture, and then dry him.

Messrs. Heyward of Lincoln have a cattle wash preparation which is also very useful for the removal of parasites, and of all kinds of itchings in the skin.

Oiling and shearing

In connection with this subject of cleaning and grooming camels there is another matter of great importance, from a hygienic point of view especially, and that is shearing and oiling them. The former is particularly applicable to hot climates, and during the hot and dry seasons, and should be done periodically to prevent the hair from growing. This keeps him cooler, and helps his skin to act more freely, because he can be kept cleaner much more easily. If the nights are at all cool, or the difference between them and day considerable, precautions should be taken to clothe or shelter the animals. The oiling ought to be done frequently and regularly—once a week or oftener if possible. Previous to this the animal should have a thorough good cleaning, and in hot weather a good wash and swim, rubbing the oil well into his skin when dry. One shear to twenty-five camels is a fair proportion, while 4 lb. of mustard oil, and 2 oz. of brimstone mixed with it, is required for each animal. During stable hours, and preparatory to a march, particular attention should be paid to the saddles. These ought to be shaken, beaten, and dusted before putting them on, as it is another preventive against galls, which can be caused by dirt or any hard substance getting in between the pad and the back. Besides, it prevents the padding from getting hard and lumpy, and keeps it soft. The hair on and round the hump should never be allowed to grow long, but must be clipped quite close at all times, as it only becomes tangled and matted, and, especially with a badly-fitting saddle and clumsy load, is certain to chafe the skin.

Camels should be branded on the near side of the neck, and these marks ought to be frequently examined. When an animal is considered or declared unserviceable, the best place to brand them as such is on the near buttock. Branding

Camels that are once pulled down and that have lost their condition from neglect and overwork never Treatment of over-done camels recover, and eventually die from the effects. Those that have fallen into a condition which requires from six months to a year to pick up in should be sold, for even at the end of this time they will be soft and quite unfit for hard work. If they are in the past-recovery stage, it is better and kinder to shoot them. Why let them linger and suffer and die by inches? Besides, their food, medicine, pay of drivers to look after them, cost money, though you have another alternative—turn them out in the desert to graze, and let them take their chance. In a humanitarian sense, keep them; in a transport sense, sell or shoot them, for they are useless, and always will be should they survive, which is doubtful. Most of our expeditions are short-lived, but even when they do exceed the limit these animals, if worked again—most likely before they are thoroughly fit—would in the second instance join the ranks of the majority. And to show how camels of this sort die off, I will quote an instance that occurred in the Afghan campaign on the Candahar side. It was on the line of communication—at Dadur, I think—that the transport officer in charge decided on sending his sick camels back to Jacobabad to graze, rest, and recover. From 1,800 to 2,000 of these animals, in charge of a native cavalry officer, left Dadur, and were driven, unloaded, of course, arriving at Jacobabad, a distance of 116 miles, in a week, with a loss of over 700 on the road. At Suakim, when the campaign was over, the remnant of our camels were in a mangy, emaciated state. Some contractor offered 30*s.* apiece for them all round, but it was refused—foolishly, I think. It would have been better to have taken this low offer, for all, or nearly all, that were used in the Nile expedition very soon died. On the other hand the mules, which in some cases had not been worked at all, and in others only to a very limited extent, that were sold by contract after Tel-el-Kebir, realised large prices—not to Government, but to contractors. A certain Baron de Stein purchased 1,000, and sold most of them on the spot, in batches of from five to fifty, to other people, clearing 100 per cent. on the transaction. The transport officers could have done the same thing, and put the money into the Government coffers; but this practice being strictly forbidden, we were obliged to send away scores of would-be purchasers, who were offering twice, and in some cases three times, the contract price.

Every sectional, divisional, and company commander should keep a diary, especially on service. This ought to be officially insisted on, as the importance of a well-kept diary cannot be overrated. It should be inspected on completion, and the writer judged impartially on its practical merits, as well as on the amount of actual work performed by him.

CHAPTER XIII

COMPARISON WITH OTHER ANIMALS

This is a subject not to be entered on too lightly, for a difference of opinion seems to exist as to the capabilities of the various animals used for pack transport, some asserting the superiority of the mule, others of the camel. These opinions are most likely founded on the fact that the holders of them have worked exclusively, or at least oftener with one animal than with the other, or that they have not had an opportunity of instituting a comparison between them. One fact must not be lost sight of, and that is, that when you have various kinds of animals doing transport work, as we had in Afghanistan, where the conditions of climate and food did not suit all alike, it is hardly fair to depreciate any one kind, which, like the Sind and Panjab camels, from the hot dry climate of sandy plains, accustomed to graze on leaves and saline herbs, were suddenly brought into an intensely cold mountainous country, entirely destitute of covering, and deprived of their natural food, &c. Or would it be just to compare them with the mules, who were in their element in the long rocky defiles and mountain passes? No, here as elsewhere the camel had hardly a chance given him. He—I do not, of course, include the hill camel, of which a number were employed—was quite out of his element, like the proverbial fish, who has been ruthlessly snatched by some ardent angler from an element which is life itself to him and thrown high and dry on to another which means but death. It would, therefore, be needlessly unfair to criticise and condemn him. He was misunderstood, consequently mismanaged. To get at his true working capacity he must on no account be judged from our past experiences of him, and yet it has no doubt taught those who had their eyes open what his real value is.

Let us take a rapid glance at the eligibility of each animal for military pack and draught transport, and begin with the elephant.

The elephant is up to great weight, from 2,000 lb. to a ton, but in spite of his great size and strength he is not well adapted for transport work, and should never be used except under the most favourable conditions. He requires good roads, abundance of food and water (not only for drinking but for washing purposes), and a temperate climate. He eats too much, and is costly to maintain; is very delicate, and highly susceptible to climatic changes—cannot stand cold, and altogether requires a lot of mollicoddling. Lives, as a rule, to a great age. In 1878, marching from Jacobabad to Candahar, my company was escort to a heavy battery, drawn by 11 elephants and 300 oxen. We only lost one of the former—within sight of Candahar, too—but this was due to the extreme care and attention lavished on them by the officer in command, and the amount of good things—'chapatties' (cakes of unleavened bread), rice, sugar and rum (a couple of bottles at a time)—given to them of an evening after a march. The

The elephant

faces of the men, and their remarks as they looked on with watering mouths and overpowering envy, were worthy of a camp ballad by Rudyard Kipling, or a picture by Simpson. The other heavy battery, which had the same number of elephants, lost four or five on the same march. Elephants are inclined to be lazy, and will not pull if they take it into their heads not to do so. They are also uncommonly sharp, and possess a large amount of reasoning power. I had frequent opportunities of judging on this march, but will quote only a couple of instances to bear out my statement.

'*Sir-i-Bolan. Dec.* 26, 1878.—The elephants riled me to-day. There were three of them in a gun, which any one of them might have hauled by himself had he only chosen to do so, but no coaxing or persuasion on the part of the "mahout" [driver] would make them exert themselves. They simply would not pull, whether it was from stubbornness or laziness I can't quite make up my mind, the latter I am inclined to think. I picked up a pebble and threw it at the one nearest to me. He felt it about as much as he would have a fly, but the cunning old brute resented it, and turning his near eye on me with a kind of roguish twinkle in it, and his trunk at the same time, he singled me out from among several men who were close to me, and soused me all over with water—about a gallon—which he had in his trunk.'

Another instance of this sagacity occurred on the first march out from Dadur, when the leading elephant in one of the guns, while crossing the river, suddenly stopped, and would not go on, in spite of several blows which the driver gave him on the head, until he had lowered his trunk into the water and pulled out a pannikin, of the same pattern used by the men, and raising his trunk handed it to the mahout. Then he went on again. An elephant is better for draught transport, and can draw about 8,000 lb., or four times as much as he can carry, and he is useful for siege trains and heavy ordnance; but he will not stand fire at all. His feet are very tender, and easily knocked up. The conclusion I came to before reaching Candahar was that they were not the animals for the country. They are not fitted for this work; for in crossing the deep heavy sand of the desert between Jacobabad and Dadur they floundered along, sunk deep into it, and were frequently done to a turn if it happened to be exceptionally heavy; while in the Bolan Pass the rough stony shingle completely knocked up their feet, which seem to be tender at all times.

Bullocks

The opinions that prevail about this beast are very contradictory. Some say he is an excellent pack animal with great patience and endurance. Others condemn him *in toto* as least suited, because he is a slow mover, loses condition when underfed (but what beast, after all, does not?), is easily knocked up, is timid, and given to falling down with his load. He carries only 160 to 200 lb., very little in proportion to his size and strength, and at his best moves but slowly. He is better in draught. Is not long lived. My own personal experience of an Indian bullock inclines me to agree on most points with the latter statement. Like ponies and mules he must be regularly shod. He is specially unfitted for stony country, and soon gets footsore and bruised. I do not know so much about his patience and timidity, but I can answer for his obstinacy. For downright sheer obstinacy commend me to an Indian bullock. The mule is not in it with him, and is a paragon compared with him. You may have trouble in loading a mule, but once loaded he will go until he can go no further; but the bullock will quietly lie down—not from weakness, but of his own accord—and nothing on earth will move him. To quote again from my Diary:—

'*December* 24, 1878.—Here we had some trouble, as the leading bullocks in one of the mortars lay down and refused to budge an inch. After making every effort to induce them to rise, we had to unyoke the stubborn brutes and haul them out of the way with drag ropes. Then the remaining pair would not pull an ounce, so, putting all the men on the ropes, we dragged the gun, bullocks and all, up the incline.'

One more instance:—

'*December* 26, 1878.—We had not gone more than two miles, during which we had crossed the river three times and found the road very heavy, when we came across four wagons belonging to the left half-battery, which we literally dragged into camp the whole way—about seven miles—because the bullocks would not pull. One leading bullock, in particular, gave no end of trouble. He lay down six times, and each time but the last we got him up with the greatest difficulty, only to lie down again. At last he would not move, and we were nearly out of our wits. However, by dint of sheer force we got him up, when, without a note of warning, this brute, whom we had thought to be in the last stage of exhaustion, rushed at Wardall (a private in my company), and tossed him about ten feet in the air, then on to the next man who was standing near, and sent him flying, and lastly at his own driver, whom he tumbled over like a ninepin, the rest of us, scattering like chaff before the wind, took refuge behind the wagons. However, we soon tackled him, and put him in the yoke again and went on; but before we got five yards he was down again, and had finally to be unyoked and driven into camp. This march, though only 8½ miles long, occupied ten hours.'

Frequently on this march between Jacobabad and Candahar we were obliged specially to halt because elephants and bullocks were entirely done up, and suffering from galls and sore feet. 'The road' (so I wrote on December 27, 1878) 'since we left Jacobabad has been dotted here and there with carcases of bullocks and camels, and since Dadur it has been worse. We ourselves [i.e. the battery] have been for the last three weeks leaving three or four of the latter daily. Three bullocks died on this day alone, a good many more are lame and done up, over thirty are sick and unfit for work, while others are suffering from the foot-and-mouth disease. Truly a pretty state of affairs before we are half way. What will it be later on?'

As a draught animal the Indian bullock is not a success, except in the plains of India, under favourable conditions; but in South Africa he has proved himself very useful. What would have been done without him it is hard to say? One bullock in a light cart on level ground can draw about 800 lb.; over hilly ground 500 lb. A pair of bullocks on the level 1,500 lb. I am speaking of the Indian animal. In South Africa, in the Colony, and more civilised parts, a team of fourteen to sixteen oxen draw up to 8,000 lb., I am told.

From Tuli to Salisbury, and even from Johannesburg and Mafeking up to Tuli, transport riders did not as a rule carry more than 5,000 lb., and occasionally 6,000 lb., as the roads were rough and heavy and the distance long.

The mule

The mule is about the handiest and hardiest of all pack animals. He can work in any country, and under every condition of climate, but is specially suited for mountainous regions. He will go over any ground, no matter how steep and rocky, he is so very sure-footed and nimble. His toughness and endurance are perfectly marvellous, and it is wonderful how long and on how little he seems to live and even thrive upon. He is less liable to sore backs and galls than any other animal, the donkey excepted. He is a fast walker, and will keep up 3 miles an hour on average ground, and on good I have known him to do 3½. Even on a bad road over rocks and hills he will do 2½ miles an hour; but of course heavy sand is very trying to him, as it is for all animals except the camel. He is accused of being obstinate and ill-tempered, but this—if it is the case—arises almost wholly from ill-treatment during juvenility, as well as from the woful ignorance of the animal's ways that generally prevails among Britishers. The mule is naturally docile and patient in the hands of those who understand him and who treat him kindly, and he will show them as much affection nearly as a horse. He strongly objects to be hit over the head and kicked violently in the ribs or stomach, as I have frequently caught Tommy Atkins doing, and naturally enough this brutal treatment by no means improves his temper or his manners, so he returns it by biting, kicking, and becoming generally refractory. It is generally supposed that they live from fifteen to twenty years, though some live to thirty, and a few beyond that age. When I was in India fifteen years ago there were mules belonging to the Commissariat who were said to have been twenty-two years in the service, and were still working. In embarking some at Suez for service in Suakim, in 1884, one baffled all our efforts to get him on board for a very long time. He was a perfect demon, and attacked the men open-mouthed when they went to sling him. He was uncommonly cunning as well, for no sooner did he make his rush than he used to slew round like a teetotum and clear the ground with his hind legs. Then when we managed to get into close quarters with him, his teeth and fore legs were brought into play. Even when we had lassoed, thrown, and gagged him it was no use, for he still made use of his hind and fore legs most violently. However, finally we managed to tie these together, and after a tremendous struggle we got him into the sling and on board; but about thirty mules could have been slung in the time. This, however, was an exceptional case. The Indian pack mule, or I should say the pack mule used in India, ranging between twelve and thirteen hands, is by far the best I have seen. I dislike taller mules for pack work. The shorter ones are handier and much easier to load, much more so when they are fresh and obstreperous, as at the beginning of a march or after a rest. In the Egyptian Expedition of 1882 I worked with 400 Sicilian mules, and splendid animals they were too, but, on the whole, they were in my opinion a trifle too tall for pack work. At Ismailia, with these same mules under Maltese drivers, assisted by a handful of commissariat and transport men, who as a matter of fact did all the work, it took us from six in the morning until 8.30 at night to saddle and load 200 mules, and it was 9.30 before we got clear of the commissariat stores on our way to the front, on a pitch-dark night too. Those first few days were an experience in themselves, and such as one wants but once in a lifetime, and I shall never forget them. It was not until Tel-el-Kebir had been fought, and our services no longer required, that we began to get shipshape and into working order. The mules had long since settled down, but the drivers—oh! the drivers—were fiends incarnate. I might give many instances of mulish experiences; but I have already said enough. As a draught animal on service I have had no experience with him, though from what I have seen of him in India and South Africa, in Cape carts and coaches, I have a very high opinion of his powers. Spanish mules are also magnificent creatures, but from what I know of them they seem to be bred nearly exclusively for draught work, some of the smaller sized ones being reserved for the mountain artillery.

Ponies

I have had a good deal to do with ponies, and have always found them excellent. They are very tough, and thrive on very little food, and country-breds, such as the Indian tats, and those of Egypt and Syria (which have a good strain of Arabian blood in them) can do—or more correctly go—without water for a longish time. At Suakim in 1884, and up the Nile in 1885, the country-breds which carried the 10th and 19th Hussars, carrying 17 to 18 stone on an average, were on one or two occasions without water for thirty-six hours in the former, and forty-eight in the latter expedition. The ponies or small-sized horses bred in Kordofan are strong, handy, and said on an emergency to travel sixty hours without water. Ponies are very plucky, and very liable to sore backs and galls, especially when in poor condition, and they require far more care than mules and donkeys. They will walk as fast as a mule, and carry on an average 150 lb. They are too small and too light for draught work.

In my estimation, the donkey is the toughest customer of the lot; but his size, therefore small weight-carrying capacity, is against him, speaking comparatively of course, for in proportion to his size he is up to great weight. Even the very smallest will carry an average of 130 lb. He is, if anything, more enduring and will thrive on less food than the mule, and he is not shod. In Nubia and the Soudan, in the deserts east and west of the Nile, the natives have a very small species, which is very tough and hardy. They make them carry from 120 to 150 lb., and often ride them through the deserts without water for fifty to sixty hours, and with just the scanty browsing they can pick up. I believe in the donkey most implicitly for transport, in spite of his smallness and the numbers that would have to be employed. This, of course, would be one of the chief reasons against him, as I doubt if sufficient could be obtained. To supply the fighting lines, and even the supports and reserves, with ammunition he would be invaluable. He can carry two boxes, can be kept out of sight, and can keep up easily; besides, the ammunition would be much easier to get at. He cannot Donkeys walk as fast as either a pony or a mule, his average pace being 2½ miles an hour; but he requires far less care and attention, fewer drivers (one to six or eight), and infinitely less rations to carry, and he is little or no trouble to look after, for he has great patience and docility. The establishment of breeding studs and the greater employment of the donkey as a transport animal is well worth the attention of the military authorities. In Europe, Spain and Portugal stand first, not only in point of numbers, but in the excellence of their donkeys, it being computed that there are over 2,500,000 in the Peninsula. They are noted for their beauty and good breeding, which naturally accounts for the excellence of the mules. Italy is likewise famous for its breeds, and numbers over 500,000; France coming next with about 400,000, and the United Kingdom with about 350,000; but I do not think either the French or ourselves take any care or trouble in breeding them.

The donkey in Southern Afghanistan is about the same size as the Nubian, and very strong and wiry. I have seen them carrying 130 lb. apiece, and sometimes up to 180 lb., without any pack, over the rough mountain passes of the Kojak. The Syrian donkeys are the finest I have ever seen, and are very strong and large, up to 13 hands 3 in., and even 14 hands. I have never used them for transport, but imagine they would answer the purpose very well. They are excellent for riding and have good paces. They would be invaluable for the stud, and would immensely improve the breed. The Berber breed would, from what I have read, be also an acquisition. The majority are black, and have a wonderfully glossy coat. They are very high at the shoulder, most comfortable to ride, and at the same time quick in their paces. They were very cheap too, costing (in 1878) from 10 to 20 dollars (2*l.* to 4*l.*). Their present price I do not know. The donkeys in Lower Egypt, which I imagine have been crossed a good deal with the Syrian, are also a fine lot, and smart in their paces. My only acquaintance with them has been in the towns—Cairo, Alexandria, Ismailia, &c.—where the donkey-boys, who are as sharp as needles, in shrill chorus almost insist on your riding such world-renowned celebrities as Lord Wolseley, Lady Florence Dixie, Mrs. Langtry, Prince Bismarck, &c., &c.

Having sketched roughly the advantages and disadvantages of the different animals, it now remains for us to decide on the one we consider the best for pack transport. I do not think I am wrong in saying that, on the whole, the preponderance of military opinion is in favour of the mule, who has been called the king of transport animals. I have worked with all of them, and personally I have no hesitation in saying that, under existing conditions, mismanaged as the camel is, and taking him all round, for military purposes he is the best, though the donkey will run him very close. His two advantages over the mule are that on an average he will carry 50 to 80 lb. more and walk quicker, whereas the donkey has three or four over him; but we have no time now to go fully into this question; and as the mule is the generally acknowledged favourite, we will endeavour to strike a comparison between him and the camel, who, though he may not be considered quite so generally useful, is sufficiently so, apart from numbers, to make him indispensable on service; and who, I maintain, if properly treated and managed, would prove, even for military purposes, a more economical and useful animal than the former.

The mule, on account of his hardiness and quickness of pace, is generally considered preferable to a baggage camel on a long and rapid march, such, for instance, as General (now Lord) Roberts's march from Cabul to Candahar, a distance of 350 miles, over a road, well watered, and through a large tract of cultivated country. His fighting force was 10,000 strong, and owing to the precarious condition of affairs at Candahar it was necessary to march as quickly as possible. For this reason, all wheeled carriages and baggage camels were left behind, and mules chiefly, also ponies and donkeys, were substituted. As regimental transport officer I remember handing over to the 2nd 60th Rifles 319 mules, all fit and in splendid fettle, in exchange for camels. Had General Roberts marched with picked baggage camels instead, I think he would have reached his destination as soon as he did, for his march occupied nineteen marching days, or only a daily average of 14¾ miles; but had it been possible for him to mount his force on riding camels—marching very light—with perhaps a very small percentage of baggagers, he would have got there in about half the time that he did.

Against this achievement I will quote Sir Herbert Stewart's first forced march from Korti to Gakdool (96 to 100 miles on the road to Metammeh), where there was a large storage of water which it was incumbent that we should seize before the enemy, and hold, so as to enable us to dash across the Bayuda desert. With 1,000 fighting men on camels, and 580 baggagers laden with stores, we reached Gakdool in 66 hours, marching 13 hours daily, halted 30 hours, returning empty in 48 hours. In addition to this (13 hours' marching), the camels were kept loaded for some time previous to marching each morning, and some were never unloaded (for 66 hours) until Gakdool was reached. The effect of this on the baggagers was simply disastrous; but in addition to this, and previous to the march, they had been worked on the lines of communication, were in a weak condition, and tolerably stale, instead of fresh. The riding camels had also marched a long way (mostly from Assouan), but were in better trim, and consequently did not suffer so badly. Of the baggagers 55 died, 12 were shot, and 43 abandoned, to say nothing of the majority who were suffering from galls and exhaustion, so much so that when Sir Herbert, a few days after, started the second time for Gakdool *en route* to Metammeh, not one of these camels could go as they were all unfit. I have given these as tolerably fair examples of the two animals; but I must ask you to make a note of the very important fact that, while in the former case the transport had been resting for a long time and was fresh, in the latter—as we have just seen—they had already been overworked, and were as stale as stale could be. As I have already remarked, in our hands the camel never gets a fair chance. Had these camels been quite fit, as they should have been for such a rapid and risky undertaking, they would have come out much better than they did without doubt. Even as it was, it is simply wonderful to think that, in spite of everything being against them, they covered a daily average of 34 miles in the first march, and of 20 in the second, which was nearly 200 miles in length, and included two days' halt, and two general actions, which delayed us another two days, so that the camels actually marched about 30 miles a day. It is my firm impression that not one of these—and other camels similarly used—ever recovered from the terrible effects of the work they were forced to do, but that one and all died eventually. One can hardly compare the two marches, not only for this reason, but also because (1) Roberts had 10,150 fighting men and 8,145 followers, ten times Stewart's force, which was mounted, even the transport, while his were chiefly infantry; (2) the distance was much greater, and (3) so were the impedimenta (guns included) and the number of followers, Stewart having no impedimenta to speak of, a few seven-pounder and machine guns, and only some camel drivers, from 100 to 150.

But though the mule actually walks faster, the baggager of the right stamp, and in proper hands, will for all practical purposes cover as much ground daily as the former, while the Sawari will jog away from him in no time. In other respects a mule has the following advantages over the baggager: (1) he can stand climatic changes, heat and cold, wet and dry; (2) on this account he is hardier and tougher; (3) can tolerate any ground except heavy sand. On the other hand, he has always to be shod regularly, in rocky hilly country especially, though ponies and mules, if never shod from their birth, can go over any ground if their hoofs are regularly looked after; (2) requires more attendants; (3) carries only half the weight a camel can; (4) requires food and water to be carried for him.' Now as to the camel: (1) he has greater powers of abstinence from food and water; (2) carries double; (3) requires fewer drivers; (4) is never shod; (5) procurable in greater numbers and more easily; (6) initial outlay less; (7) cost of maintenance less. It is asserted that a number of camels will cover half the length of road on the line of march that the equivalent number of mules will; for instance, 800 camels tied in strings will cover about from 1½ to 1¾ mile, while 1,600 mules will extend nearly 3 miles; but I doubt this very much, as the latter do not straggle so much, and, being more even-paced, keep better together.

Lieut. Massoutier, in comparing a camel with a mule, is of opinion that, because of the special treatment and management of the former, which necessitates extra supervision and greater care and attention, more trouble in fact, it is more difficult to keep order and regularity in a convoy of camels than in one of mules. Certainly, so far as we are concerned, and under existing conditions, I think he is right, because we know nothing of the camels, invariably get animals of the worst description, and place them in the hands of useless and incompetent men. But if we were to reverse this order of things, I feel quite convinced that we should attain the very best results, and find that order and regularity could be as well, if not better, kept among camels than mules. The latter, as a rule, are difficult to manage, and at times are very fractious and troublesome, especially in the hands of men who do not understand them. In fact, the whole question, no matter what the animal, depends on the drivers, and you will not obtain such good results from the very finest mules in the hands of fools and ignoramuses as you will out of moderate camels driven by good men, and *vice versâ*.

It will therefore be seen from above that, though the former for certain general conditions is superior to the latter, the latter in reality has more points in his favour, which quite equalise, if they do not counterbalance, the drawbacks, but from which I should draw the following deductions. That for certain services in mountainous districts the mule *par excellence* is the animal, and *vice versâ* in flat countries the camel. But again, for general transport purposes, in a large campaign especially, on account of the last three points chiefly the camel is undoubtedly the animal to employ. Let us compare the comparative yearly cost—approximately, of course—of a company of camel transport, and of its mule equivalent, and let us take the organisation of a company of the former to be as stated in chapter xi. :—

	£
1 captain at 400*l*. a year	400
2 subalterns at 300*l*. a year each	600
8 conductors at 150*l*. a year each	1,200
8 headmen at 6*s*. per day each=48 × 30=1,440 × 12	864
200 drivers at 3*s*. per day each=600 × 30=18,000 × 12	10,800
11 Europeans' rations at 2*s*. a day =22 × 30=660 × 12	396
208 natives' rations at 1*s*. a day=208 × 30=6,240 × 12	3,994
	18,254

Take a camel's ration at 8 lb. of grain and 30 lb.

of chaff daily, the former at 1*l.* per 100 lb., the latter at 10*s.* per 100 lb.:—

	£
Brought forward	18,254
8 lb. of grain × 30 × 12 × 800 = 2,304,000 lb. ÷ 100	23,040
30 lb. of chaff × 30 × 12 × 800 = 8,640,000 lb. ÷ 200	43,200
	84,494

1,600 mules are the carrying equivalent to 800 camels. These would have to be divided into companies of 400 each. Each company to consist of two divisions under a subaltern, each division of two sections under a conductor, viz.:—

	£
1 captain at 400*l.* a year	400
2 subalterns at 300*l.* a year each	600
4 conductors at 150*l.* a year each	1,200
4 headman at 6*s.* per day = 24 × 30 = 720 × 12 . .	432
200 drivers at 3*s.* per day = 600 × 30 = 18,000 × 12 .	10,800
7 Europeans' rations at 2*s.* a day = 14 × 30 = 420 × 12	252
204 natives' rations at 1*s.* a day = 204 × 30 = 6,120 × 12	3,672
	17,356

A mule ration is 8 lb. grain and 10 lb. chaff:—

	£
Brought forward	17,356
8 lb. of grain × 30 × 12 × 400 = 1,152,000 ÷ 100 .	11,520
10 lb. of chaff × 30 × 12 × 400 = 1,440,000 ÷ 200 .	7,200
	36,076

36,076*l.* × 4 = 144,304*l.* against 84,494*l.*, which leaves a balance of 59,810*l.* in favour of the camel transport. Now let us take the initial outlay. 800 camels at 15*l.* apiece (a high price) equals 12,000*l.* 1,600 mules at the same price will cost double this, but 20*l.* to 25*l.* each is more likely to be the price, which would mean a greater outlay of from 20,000*l.* to 28,000*l.*; while the mule equipment would also amount to about three times as much as the camels' (say 4,000*l.*

as compared with 1,500*l.*); so that, roughly speaking, camel transport is both in initial and yearly expenditure half as cheap as mule. The loss by death I have not taken into consideration, as this is difficult even to approximate. It would be in favour of the latter; but remember that, even were the rate to be double, the comparative original cost of each animal would minimise if not equalise this. Nor have I gone into the extra amount of kit and rations that would have to be carried for 800 drivers and 1,600 mules, as against 200 drivers and 800 camels; but I think I have sufficiently examined the question to show that camel transport has been unnecessarily despised and underrated, and I must again reiterate what I have so frequently stated in these pages, that a camel in his own country and climate is second to none, while in proper hands he is invaluable anywhere.

Camels for draught

Camels can be and are used for draught. In parts of Central Asia they are harnessed to wagons, and employed by the Russians to carry heavy loads. And in the Kara-Kum desert, along the Orsk Kazala high road, they take the place of the post horses, and as such carry both mails and passengers. The Kirghiz yoke their camels to a kind of cart, and in Orenburg or elsewhere yokes of four camels are used for ploughing. In winter, when the steppes are thickly covered with snow, they are employed in drawing sleighs. In Central India, also, and the North-West Provinces they are in use all the year round. I have seen them in Agra and Muttra—between which places four-wheeled carts carrying native passengers and goods run regularly—the carts are covered, and are long, low and clumsy.

They are of two sizes—the smaller, drawn by one camel, takes twelve to fourteen passengers, or from 1,200 to 1,600 lb. of goods; the larger one, drawn by two, carries sixteen passengers, or 2,000 lb. to a ton of goods. Their pace is about the same as when carrying packs; so that in draught one camel draws about four times as much as he will carry, and in comparison to an ox or mule for drawing heavily laden wagons, one camel will draw twice as much as either.

We have all through discussed the baggager only, but before concluding I should like to say a few words in favour of the riding camel. Not only is he useful for commercial and postal work, but in maintaining law and order, for police and military purposes, patrolling and flying columns, or fast work of any description, the riding camel would simply be invaluable, and far more suitable and in the end more economical than the horse, especially all over South Africa, where the deadly horse sickness has to be reckoned with. Of course he has drawbacks—viz. (1) he is essentially gregarious, and should be ridden in company; (2) is not nearly so handy as a horse or pony, but though perhaps unwieldy in thick bush, you can see farther off his back; (3) is unhandy in wet and slippery and soft boggy ground. However, in spite of these, he is a splendid animal for the duties above mentioned. The whole question, I think, hinges upon his proper treatment and management; but even throwing this into the scale, there is no doubt whatever in my mind of the vast superiority of the riding camel over the horse, and the baggager over pack-animals, and the more unfavourable the conditions, the greater the superiority. Riding camels

CHAPTER XIV

PURCHASING

To purchase camels for transport purposes is not so easy a task as might be supposed. On the contrary, it is an operation that on the part of the purchaser requires great practical experience and knowledge of the animal, as well as plenty of tact and discrimination in dealing with the wily native. It most certainly ought not to be entrusted to anyone, and yet invariably you will find this to be the case; during the late Afghan war, for instance—and especially in the Nile expedition—where many an officer had never seen a camel, except perhaps in the days of his youth, at the Zoological Gardens in Regent's Park.

Purchasing officers to be specially selected

Officers—veterinary surgeons, if available—under present arrangements should be specially selected for their knowledge and experience of transport and transport animals in general, but camels in particular, and the deeper their knowledge, and the wider their experience, the better. It is self-evident that an army cannot make war without an efficient transport. The commissariat has been very truly called the 'belly of the army'—equally so the transport is the 'legs.' Without its legs no army can move. It is crippled, helpless in fact. Even when the legs are only shaky—in other words, when the transport is inefficient—the mobility of an army is considerably diminished, consequently it is far more vulnerable, and exposed to the attack of an active and mobile force. At the outset, therefore, of our little wars, owing to a defective system, animals have to be bought here, there, and everywhere, in large numbers, and in a great hurry. For though we recognise in theory the truism of that ancient precept, quoted in more recent times by Washington, that 'to be prepared for war is one of the most effectual means of preserving peace,' and although we acknowledge the soundness of its principles, British-like we never act up to it.

I believe we mean to, but somehow or other we never do. With what results? All those who are acquainted with the history of our expeditions during the past twenty years or so could tell; or if that enterprising American, Mr. Garner, who has recently encaged himself in the heart of Africa in order to learn 'monkey language,' could only go a trifle further, and master the mysteries of the camel tongue, what an extraordinary flood of light would be thrown on the diabolical sufferings and hideous tortures that have been forced on the poor camel by stern-hearted man, especially were he to have the good fortune to drop across a survivor—which I strongly doubt—from either the Afghan or Nile expeditions! What a tale of woe, and what a lesson to us for future guidance!

Time ignored

And so men are sent out to purchase against time—make a note of this, for 'time' is an all-important factor, the most important, in fact, in war, and is ignored—men whose sole idea is to buy as many animals as they can; good or bad, old or young, it is all the same to them, so long as they can produce a large number. Quality and fitness for the work is a thought which never troubles them. They take no interest in these points. They are buying against time; their orders are to lose no time. The Government, without any warning to the military authorities, have made war. The general in command must move at once. He bullies the director of transport, who in turn worries the purchasing officer, who to satisfy his chief gets rid of the money entrusted to him as quickly as he can, and buys in the most reckless fashion. And so it will always be, so long as our system remains unchanged. I do not altogether blame the individuals. In some cases it is as I have just stated; in others the buyers are conscientious enough, no doubt, but frequently how many of them know anything about a camel—his points, characteristics, &c.? They know the points of a horse, and when buying him will know what they are about; but a camel! Why, many of them do not even know that he has a point. Whereas in reality a camel has more points to look at and consider than a horse; therefore a buyer cannot be too careful and too particular in his inspection, for camel owners all the world over—like the horse-selling fraternity—are only too ready to plant on the unsuspecting 'griff' their most worthless screws, only too anxious to get rid of the extremely old and the very young to ignorant and careless buyers. No, I do not blame the individual officers so much as the system that admits of such an entire want of system, and that employs such material. If, as in the Afghan and the Nile campaigns, these animals have to march a long distance—very probably before they are inspected by a veterinary surgeon or competent transport officer—they are found to be too young, or too old, therefore unfit for work—in fact, totally useless. They are a dead loss to the Government, for the natives who have sold them have only done so to get rid of them. Naturally they always sell their worst animals; in fact, the carrying tribes in India and the Soudan are averse to selling, and if they buy at all—which I doubt—they would only give a nominal price for juveniles, while the older and worn-out ones only fetch a mere song from the butchers, who convert them into meat. One of the real reasons that breeders and owners will not sell or hire to us on service is on account of the enormous death rate among the camels, which is a distinct loss to them in point of yearly revenue. They are bound to lose by it either way, unless in the latter case compensation was given them on the death of each camel, which would be an immense expense, but the only way out of the difficulty. It was only by giving liberal compensation in the case of loss of camels that the French in Algeria were enabled to cope with native prejudice against parting with their camels. Besides this, they found it necessary (1) to humour the headmen, (2) to make requisitions bear as lightly and equably as possible on the different tribes, (3) and to issue payments regularly without deductions. But in spite of all these advantages they have never overcome the native unwillingness.

But this is by no means the worst feature of the question, for both in Afghanistan and up the Nile a great many camels under three years, and even two years old (and without their permanent teeth), which

The worst feature

were passed (or, what is more probable, had never been inspected at all), were made to work. If this is not going out of the way to be unjustifiably and unnecessarily cruel, I do not know what is. None of these poor beasts did any real work, because from the very beginning they were unfit, and they were very soon broken down or killed. In the march from Sukkur to Candahar in 1878, and in keeping up supplies on that side during 1879, numbers of juveniles were worked; and it is a fact that in some convoys 37 per cent. of the camels were two years old and under three. In the march from Korti to Metammeh a large percentage were under four years old, and out of fifty camels that my company got from the Remount Depôt, which were placed on the rearguard under the sergeant-major, not one carried a load. They were all snippets—between two and four years old—too young and too feeble. There were no spare animals with the column except these, so extra loads had to be placed on other camels in order to supply the rearguard with a few spare mounts; and as a matter of course many of those which carried the extra light weight succumbed.

Cause of failure in Afghanistan

I do not attribute our failure of the transport in Afghanistan entirely to the Indian Commissariat or to the lack of system on their part, but in a great measure (1) to want of system generally; (2) to the Indian Government, who did not give them timely notice; (3) to the fact that Sir Donald Stewart's orders were to march to Candahar without delay. And although he did not get ahead of his transport, as Lord Wolseley did in 1882, yet he marched 400 miles in the depth of winter, through a barren country, with a hastily improvised transport—a scratch pack, one might almost say—a transport composed principally of camels, which rapidly dwindled away from the causes which I have so often reiterated in these pages—starvation, cold, overwork, &c., &c., and yet again &c.

What we shall do if a big war were to break out on our north-west frontier—say, against the Afghans, or to repel a Russian advance—it is hard to say, but camels would, I imagine, be very difficult to obtain—(1) because our losses in Afghanistan were so enormous; (2) distinct loss of revenue to owners, and their aversion to selling; (3) their preference to hire their camels for trading purposes; (4) the stories in circulation of the countless hardships and miseries that camp-followers had to endure during the late Afghan war, which have done incalculable mischief; (5) loss of ordinary carrying trade.

Effect of demand for camels, and remedy

The demand for a large number of camels naturally enough causes a rise in the tariff for transport of traders' goods whether the authorities buy or hire, for in either case a sensible reduction is made in the number of animals available for the trading caravans, and prices immediately go up. To obviate this, and to render themselves entirely independent of native owners, should be a sufficient inducement for the Government to breed its own camels.

Failure in supply on expedition for Gordon's relief

The remarks as to the failure of our transport in Afghanistan apply in like measure to Egypt. In the expedition for Gordon's relief, whatever the reasons were, we were distinctly short-handed all through the campaign, and could have done with double the number of camels from the very commencement. That this was not due to scarcity of animals anyone with a knowledge of the country would at once admit, and dismiss the very idea as a thought of the idlest description. That the price had nothing to do with it can also be put to one side as equally idle, considering we were paying treble the ordinary value for a common baggager. Nor was it due to animosity; for the great Bedawin tribes in Upper and Lower Egypt, if not in sympathy with us, were at all events not openly hostile or even neutrally inimical to us. Besides, this would not have influenced them in any way; for though co-religionists with the Dervishes, there their sympathy ended; and being an avaricious, grasping lot, they would not have lost an opportunity to sell, and so make money. Economy on the part of the authorities—not to spend more than a certain amount on transport—may have had a little to do with it; but in reality the deep-rooted aversion, on the same grounds as above, that all camel owners have of parting with any animals but those which are useless to them, had much more to say to it. This, at least, is the only reasonable conclusion that I can come to, and ought to be a warning to us for future guidance.

Should, however, no attempt be made to form a Remount Establishment—a formation which cannot be too strongly advocated—for the purpose of breeding camels, and of instructing soldiers in all their habits and characteristics from birth to maturity; if we prefer to remain in a state of unpreparedness—the same unsystematic state that we always have been in—I can arrive at no other conclusion but what we came to in the first few lines of this chapter, that purchasing officers will have to be men of the greatest experience, otherwise in the next war the collapse of the transport, as heretofore, may well be anticipated.

It is no easy matter to formulate a system of transport, and it would be presumption on my part to put forward a scheme, which—in order to meet the varied requirements, under diverse conditions of climate, country, circumstances, and warfare, that our troops are called upon to cope with in all parts of the globe—would have to be based on such broad lines as would enable a peace establishment to be rapidly expanded and readily concentrated in time of war.

Formation of remount depôts

In fact it seems to me—fighting, as we have to, in countries where wheeled transport cannot, and pack animals have to, be used—that the formation of an establishment such as I have suggested, where officers and men could be taught the ways, not only of camels, but of mules, donkeys, bullocks, &c., would be not only practicable but feasible; for I maintain that a transport officer, to be competent, ought to thoroughly understand all animals that he is likely to come in contact with. In fact, I go further and say, as I remarked before, that all transport officers should go through a proper veterinary course and become qualified vets. For where on service can you ever obtain the services of a vet., and when do you ever have any medicines given you? I have often been in charge of a large number of animals, sometimes over 500, in the wilds without a drug of any sort. What we want in peace time is the nucleus of a proper transport department, which on the advent of war would be capable of immediate expansion and development; and to my thinking there is literally nothing to hinder a scheme of this kind being carried out, with the formation of depôts and schools of instruction in England, Cyprus, Egypt, India, South Africa, and Australia. We might very well learn a wholesome lesson from the Germans, by copying their *etappen* system in principle and spirit, but not in blind imitation, as the conditions under which the two armies fight are so diametrically opposite. The whole essence of their system lying in the fact that during peace time their transport train is only maintained to a modified extent—sufficient to meet ordinary requirements—but capable of extreme expansion at any moment, because the nucleus is already there, while each train battalion belonging to an army corps is nothing but a nursery or training depôt for young soldiers, who for six months of their service are instructed thoroughly in all transport duties before they are sent back to their homes. Bactrian camels, and those from Afghanistan or any such cold climate, would thrive just as well in a remount depôt in England as in the Zoo. What in the world is there to prevent their introduction, and the formation of camel and mule transport? Nothing, that I can see.

The sensation on seeing the great awkward beast, with his long neck, big hump, gawky legs, and prominent but beautiful eye swinging along the streets of a garrison town might at first be strange, but it would soon die away, and—as with lions of the Stanley and Cetewayo type, and other curiosities—we would soon become accustomed to him. Of what earthly use, except perhaps in England, are those clumsy, lumbering transport wagons and those great fine horses? Those who were in Egypt in 1882 could answer this, and could tell you how, on the way to Kassassin, the wagons stuck in the deep loose sand, and how the poor unacclimatised horses broke their hearts in struggling to haul them out under a hot sun! Even at home these wagons should be done away with, and in their stead wheeled mule transport be substituted, but only to a certain extent, for a good proportion of camel and mule pack transport should be maintained also. Then, as in 1882, if we were to have a row in Egypt, or elsewhere in a country of a like nature, according to the strain brought to bear upon it the system would expand sufficiently to meet the strain, and we would at all events have a transport fit to cope with the natural characteristics of the country in the hands of men who thoroughly understood their animals.

Objections on financial grounds can readily be advanced against this or any other system, but I do not think the expense would be any greater than the present one. Even were it ordinarily greater by a few thousand pounds a year, in the end it would be more economical, when the enormous losses in animal, especially in camel, flesh that occur on active service are taken into account. But here we are brought face to face with the real obstacle that prevents change of system—party government, with its fears of unpopularity, and loss of power through increased estimates. In peace time they are afraid to spend a few thousands on a cause no matter how worthy; in war time thousands, even millions, are thrown away, while the ugly fact is glossed over and the confiding public gulled. Besides, the difficulty of obtaining

Financial objections

sufficient animals for a war on the same scale as the late Afghan and Egyptian (1882) has greatly increased, and, as I previously pointed out, even if ample time were given, India would be hard pushed to get an adequate supply. This, more than anything, would seem to me to point to the adoption of some such system the framework of which I have already hastily outlined, and especially to the breeding of camels and mules. Not only would this make us independent of buying and hiring from owners and breeders; not only would it give us more efficient transport, immediately ready, and fit for any emergency or crisis; but in peace time the animals that were not required for garrison use and the ordinary service routine could be used to advantage and hired out for work. Should there be any objection to this for financial or other reasons, the system might be modified as follows: Let Government urge the breeding of mules in England, and of mules and camels in Cyprus, Egypt, India, and Africa, and offer a yearly subsidy or premium to breeders, on the distinct understanding that in case of war the animals should be sold or hired to them. But though there is much more to be said on the subject, space and time prevent me.

No one will deny that the difficulties of purchasing or hiring and maintaining good transport, if not insuperable, are at all events so great as to be almost impossible to cope with on a sudden emergency, much more so to the attainment of any excellence, which is invariably the case in all our wars, where we have to battle, not only with the enemy, but with time, which is, in ninety-nine cases out of a hundred, a far more formidable opponent than the former. And that these difficulties will increase instead of diminish in the future appears likely, so far as one can look ahead, unless we make a complete and radical change in our system.

The remedy lies in our own hands, and in the face of such bitter experiences as ours have been in the East and in Africa, it is almost incredible that we do not set to work in earnest to grapple with this bugbear, and settle it at once and for ever. If, for reasons best known to itself, that kernel of centralisation the War Office will not adopt a permanent system, it ought at least to follow the example of the French in Algeria, and hire camels, or any transport animals, on the same principle. This would, at least, have one advantage, which in itself is sufficiently powerful to recommend its superiority over other temporary systems, and that is, having owners as supervisors and professional men as drivers, which, at all events, ensures better treatment and management of animals, and, as a consequence, a greater return of work on their part. Remedy

And there is yet another alternative which is worthy of attention, but which, while providing for transport, would not succeed in the question of drivers. In all possessions and colonies where necessary, keep a register in each province or district, under the responsible civil officer in charge of such, in which the owners of all vehicles and transport animals of every description should be compelled to register annually (or every six months) the number of animals and carts in their possession, showing the individual value of each, with a strict proviso that, in the event of an Another remedy expedition, the authorities could impress a certain percentage of such transport, wheeled, draught, or pack; but so as not to seriously interfere with the ordinary trading and agricultural operations.

Its value to India

This scheme, if properly organised and fostered, ought, in India at all events, to assist in enabling the transport system which the Indian Government have established to meet a crisis better than hitherto; though, as pointed out, its weak point would be drivers, and there would always be a certain amount of difficulty in obtaining good animals, for owners would naturally try and get rid of the worst. Whether our Afghan experiences have sufficiently impressed the Indian authorities to persuade them to organise and create a thorough system, capable of coping with a big war, I cannot say, as we have had no serious undertaking out there since then. But no matter how elaborate and seemingly perfect the working of the system may appear, without a sufficiency and efficiency of animals and drivers where shall we be? No nearer, I imagine, than before.

Hints to intending purchasers

A few hints that I have picked up in my wanderings will not be out of place here, and may prove of some use to intending purchasers. It is a mistake to suppose that all, or nearly all, breeds of camels make good baggagers, and, as I have previously pointed out in chapter iv., there is a vast difference between breeds in carrying capacity and endurance, those bred in civilised and cultivated districts being, as a rule, larger animals and greater weight-carriers, but far less enduring and abstaining than the desert breeds. On the whole, therefore, the latter are by far the best for a sudden rapid march under hard conditions—in fact, for all emergencies—while the former are better adapted for slow heavy work, where food and water are obtainable in plenty, and where the roads are good.

Object and class of work the guiding principle

It is very clear and evident, then, that in purchasing an officer must bear in mind the object for which he requires an animal, and the class of work that it is to be subjected to. This undoubtedly is the first principle that should guide him previous to examining a number of camels, and before making a selection. These remarks apply equally to Săwārīs, the points of which, by the way, are identically the same, with this broad distinction, remember, that, like the racehorse, he is built for riding and speed, combining agility and swiftness of movement with strength and endurance, in spite of his light spare frame, which is none the less wiry and hardy. While the baggager has a frame which was made simply to draw or carry weight.

Qualifications of purchasing officer

A purchasing officer should also be acquainted with all the various breeds belonging to the district which has been allotted to him, as well as the different features and characteristics which distinguish them, so as to be able to detect one from the other. A knowledge of the native language is, as a matter of fact, more or less indispensable, as he can get through the work far more satisfactorily and economically than through an interpreter or middleman.

Points

The first thing to do when you have decided on the class of animal, and before purchasing a camel, is to see to his points, which are—(1) general condition, (2) fulness and firmness of hump, (3) depth of chest, (4) muscular development of fore-quarters, (5) breadth and firmness of hind-quarters, (6) breadth in proportion to height. Also to the absence of the following defects—viz. (1) shallowness of callosity under chest, (2) wideness of chest, (3) skin of belly coming in folds, (4) brushing, (5) leaning hump, (6) swelling in groin, (7) a lump near shoulder, (8) mange, (9) thickening of skin, accompanied by mange between fore legs and outside of hind legs.

And now a few remarks on some of the chief points and defects will help in guiding the buyer.

The hump

A camel when in first-rate condition, as we have seen in chapter i., has a round full hump, which falls away when he fails in condition, and which is considered a bad sign; but do not forget the fact that certain of the desert breeds have scarcely any hump, but what little there is should be firm and hard; so be careful to examine this feature, and the state of the skin also, very minutely and closely.

Leaning hump

A camel with a leaning hump is apt to get a sore back far more easily than one with a full hump, and if possible should be avoided.

Height and depth

I cannot too strongly impress upon buyers the fact that the largest or tallest camels are by no means the best. Height alone is no criterion, only consider height when the camel is made in proportion. Short, deep-chested, thick-set animals are the best weight-carriers.

Class of camels to avoid

Shun a wide shallow-chested camel as you would the devil, and needless to say a narrow-chested one likewise. These are signs of weakness, and a camel with these serious defects is not up to hard or heavy work. Always look for depth of chest, which is a certain criterion of stamina and strength. See that the limbs are strong and well attached to the body, and that the muscular development is good. An animal with bent hocks, or one that stands well over on its hocks, especially if long shanked, is not up to much weight, and in ground which is at all rough or heavy is liable to come down if well loaded. These should also be avoided.

The callosity under the chest is a provision of nature, upon which the camel rests when kneeling for the imposition of a load. It should be large, well rounded, and deep. Examine this well, for he often gets a bruise here which turns into a nasty sore. Callosity under chest

'Brushing' and 'thickening' of the skin under the fore legs go together—for the former is really the result of the latter, consequent on the friction which takes place when the animal is walking. The surface gets rubbed and terribly raw, and if the camel is kept working develops into sores and incapacitates him. Many camels are liable and predisposed to this most serious fault; and it is a point that requires a very close inspection also, as camels which suffer from it are more or less useless. For this reason never fail to look under the elbows, to see if a camel has any marks of brushing on the body; for if it is a young one, or one which has been little worked, it is not so easy to detect as on old ones that have been hard worked. Should the animal be at all narrow-chested, and have folds of loose skin underneath the elbow, have it walked past you, with a load on if possible, as one of this kind is prone to brush. A practised eye will at once detect this, and will on no account buy the animal. Brushing and thickening of skin

Examine a camel's paces carefully, as well as his

Examine paces — action in kneeling and rising. With an average load on he ought to kneel and rise without any difficulty, and if he does it is a bad sign, and arises either from weakness or debility.

Firing — Orientals and Africans resort to firing as a cure or remedy for many ills, so do not unnecessarily underrate a camel so marked, unless the marks are very recent, and on the tendons of the legs, between the knees and hocks.

Eyesight — Should you be at all in doubt as to an animal's sight, move or pass your hand within a few inches of his eyes, and if he does not flinch, or only very slightly, you can form your own conclusions. If you are not satisfied, as a further test hold out a bunch of green or tempting fodder, of a kind that he relishes, a short distance away, say about two or three yards in front of him; but you must watch him very closely, as at this distance he may be guided by the smell.

Always be suspicious of a camel that is off his feed or drink, for this is one of the surest signs that he is ailing, although it may of course arise from temporary indisposition only, still, if you are buying against time you cannot tell. A camel in good condition should have a healthy appetite and drink well, and as a general rule most camels in this state border on the ravenous. The stomach of a well-conditioned animal should be well rounded, in addition to a full firm hump.

Mange — This of course is serious, because it implies impurity of blood and general unhealthiness of condition, besides being infectious; but it can be cured easily enough, and ought not to stand in the way if animals are required in large numbers, unless sufficient for the purpose are easily procurable.

Again, it is as well to know something about the approximate measurements and weight of camels, as it will to a certain extent enable you to arrive at the animal's weight-carrying capacity, because you may accept as a hard-and-fast rule that for hard and continuous work he will only carry one-third of his own weight, or a very trifling amount over it. Measurement and weight

The last thing to do—but by no means the least, for it is equal in importance to the first—when you have decided on your camel is to ascertain his age, and the vital importance of this cannot be overlooked. A camel may be worked at four years of age; but when you are buying him for service never get one under five or over fifteen years old, though at a pinch you may go up to twenty. He can be worked up to twenty, and some authorities assert up to twenty-five years of age, and I see no reason, if not worked too young, why he should not work up to that age. It is stated that he lives up to forty and fifty, and even beyond that, and the Russian writer that I once before have quoted says that the Kirghiz camel lives to fifty years. I cannot speak on this point from my own experience, but from all I have gathered am of opinion that he is a long-lived animal. A camel when rising five years sheds his two front sucking teeth—one on each side of the first ones—these are full grown at six years, and he also gets two more teeth when rising seven, which become full grown at seven years. When he is eight years old his tushes appear; and by the time he is nine years old his full set of teeth is complete. After this the Age Teeth

teeth get gradually worn away, and the marks are obliterated, so that you can only judge a camel's age approximately, for of course the older he grows the more worn away his teeth become. When he is in his sixteenth or seventeenth year the hair on his tail, as a rule, begins to turn white; and when he has reached his twentieth or twenty-first year the holes about his eyes become very deep. Above all things, in dealing with the oily Oriental, keep not only your weather eye, but both eyes wide open, and be on the alert the whole time, for the art of filing and disfiguring the teeth and of deception in general is not unknown to them, and if they can get rid of their most useless animals—the youngest and the oldest—be sure they will.

Two points to be noted

In examining the teeth to arrive at the age be very careful on two points, and be guided by them, viz.:—1st. Take into consideration the fact that, owing to the rough quality of the food which camels are obliged to eat, particularly in salt and sandy places, the marks are frequently obliterated or worn out sooner than would otherwise happen, so that an indication of the age according to ordinary rules would often mislead one.

2nd. Look well at the molars. If they are in a very decayed state you may rightly conclude that the beast is aged; but if necessary you must take the above point into consideration, and if doubtful look well at the holes over his eyes, and at the hair about his rump. In any case, however, it would be wiser to have nothing to do with him, for without the molars he cannot properly masticate his food. Consequently, even if in fair condition at the time, hard work will soon reduce and quickly dispose of him.

Another point and I have done: avoid middlemen or go-betweens, and buy direct yourself from the seller. This course will meet with opposition at the outset, but be firm and do not give in, and you will be the gainer in the end. However, let us earnestly hope that the day is not so very far distant when we shall have our own camels, and not be obliged to purchase any more.

CHAPTER XV

GENERAL REMARKS

Employment of first line of transport on lines of communication

HAVING practically finished my remarks, there is little more left to say, as I think I have discussed the camel in all its bearings as a transport animal. I have not treated the riding camel separately, because, with few exceptions, which have been noted, its treatment and management are exactly similar. Before concluding, however, I should like to make a few remarks on the employment of the first line of transport on the lines of communication—or, to be nearer the mark, making no distinction between the two, owing to a paucity of animals. To do justice to a subject of such vast and vital importance as this, one should discuss it in all its details and from every point of view; but here it will be sufficient to take only a cursory glance at it, and condemn it as the most fatal error that can be committed. We have seen in these pages, in one or two instances, the terrible consequences of it. It is essential that camels, when called upon suddenly to cope with any unusual fatigue or exertion, should be perfectly fresh and fit. Those that are stale—in other words, that have been worked off their legs on the way up—may, as in Stewart's march, get through, but with what result we have seen. Immediate collapse; final death. It was manifestly unfair, to say the least of it, to make camels in their condition undergo so severe and rapid a march—especially in a country like Egypt and the Soudan, where camels are bred in tens of thousands, and where there would have been no difficulty whatever in having 3,000 fresh animals concentrated at Korti. Besides, it is opposed to all principles of transport and common sense to use animals on lines of communication for any other purpose but working from stage to stage on those lines. But where, oh! where, is common sense to be found, especially in connection with one of the chief portions of our military machine? 'Common' sense, I am afraid, is a misnomer; 'uncommon' would be far more applicable. Further argument, however, is unnecessary. It is not from want of experience that we commit such glaring faults; it is because we conveniently forget the lessons it has taught us. It is almost fifty years ago since Sir Charles Napier—whose views on transport were very profound, and whose knowledge of camels was sound—took the most vigorous and effective measures to form a Camel Corps and a baggage or Land Transport Corps; but, to quote from his 'Life': 'These two corps, so admirable in conception, and afterwards found so well adapted for actual service, were by Lord Dalhousie and the Bombay Government abolished—as their avowed organs of the Press asserted—to vex Sir Charles Napier.' It seems almost incredible to think that this could have happened in an enlightened country such as ours, and in the face of so thoroughly practical an experience such as Sir Charles had brought to bear on the subject; yet here we are, towards the end of this very advanced nineteenth century, in as rotten a state of unpreparedness as ever we were! For in all our recent expeditions the transport has been nothing more than a mere hasty collection of animals, bought not for their special fitness, but by the gross, looked after by men totally inexperienced and ignorant of the work, without any organisation, and with improvised administration. Such it will remain as long as the system is unchanged. As Lord Strathnairn said, it would be 'wiser to have ten thousand men with perfect transport, which ensures their efficiency, than twice that number with imperfect transport and all the evils which follow in its train—an embarrassed strategy, neglected sick, and an ill-supplied soldiery.'

Advantages of permanent over temporary transport

A permanent camel transport has indisputably in every way the advantage over a temporary train, the main features of which, in summing up, are: (1) The quicker and easier method of obtaining a large supply of animals; (2) the supply of a superior stamp of animals; (3) improvement of class and breed; (4) a decided diminution in casualties on service; (5) a considerable increase in the weight-carrying capacity of the animals, thus adding considerably to the mobility and activity of an army; (6) a state of preparation and readiness which, if it does not immediately secure a moral victory, at all events secures the initiative, and gives a force all the moral superiority which the attack has over the defence; (7) an immense economy of (*a*) money and (*b*) time—both of which are of inestimable value, the latter especially, plunged as we so often are into war without a moment's warning. While in peace time the following are some of the sources by which profit may accrue: (1) Yearly increase of animals by breeding; (2) yearly revenue to be derived, (*a*) by hiring out the camels to the public, (*b*) by the sale of the hair, (*c*) and of the skins of the dead animals. This, after the numerous examples that we have before us in the past, should seem self-evident, but whether or no we make no effort to move in the right direction. Let us hope, however, that before long our national indolence will be awakened, and the vital importance of the fact recognised by those deep-thinking men who take a real interest in the welfare of the mother country and in the growth of that Greater Britain outside it; and let us trust sincerely that on the 'better late than never' principle they will lose no time in boldly taking the initiative.

Suitability of Australia for employment of camel

Nor can I conclude without reference to the undoubted suitability of Australia and South Africa, regarding the employment of the camel in its threefold capacity of riding, carrying, and drawing. I have never, I regret to say, been to Australia, but from the second-hand knowledge of it that I have gleaned from men and books I am firmly convinced that the colonies of Western and Southern Australia and Queensland are splendidly adapted for the animal in every way, and that if properly worked and managed the interior can and will be opened up and expanded through its medium into self-supporting districts; while it is evident that the comparative cost of maintenance between camels and oxen in a country like Australia, where the former are a recent importation, would in a few years tell in favour of the camel, the advantage being entirely on its side. That the Australians have already begun to appreciate its value is proved by the great increase latterly in the numbers employed. And with the usual energy and determination that they infuse into everything they take in hand they will, I have no doubt, pay the serious attention to the question of which it is deserving.

Also of South Africa

As to South Africa, I have no hesitation in saying that, from what I have seen of it, the whole country is eminently suitable. When I landed at Cape Town four years ago this was the first thought that struck me as I passed through—the Karoo especially—on my way to Kimberley. The same idea prevailed when I drove in a Cape cart from the latter town up to Macloutsie, a distance of over 800 miles (1,500 from Cape Town), and also when I subsequently rode up from Macloutsie to Salisbury—close on 500 miles—and on to Umtali, another 190 miles further on. After a residence of a year in the British South Africa Company's territory, and when I had traversed the veldt in every direction, and become acquainted with its botanical, climatic, and geological conditions, my first impressions were confirmed, and I spoke on the subject to Dr. Jameson, the Administrator of Mashonaland. At his instigation I wrote to Mr. Rhodes, proposing a scheme for introducing camels into the country; but, whatever his reasons, he did not take it up. At the same time I suggested to him the importation of Syrian donkey stallions for the improvement of mule breeding; also the utility of attempting to tame and employ the African elephant as a means of transport, &c. A reversion to the old order of things purely and simply, for Schweinfurth tells us in his 'Heart of Africa' that there is evidence beyond doubt to show that the African elephant was *once* employed as a domestic animal.

First impressions

Confirmed after residence

In October 1892, learning that his Excellency Sir Henry Loch, G.C.B., G.C.M.G., was considering the question of adopting camels in Bechuanaland, I called on him, and finding that he took a deep interest in the subject I wrote him a *précis* on it. So far, however, the Imperial Government, to whom Sir Henry Loch submitted a scheme for introducing them, have taken no steps. This, apart from every other consideration, is a great pity. In Cape Colony, the Orange Free State, Transvaal, Natal, outside the railway sphere camels would be very useful, though the sluggishness and deep-rooted conservatism of the people in favour of the ox, with which they have always worked, would be extremely difficult, if possible, to overcome. In Namaqualand, Bechuanaland, the Protectorate, Kalahari Desert, and in the British South Africa Company's territories, the uses of both Sawari and baggager, the former especially, cannot be exaggerated. From a purely practical, and eventually economical, point of view it would be almost impossible to place a value on them.

A practical comparison between the camel and ox wagon

To make the matter as clear as possible, I will draw as practical a comparison as I can between the ox and the camel, showing their relative advantages and drawbacks. To begin with. Until January 1893 I was doubtful as to the liability of the latter to lung sickness. Then, by the kindness of his Excellency Sir Henry Loch, I was enabled to read a Report on the Employment of Camels in South-West Africa, by Major von François, the German Commissioner in those parts, a Report to which I intend to refer in the following pages. After two years' experience with some camels that he had imported from Teneriffe (an inferior breed,

Non-liability of camel to lung sickness

by the way), Major von François found that they had in no way been affected by cattle diseases or horse sickness. As the climatic, botanic, and geological conditions of Damara- and Namaqualands are very similar to, if not identical with, Bechuanaland and the Protectorate, this removes the only obstacle that might have been advanced against the introduction of the animal into those parts.

Utility in damp climates

A doubt also exists as to the employment of camels in a wet climate. As a rule, of course, a dry climate is essential for breeds of the Arabian species, though with a little care they will stand the exposure, and prove quite serviceable. And, as I have pointed out, if necessary the feet can always be protected—a protection causing less trouble and expense than shoeing. Camels of the Bactrian breed are better suited for damp, as they are accustomed to it, and their feet are more adapted to wet and slippery soil.

Superiority over Damara cattle

In his Report, Major von François alludes to the superiority of the camel over the Damara oxen in abstinence from food and water. But this is by no means extraordinary, as a knowledge of his internal machinery will quickly demonstrate, and because, as I have endeavoured to explain in this work, his powers in this way, although exaggerated, are greater than those possessed by other ruminants.

He also refers to their not becoming footsore in the stony ground of the border regions of Damaraland. Camels are tolerant of shingle and stones, and, provided you are careful of them, will march for days over such country. Both in Afghanistan and the Soudan I have taken camels over very broken stony ground without knocking up their feet. In fact, they will go anywhere that an ox can, and the more sterile the country, the greater their advantage over the ox or horse.

Of their relative weight-carrying capacity I have already spoken in chapter ix., while, slow as a camel is, he can walk faster than an ox, either in draught, or under the pack. I can lay my hands on several breeds of the former that will carry a minimum load of 400 lb., and cover 25 miles a day. In proper hands, and in the country stretching from Vryburg and Johannesburg up to Salisbury, they could make eight journeys of 400 miles a month. Rest them for three or four months during the rains, and they will be as fresh as ever for the ensuing season. Should the herbage be scanty and the water scarce in districts such as the Kalahari is reputed to be, a monthly average of 300 miles would be enough to expect. Or look at it in another way. A baggager walks 2½ miles an hour, and can be worked 10 hours in the 24, or 25 miles a day. Rest him every fifth day, leaving 24 working days in the month, which, multiplied by 25 miles (a day), equals 580 miles. Relative marching powers of the camel

Now compare this with an ox. Taking his average pace at 1½ mile (in the shafts) an hour, and say he can work 12 hours out of the 24, you get an average of 18 miles per diem; a *most exceptional one too.* Rest every fifth day gives 24 working days, which, multiplied by 18 miles, equals 432 miles in the month. The question, however, naturally rises, How long will the same team of oxen keep up this rate? Granted they make a similar journey in the second month, could they accomplish a third? and would it be possible for even an exceptional team to make a fourth? I say, most and of the ox certainly not. Two successive journeys would be their limit, and then with a heavy loss.

Daily average of oxen

I know that in Mashonaland in 1890–91 the average rate all through for wagons, coming either from the Transvaal or from Bechuanaland to Salisbury, was ten miles a day. Of course there were certain exceptions, under the most favourable conditions of forage and water, and with light loads; but in most cases it was as I have said, the oxen only being fit to return empty, while in others they were so completely knocked up that they had to be rested for long periods. The death rate too, from various causes, was very high; while, in proper hands, the mortality among camels would be very small.

Carriage of heavy bulky goods

The carriage of heavy and bulky goods—say, machinery—would necessitate the use of wagons. But here, again, do not forget that the camel can be, and is, used for draught purposes, and he can draw just twice as much as a bullock, so that eight camels will do the work of sixteen oxen.

Number of attendants

Taking into consideration the question of attendants, the advantage is in favour of the latter animal. But not so very much. Sixteen camels can be looked after by two men, but for loading purposes two more are necessary. The proportion of attendants to an increase of animals would, however, be in inverse ratio; or, in plainer language, on increasing the number of animals, an equal increase of drivers would not be necessary, 6 men being sufficient for 32 camels, 10 for 64, 20 for 128, &c. That these drivers should be of the best class I need not add after what I have said in chapter xii. Naturally enough, to induce such men to leave their homes, and to come all the way to South Africa, a high rate of wages and other inducements would have to be offered. But in the long run this would be advisable, and with their help the natives of these parts could be instructed.

Breeding the best plan

In face, however, of the objection to the camel on the grounds of expense, Major von François, I am pleased to say, recognising its high utility, has recommended his Government to adopt the breeding of camels in Damaraland. Let us hope that our Government will lose no time in setting the example, or even in following it. That he is right goes without saying, for this is from every conceivable standpoint the best and most practical method to adopt, and I am certain that camels thrive better in a climate and country in which they have been bred. The best plan would be to import females six months pregnant, so as to give them ample time to recover from the journey before giving birth. Ten is too small a number to begin with, and fifty would enable one to arrive at a sounder opinion, besides proving a more suitable investment; and of course, either for breeding or working, it would in the end be far cheaper to import the best breed, a question that does not in any way admit of argument.

And now in a few words let us sum up the special advantages of camel over ox transport.

The advantages of the camel over the ox wagon

1. Can carry or draw twice as much.
2. Faster, and able to cover more ground daily.
3. Can do from 20 to 25 miles in one stretch.
4. Will make many more journeys in a year and in their respective lifetimes.
5. Able to traverse ground that a wagon will stick in.

6. No trouble fording rivers, where wagons would have to be unloaded.

7. Not subject to the diseases so fatal to cattle up country.

8. Live and work four times as long.

9. Greater powers of abstinence from food and water.

10. Greater tenacity and endurance.

11. Wagon liable to break down, upset, or stick. Consequent loss of time and additional expense in former case, besides inability or want of means to repair.

12. Lastly, the additional dead weight of the wagon, which is considerable—at least a ton, I should say.

Another very noticeable point is, that in the dry season preceding the rains, when grass and water are scarce in the veldt, oxen lose condition and fail considerably. This would in no way affect camels, for there would always be a sufficiency of water for them, while they would get ample grazing among the different kinds of prickly thorny bushes and trees in which the veldt abounds.

Against these the only two disadvantages that can be advanced are (1) greater expense, (2) daily loading and unloading, (3) more attendants. As to the first, taking this into account, the greater returns, as I will show later on, will more than counterbalance the excessive expenditure, and time will reduce even this to its proper level. As to the second, it is, after all, a trifle, and with loading nets the trouble and delay can be reduced to a minimum. Besides, once loaded, a camel can, as a rule, accomplish his journey in one stretch, while with an ox wagon you have to collect the oxen, inspan and outspan at least three times in the twenty-four hours, which, if anything, is worse. Of the third we have already spoken.

Most of these advantages apply, if anything, more forcibly to riding camels; but, as I have alluded more than once to their wonderful speed and endurance, and to the terrific death-rate among horses in these regions—facts which in themselves are the most convincing proofs of their superiority over the horse for any kind of police, military, or commercial work. Besides, they are cheaper to feed than horses, and are altogether more economical once the initial expense of importing them has been surmounted—say in ten years—and they do not require shoeing.

The financial aspect of the question

Lastly, let us glance at the financial aspect of the question. In calculating the cost, we must not overlook the fact that the initial outlay of most undertakings and commercial transactions is invariably large, and in this particular instance it is hardly fair to institute a comparison between a camel imported from a long distance and an ox which is native to the country. Every venture must have a beginning, and one such as this is bound to be expensive at the outset, besides requiring time for development. When in working order, however—say, in ten years' time—the price of an average baggager, bred in this colony, ought to be from 8*l.* to 10*l.*, and of a riding camel about 20*l.*; while in twenty years the former should drop to 6*l.* and the latter to 15*l.*, providing the scheme was successfully carried out in its entirety, against which I can see no objection. Of course, this result would depend entirely on the amount of the original outlay and capital. And in a scheme of this nature, if worked properly, and from a commercial point of view—say, for trading purposes in competing against the ox wagon —a large initial outlay would be followed eventually by a corresponding profit that would justify the original risk; and the larger this expediture—to a reasonable extent—the quicker would be the returns.

An approximate calculation

I have so far abstained from entering into any calculations, because for various reasons—frequent changes in the rates of transport, and fluctuation in commercial tariffs—it is almost impossible to give anything but an approximation.

Say, however, that 16 camels landed in Bechuanaland cost 75*l.* each:—

16 × 75*l.*	1,200*l.*	
16 oxen at 8*l.* apiece	128*l.*	} =228*l.*
1 waggon cost 100*l.*	100*l.*	

16 camels, carrying 6,400 lb. at 1*l.* per 100 lb., and making 8 journeys in the year=	64*l.* × 8=	512*l.*
So that in 4 years	512*l.* × 4=	2,048*l.*
Deduct 200*l.* yearly for expense of attendants, &c.	200*l.* × 4=	800*l.*
Leaving a balance of		1,248*l.*
One wagon, carrying 6,000 lb. at 1*l.* per 100 lb., making 6 journeys (with fresh teams) in the year	60*l.* × 6=	360*l.*
And in 4 years	360*l.* × 4=	1,440*l.*
Deduct 100*l.* a year for expenses .	100*l.* × 4=	400*l.*
And we have a balance of		1,040*l.*

It will be seen that I have overestimated the work of an ox wagon, for, as a matter of fact, even with a large percentage of spare oxen or fresh teams, it would not do more than four long journeys at the outside; but I have done this purposely, so as to show the actual difference between the two systems.

Thus in four or six years, allowing for a deficiency of trade, sixteen camels would pay off their original cost. And with a first-class breed, even supposing fewer journeys were made in the year, greater loads could be carried, and about the same result arrived at. At the end of this time the profit realised by the camels would be quite double that brought in by the wagon; to say nothing of the heavy loss that would have been incurred among the oxen; whereas with care there should be little or none among the camels—an item which would still further increase the earnings of the latter. Besides, camels are long-lived, as we have seen, so that in the ordinary course of events you would get twenty years' work out of them. While with superior breeds, with great care, you might expect from twenty-five to thirty years. On the other hand, a bullock's life up country, running the gauntlet, as he has to, of so many risky diseases, many of them rapidly fatal, is decidedly precarious, and on short rations and hard work they do not on an average last much longer than six or seven years, if so long.

When we take into comparison the great advantages of the Sawari over the horse and the baggager over the ox in the country we have been discussing, it seems impossible to hesitate in deciding on the introduction of an animal which would be so valuable and useful in its expansion and development. But I have said enough.

It might reasonably be asked why, in the face of

such a sweeping condemnation of his mental powers (*vide* chapters ii., iii.), I place such marked importance on the extreme value of the camel as a riding and baggage animal? But it is on this very account that I base my opinion. He is simply a living automaton, that moves when and where he is required to; a patient, submissive, if not willing slave, and a faithful drudge who does his best, even when ill-treated, and whose best is by no means contemptible under the cruelest of conditions. But, accord him humane treatment and careful management, and his value and uses will increase, as I have endeavoured to show, in a corresponding ratio, repaying our care and attention a hundredfold, and it will be evident to any unbiased reader, after a careful perusal of the work, that (1) By a judicious system of elimination of inferior, and by the strict selection and blending of the best breeds, a superior race of camels could be produced. (2) In addition to this, through proper management, a far higher maximum of work would be obtained. (3) And finally, that, with this increased improvement especially, Sawaris and baggagers would prove infinitely superior to any other class of riding or transport animal.

I am afraid that, instead of confining my remarks simply to the camel and his characteristics, I have touched rather more fully than I had originally intended on other questions in connection with transport generally. If, however, I have made it clear (which has been my object all through) that the baggager is invaluable on his native soil, and with proper management is useful at all times and in all climes, while the riding camel is unequal for certain duties, and that both are really indispensable to us, I shall be satisfied. And should I have elicited any sympathy for the poor patient creatures which in future years will bear the fruit of kinder and better treatment, and help in any way to ameliorate their lot, I shall feel that I have at least done some little good.

In conclusion, I recognise and regret the fact that there are many shortcomings in this work: deficiencies in technicalities, anatomical, botanical, and otherwise, especially on the subject of breeding and in the information concerning species and breeds. But I trust, on some future occasion, after further experiences and fresh research, to add really valuable and useful information on such an important but much neglected subject as this. Conclusion

If, however, this work will have no other effect but to raise sufficient interest in a hitherto despised and neglected animal, which will result in the inculcation of a humaner treatment and better management—including a wider spread use of it—I shall consider it a decided gain, and feel that its production has—in a certain sense at all events—been fully justified.